T0331097

Regional Economic Development and History

Regional Studies is inextricably intertwined with history. Cultural and institutional legacies inform choices between different policy options, meaning that the past plays a crucial role in how we think about regional economic development, planning and policy.

Through a selection of accessible theoretical, methodological and empirical chapters, this book explores the connections between regional development and history. Drawing on the expertise of scholars in several disciplines, it links history to topics such as behavioural geography, interdependence, divergence and regional and urban policy.

This innovative book will be of interest to researchers across regional studies, planning, economic geography and economic history.

Marijn Molema is a historian and working as programme leader at the Frisian Institute of Social Research. He is also a guest researcher at the Fryske Akademy, a research institute in the city of Leeuwarden of the Royal Netherlands Academy of Arts and Sciences.

Sara Svensson is a political scientist specializing in regional collaboration across national borders. She is Senior Lecturer at Halmstad University in Sweden and Research Fellow at the Center for Policy Studies at Central European University in Budapest (Hungary).

Regional Studies Association

THE GLOBAL FORUM FOR CITY AND REGIONAL RESEARCH, DEVELOPMENT AND POLICY

Routledge
Taylor & Francis Group

Regions and Cities

Series Editor in Chief
Joan Fitzgerald, *Northeastern University, USA*

Editors
Ron Martin, *University of Cambridge, UK*
Maryann Feldman, *University of North Carolina, USA*
Gernot Grabher, *HafenCity University Hamburg, Germany*
Kieran P. Donaghy, *Cornell University, USA*

In today's globalised, knowledge-driven and networked world, regions and cities have assumed heightened significance as the interconnected nodes of economic, social and cultural production, and as sites of new modes of economic and territorial governance and policy experimentation. This book series brings together incisive and critically engaged international and interdisciplinary research on this resurgence of regions and cities, and should be of interest to geographers, economists, sociologists, political scientists and cultural scholars, as well as to policy-makers involved in regional and urban development.

For more information on the Regional Studies Association visit www.regionalstudies.org

There is a **30% discount** available to RSA members on books in the ***Regions and Cities*** series, and other subject related Taylor and Francis books and e-books including Routledge titles. To order just e-mail Emilia Falcone, Emilia.Falcone@tandf.co.uk, or phone on +44 (0) 20 3377 3369 and declare your RSA membership. You can also visit the series page at www.routledge.com/Regions-and-Cities/book-series/RSA and use the discount code: **RSA0901**

138. Metropolitan Economic Development
The Political Economy of Urbanisation in Mexico
Alejandra Trejo Nieto

139. Regional Economic Development and History
Edited by Marijn Molema and Sara Svensson

For more information about this series, please visit:
www.routledge.com/Regions-and-Cities/book-series/RSA

Regional Economic Development and History

Edited by Marijn Molema
and Sara Svensson

Routledge
Taylor & Francis Group
LONDON AND NEW YORK

First published 2020
by Routledge
2 Park Square, Milton Park, Abingdon, Oxon OX14 4RN

and by Routledge
52 Vanderbilt Avenue, New York, NY 10017

Routledge is an imprint of the Taylor & Francis Group, an informa business

First issued in paperback 2021

© 2020 selection and editorial matter, Marijn Molema and Sara Svensson; individual chapters, the contributors

The right of Marijn Molema and Sara Svensson to be identified as the authors of the editorial material, and of the authors for their individual chapters, has been asserted in accordance with sections 77 and 78 of the Copyright, Designs and Patents Act 1988.

All rights reserved. No part of this book may be reprinted or reproduced or utilised in any form or by any electronic, mechanical, or other means, now known or hereafter invented, including photocopying and recording, or in any information storage or retrieval system, without permission in writing from the publishers.

Trademark notice: Product or corporate names may be trademarks or registered trademarks, and are used only for identification and explanation without intent to infringe.

British Library Cataloguing-in-Publication Data
A catalogue record for this book is available from the British Library

Library of Congress Cataloging-in-Publication Data
A catalog record has been requested for this book

ISBN: 978-1-138-33413-7 (hbk)
ISBN: 978-1-03-208754-2 (pbk)
ISBN: 978-0-429-44554-5 (ebk)

Typeset in Bembo
by Newgen Publishing UK

Contents

Contributors

Martin Åberg is Professor of History at Karlstad University (Sweden), and specializes in 19th and 20th century political organization and mobilization in a comparative perspective.

Kevin Cox is Distinguished Emeritus Professor of Geography at the Ohio State University (US).

Armando J. dalla Costa is an economist at the Federal University of Paraná (Brazil) and Research Productivity Scholar at the Brazilian National Council for Scientific and Technological Development (CNPq).

Thomas Denk is Professor of Political Science at Örebro University (Sweden). His research focus is on comparative interdependence, state formation, democratization and political culture.

Kerstin Enflo is Associate Professor at the Department of Economic History at Lund University (Sweden) and is a leading expert on long-term regional development.

Emil Evenhuis is a researcher in the Department of Urbanisation and Transport at the Netherlands Environmental Assessment Agency (Planbureau voor de Leefomgeving, Netherlands).

Tomàs Fernández-de-Sevilla was the Kurgan van-Hentenryk Postdoctoral Fellow in Business History at the Université Libre de Bruxelles (Belgium) from 2015 to 2018.

Mikołaj Herbst is Assistant Professor at the University of Warsaw, the EUROREG Centre for European Regional and Local Studies (Poland), specializing in regional studies and the economics of education.

Robert Huggins is Professor of Economic Geography at the School of Geography and Planning at Cardiff University (UK).

Justyna Kościńska is a PhD candidate at the Institute of Sociology, University of Warsaw (Poland), working on the spatial accessibility of educational services and urban sociology.

Ron Martin is Professor of Economic Geography at University of Cambridge (UK) and President of the Regional Studies Association.

Anna Missiaia is a post-doctoral researcher at the Department of Economic History of Lund University (Sweden) and her main research interest is on regional industrialization and regional development in the long-run.

Marijn Molema is a historian and working as programme leader at the Frisian Institute of Social Research, Leeuwarden (Netherlands).

Peter Sunley is Professor of Economic Geography at Southampton University (UK).

Sara Svensson is a political scientist specializing in regional collaboration across national borders. She is Senior Lecturer at Halmstad University in Sweden and Research Fellow at the Center for Policy Studies at Central European University in Budapest (Hungary).

John Tomaney is Professor of Urban and Regional Planning in the Barlett School of Planning, University College London (UK).

Piers Thompson is Associate Professor of local and small business economics at Nottingham Business School, Nottingham Trent University (UK).

Bas van Leeuwen is an economic historian working on global history at the International Institute of Social History, a research institute of the Royal Netherlands Academy of Arts and Sciences.

Meimei Wang is a PhD student working on Chinese economic and social history at Utrecht University (Netherlands).

Acknowledgements

This volume could not have been produced without the Research Network Regional Economic and Policy History (ReHi-Network), supported by the Regional Studies Association. We want to thank the RSA and their dedicated staff members Klara Sobekova and Daniela Carl, among others, for their involvement and interest. Conversations and cooperation with the co-founders of the ReHi-Network, Arno van der Zwet (University of the West of Scotland), Martin Åberg and Silke Reeploeg (Karlstad University), helped to shape this volume as well. John Tomaney (University College London) was a valuable advisor in the early stage of the network, and hosted its inaugural meeting in April 2017. Lilla Jakobs at the Center for Policy Studies at Central European University gave valuable advice on the practicalities of producing a book. The Center as well as the Fryske Akademy also provided intellectual stimulating environments for the duration of the work on this book. Lisa Lavelle and Natalie Tomlinson at Taylor & Francis have been helpful throughout. Ruth-Anne Hurst did a good job as production editor. This book was edited by a historian and a social scientist (political science). We are grateful to each other for the additional insights brought together by this cooperation, all of which we will take with us in our further research work.

The editors, 17 September 2019

Prolegomenon

Bringing the past back in

Taking history seriously in the study of regional development

Ron Martin, Peter Sunley and Emil Evenhuis

We want to start in the past by recalling Sidney Pollard's (1981) classic regional economic history *Peaceful Conquest* that explained how industrialization spread across European regions. As it did so, industrialization was influenced by timing and by the pre-existing conditions and policies in each region and state, but it was also reinforced and invigorated by regional processes. Just as regional economies were formed by industrialization, so they in turn shaped the course of industrialization itself. The current phase of capitalist development, characterized by a deepening crisis of carbon-based industrial production, the disruptive effects of new economic and technological paths, and the faltering of globalization, involves a different set of creative and destructive forces, and associated policy problems. But these transformations and challenges are also profoundly regional in nature and impact, involving new relationships and interactions between regions within and between nations. As many of the contributors to this timely collection of essays argue, a regional-historical approach is no less essential to understanding contemporary economic and societal change as it is to explicating previous phases of capitalist development.

How then might history fruitfully contribute to a better understanding of regional socio-economic development? And indeed, how might the study of regional socio-economic development inform not just the practice of historical enquiry but also our understanding of the process of social economic evolution and progress? Not merely by knowing more about particular places at particular times under particular circumstances, and then adding it to the discussion – though that would certainly be useful. More fundamentally, it can be argued that by adopting a historical perspective – or perhaps better termed a historical epistemology – in which the aim is to reveal how at any particular time an observed pattern of regional socio-economic differentiation has come to be what it is, we not only improve our understanding of regional development as an inherently historical process, but also derive a clearer view of how far and in what ways policy interventions might help to steer future regional development along some more favourable path. In this respect, policy-makers would then need to be more realistic about the way in which policies mix into the flow of an economy's spatial history and not simply imagine policies will achieve the "experimental" results they wish for them.

No doubt several alternative views might be proffered as to how we should go about taking history seriously in regional development studies. But a fruitful starting point is to turn to Charles Tilly's (1984) brilliant exegesis on the uses of history, on the critical role of time in affecting development, and on the value of time and place comparisons in arriving at plausible explanations. He distinguishes four main research strategies, or "ways of seeing". We might for example adopt an "individualizing" approach, and focus on the historical processes, events, path dependencies, reactive sequences and key decisions that explain a given region's development as a means of grasping the peculiarities of that case. Such an approach might, for example, help to explain the divergent development of, say, two regions or cities in terms of, for example, their different and distinctive structural, institutional and governance set-ups. Secondly, we might adopt a "universalizing" approach in which comparison is made across several regions in an effort to reveal how regional socio-economic development over time is driven by some key common factors, forces and processes, regardless of the specificities of local context. One such common force frequently referred to in the literature is the tendency for regions to specialize to some degree in one or other particular economic activities in which they have some natural, contingent or constructed comparative advantage. Essentially, the aim here is to search for what is "universal" in the "particular", with a view to formulating or confirming some generalizations about the historical processes and forces of regional socio-economic development.

A third strategy is that of "variation-finding" comparison. Here the aim is to establish some key principles of variation in the character or pace of regional development by examining systematic differences among the histories of different regions. It might be, for example, that there are systematic differences across regions in their social-political class histories, including their propensity to trade unionism, which in turn have impacted on their economic evolution. Fourth, and most ambitiously, we might embark on an "encompassing" comparison approach. This seeks to place the development experiences of different regions within a larger system on the way to explaining those development histories in terms of the varying relationship of the regions to the larger system as a whole. Can we explain the diversity of regional development experiences over time as deriving from their (changing) roles and interdependencies within, say, the overall national economic system to which they belong? Or even more broadly, in relation to the international system? To what extent have the different regional paths of socio-economic development been shaped by big historical processes of capitalist progress and accumulation? Encompassing comparisons typically begin with a large structure or process and then explain similarities or differences among cases – in our instance, regions – as consequences of their relationships to the whole. Such an approach can yield invaluable insights. But it also carries two potential dangers: first, the presumption of a pre-given "whole" that "governs" its parts (regions), and second, a functionalist trap, wherein a region's economic development is explained in terms of its functional role in that pre-given whole. In certain respects, these were two of the problems that characterized the idea of "combined and uneven geographical development" that was a key Marxian research paradigm in economic geography and regional studies in the late 1970s to the late 1980s. That paradigm then fell out of favour from the late 1980s onwards, in part because of the general intellectual shift away from top-down grand theory and meta-narratives that swept through the social sciences.

To avoid these potential dangers, McMichael (1990) advocates a revised encompassing approach which he calls "incorporated comparison", a mode of historical enquiry in which the "whole" – such as a big historical economic process, say the industrialization of a national economy – does not exist independently of or pre-given to its parts, say the regional economies that make up the national system, but itself emerges via comparative analysis of those parts, as moments in a self-forming "whole". Large-scale historical meta-processes of capitalist development are not, therefore, "out-there", independent of individual, pre-given regions which they (differentially) impact, but are themselves historically constituted by the processes and patterns of "regionalization" of economic activity and relations at any given historical moment. However, at the same time, while such (time-specific) self-forming "wholes" (meta-processes and metasystems), emerge from their (regional) parts, they are not simply reducible to the latter, but themselves develop macro- and meta-level emergent effects that can then exert "downward causation" on those parts (see Martin and Sunley, 2012). This could open up possibilities for a more multi-scalar and recursive relational approach to the notion of combined and uneven geographical development.

All the above strategies will work for some purposes. There will be instances when what we are most interested in is a clear understanding of the singularities of a particular region's historical experience. Getting those singularities right can provide considerable theoretical insight, either by confirming existing theoretical or conceptual schemas or by serving as a firm basis for the construction of new grounded theory. A universalizing approach to revealing the importance of history can be especially illuminating. To show that regions in widely separated settings undergo the same sequence, pattern or conjunction of development forces and processes over time not only has highly positive implications for theory-building, but potentially also helps to identify suitable forms of policy intervention that have wide applicability. As Tilly argues, however, variation-finding research strategies can help make sense of socio-economic structures and processes that never recur in the same local form across regions, but which appear to vary in some systematic or regular way, which systematic variation then calls for an explanation. Such research also has immediate value for designing policies intended to reduce regional economic disparities. Exploring the role of history in regional development by means of an encompassing or incorporated research strategy, though certainly the most challenging, is arguably ultimately the most rewarding. It not only has the advantage of assessing the role of the interconnectedness (and patterns of economic dominance) between different regions in explaining their historical experiences, but also in helping to understand the historical evolution of larger socio-economic systems in terms of the differing but interrelated histories of their constituent regions. Of course, mixed research strategies are also possible, indeed perhaps desirable, depending on the specific purpose of the study in hand.

Elements of these different approaches to taking history seriously in regional development studies can be found in this welcome and timely book. As the editors note, the chapters provide some defining points for interdisciplinary conversations about the principles, aims and methods of a "new regional history". In doing so, they discuss aspects of comparative research design and exemplify the value of some of the regional-historical strategies of the sort suggested by Tilly's work. They also discuss and reflect on a further set of key questions. As several of the contributors emphasize, a key challenge is to avoid both ahistorical theory and atheoretical, purely descriptive history. But what exactly does historical or historically-appreciative theory mean, and how best should theory incorporate the significance of time and history at different paces and rates of change?

These are also questions we have grappled with in our own work, as part of our endeavours to broaden and develop the conceptual, methodological and empirical basis of Evolutionary Economic Geography (Martin and Sunley, 2006; Martin and Sunley, 2007; Martin and Sunley, 2012; Martin and Sunley, 2015; Evenhuis and Dawley, 2017). In the past two decades or so, Evolutionary Economic Geography has come to the fore as an influential "paradigm" in regional studies and economic geography. It seeks to examine "the processes by which the economic landscape – the spatial organization of economic production, circulation, exchange, distribution and consumption – is transformed from within over time" (Boschma and Martin, 2010, pp. 6–7). Much of the existing work within this paradigm has however been particularly concerned with the micro-level dynamics explaining the development of patterns of "innovation" across regions and cities over time (and the spatial configurations of firms, industries, clusters, technologies, capacities and networks involved). Together with others, we have attempted to develop a more holistic, socialized and multi-scalar approach that places these micro-level dynamics within a larger perspective, taking account of macro-level structures and processes, such as developments in national economic policies and governance, structural changes in economies (like deindustrialization and financialization), and changes in global competitive pressures (also see MacKinnon et al., 2009; Hassink et al., 2014; Pike et al., 2016). In extending this approach to Evolutionary Economic Geography, not only have we sought to look at developments over a much longer timeframe, tracing current patterns and issues back to important critical junctures in the past (also Henning, 2019), but have also stressed an important role for comparisons, as these help to uncover the various "mechanisms" by which economic evolution takes place in regions, how these are tied up with structures and processes at different scales, and the role that particular contextual factors, unique events and decisions may have played.

In advancing Evolutionary Economic Geography in the directions outlined above there is a key role for the sort of theoretical explorations, methodological innovations, and empirical case studies, contained in this volume. Indeed, in our view, the volume helps to lay the groundwork for bringing the approach to Evolutionary Economic Geography that we champion, and regional history – perhaps reformatted as "new regional history" – much closer together. We should clearly not underestimate the challenges involved in developing a historically-oriented, interdisciplinary, comparative approach, combining an enhanced geographical sensitivity with a profound historical epistemology. Breaking down old institutionalized walls between social sciences and history will be difficult, but this book provides us with a very valuable set of steps towards that multidisciplinary endeavour.

References

Boschma, R. and Martin, R. L., 2010. The aims and scope of Evolutionary Economic Geography. In: R. Boschma and R. L. Martin, eds. *The Handbook of Evolutionary Economic Geography*. Cheltenham: Edward Elgar, pp. 3–39. https://doi.org/10.4337/9781849806497.00007

Evenhuis, E. and Dawley, S., 2017. Evolutionary perspectives on economic resilience in regional development. In: N. Williams and T. Vorley, eds. *Creating resilient economies: Entrepreneurship, growth and development in uncertain times*. Cheltenham: Edward Elgar, pp. 192–205. https://doi.org/10.4337/9781785367649.00020

Hassink, R., Klaerding, C. and Marques, P., 2014. Advancing Evolutionary Economic Geography by engaged pluralism. *Regional Studies*, 48, pp. 1295–1307. https://doi.org/10.1080/00343404.2014.889815

Henning, M., 2019. Time should tell (more): Evolutionary Economic Geography and the challenge of history. *Regional Studies*, 53, pp. 602–613. https://doi.org/10.1080/00343404.2018.1515481

MacKinnon, D., Cumbers, A., Pike, A., Birch, K. and McMaster, R., 2009. Evolution in Economic Geography: Institutions, political economy, and adaptation. *Economic Geography*, 85, pp. 129–150. https://doi.org/10.1111/j.1944-8287.2009.01017.x

Martin, R. L. and Sunley, P. J., 2006. Path dependence and regional economic evolution. *Journal of Economic Geography*, 6, pp. 395–437.

Martin, R. L. and Sunley, P. J., 2007. Complexity thinking in Evolutionary Economic Geography. *Journal of Economic Geography*, 7, pp. 573–601. https://doi.org/10.1093/jeg/lbl012

Martin, R. L. and Sunley, P. J., 2012. Forms of emergence and the evolution of economic landscapes. *Journal of Economic Behaviour and Organisation*, 82, pp. 338–351. https://doi.org/10.1016/j.jebo.2011.08.005

Martin, R. L and Sunley, P. J., 2015. Towards a developmental turn in Evolutionary Economic Geography? *Regional Studies*, 49, pp. 712–732. https://doi.org/10.1080/00343404.2014.899431

McMichael, P., 1990. Incorporating comparison within a world-historical perspective: An alternative comparative method. *American Sociological Review*, 55, pp. 385–397. https://doi.org/10.2307/2095763

Pike, A., MacKinnon, D., Cumbers, A., Dawley, S. and McMaster, R., 2016. Doing evolution in Economic Geography. *Economic Geography*, 92, pp. 123–144. https://doi.org/10.1080/00130095.2015.1108830

Pollard, S., 1981. *Peaceful conquest: The industrialization of Europe 1760–1970.* Oxford: Oxford University Press.

Tilly, C., 1984. *Big structures, large processes, huge comparisons.* New York: Russell Sage Foundation.

Introduction

1 The importance of history for regional economic development

Sara Svensson and Marijn Molema

It is perhaps deeply human to feel that the time in which we happen to live is unprecedented in multiple ways. As this volume was being prepared, we still witnessed aftershocks of the 2008 financial crisis and the further rise of populist parties, and, in some places, governments. In Europe, the decision by the United Kingdom to leave the EU and the political and policy uncertainty related to that, caused many to worry, as did the regional conflict between (parts of) Catalonia and Spain. In the US, the election of Donald Trump as President increased uncertainty. These current, complex and to some extent unforeseen processes have regional dimensions in common, in the sense that the processes have much to do with geographical "cold spots". These are regions that find themselves below average and falling further behind in social, economic and sometimes cultural, terms. This was demonstrated by voting patterns in British and US elections, and have caused what some refer to as "touring journalism" in which reporters seek out small places to try to "understand these people". What we argue though is that understanding regional problems and how they have political, social and economic ramifications at the national level asks for "deep explanations" in which the historical dimension cannot be absent. This is a view that is gaining currency within Regional Studies, and to which we adhere as well.

Aim and key questions of the book

The past plays a crucial role in our understanding as well strategically supporting regional economic development. History signifies the role played by institutional and cultural legacies that inform choices between different policy options. In that respect history becomes crucial for both Regional Studies and the practice of regional policy. However, while regional economic evolution and development policies are the object of research in both the social sciences and the humanities, interdisciplinary connections are scarce. To develop this a bit further, this book is based on two empirical premises reinforced by our observations as researchers and teachers on regions. First, academic teaching and research on regions is often bound up in either nationalist methodologies, or very localist/local government issues. In our own teaching and professional lives, we have observed the need for works dealing with regions that can be used in courses directed towards undergraduate and graduate students, but also for researchers in the field. Second, while disciplinary walls sometimes cause problems within the social sciences (geography, sociology, political science etc.) those walls are thicker and more persistent between social sciences and the humanities. In order to develop our understanding of regional development and regional policy, multidisciplinary perspectives are needed.

Through this volume we wanted to explore the connections between both domains, extracting benefits of interdisciplinary cooperation for the development of Regional Studies as a field. As editors this meant we also had to question our own assumptions about ways to think about and approach knowledge, since one of us is a trained historian, the other a political scientist. We experienced ourselves how scholars from the social sciences can learn from historians that a longer time perspective is crucial to understand how regions develop, and what the impact of regional policies are. Likewise, we saw how historians can benefit from the theoretical and conceptual strengths of social science. It was our hope that this collection of theoretical and empirical essays should stimulate the study of regions across disciplinary boundaries, and we set out the work with three aims in sight:

- to stimulate the study of regional development and its accompanying policies across disciplinary boundaries.
- to connect the study of history with the social sciences through examples that both illustrate its usefulness and give directions for the future.
- to show how understandings of the past (history) is vital for shaping policies for the present and the future, thus fulfilling the promise of regional studies not only to be multidisciplinary but also to span the gap between research and policy practice.

This volume critically investigates theoretical approaches to regional studies in the intersections of social science and history, explores possibilities that can open up through methodological innovation and cooperation between the disciplines and showcases the values of improved theory and methodology through a series of case studies. Thus, the first part of this book (Disciplinary and theoretical explorations) critically reviews analytical approaches that incorporate elements of the past, such as evolutionary economic geography, historical institutionalism and behavioural psychology. The second part (Innovations in research design and methodology) engages with different analytical frameworks, including attention to methods and data like time series. Finally, the third part marks the interdisciplinary field with the help of case studies in several countries, regions and sectors.

This book would not have happened without the stimulus provided by the Regional Studies Association (RSA). As part of the 50th anniversary celebration of the Regional Studies Association, the Research Network on Regional Economic and Policy History (ReHi) was launched as one of several supported research networks. The aim of the network was similar to the broader aim of this book; to connect social scientists and historians within the field of regional research, which would in turn facilitate a deeper understanding of the roles played by history in regional development in general, and in regional policy-making specifically. Many of the contributions to this book have as their origin presentations that took place at the inaugural workshop of the network, held in London on April 25–26, 2017. The workshop focused on "stock-taking" of the connections that already exist between history and regional studies, and explored existing points of contact between historians and social scientists involved in regional studies, including geographers, political scientists and sociologists. Many geographers, political scientists and economists include historical perspectives in their work. This can include an occasional sketch of the historical context of economic and/or political processes. Additionally, concepts such as "learning region" or "regional resilience" are closely related to historical studies and analyze long- or medium-term processes which have a historical dimension. Simultaneously, the historical sciences have a long tradition of studying regional economic development and a vast body of work exists. Agglomerated economies are an important subject in the historiography about economic growth. Besides, historians make use of concepts borrowed from economic geography. For example, business historians have operationalized concepts such as "industrial districts" and "clusters" in order to explain the dynamics of regional economies. Furthermore, planning and economic policies also include themes for historical analysis. These and other dimensions of the social sciences provide a point of contact between historians and scholars with a regional studies background. The two days were divided into the guiding themes of ideas, methodologies and case studies, with four panels exploring theory, conceptual developments, variations in measurements and regional policies. That and subsequent workshops organized by the network have also inspired the editors when looking for complementary contributions to the volume.

Content of the book

Disciplinary and theoretical explorations

The benefits of interdisciplinary collaboration for theoretical development of Regional Studies and History, is explored in the first part of the book. The scene of the book is set in Chapter 2, in which Marijn Molema and John Tomaney demonstrate how a particular lens – a focus on analysis of institutions – can serve as a binding agent between regional and historical studies. Together, this duo, consisting of a historian and an urban planner, show that research objects of both regional and historical studies are situated in a (regional) *society*, and that the societal basis of both sciences makes it possible to find a middle way between atheoretical histories on the one hand and ahistorical social science on the other. The chapter sketches the relationship between the two domains of the sciences, arguing that a period of divergence (1890–1945) was followed by a period of convergence (1945–1980). In this period historians were inspired by social scientific approaches and introduced explanatory models, as well as classifications and typologies in their methodologies. After the advances of regional and historical studies, institutional thinking became influential during the final decades of the 20th century in disciplines like sociology, economy and political sciences. The authors argue that this opens up new possibilities to strengthen the connection between regional and historical studies. Through institutional analysis, scholars from social sciences and historical studies can cooperate in order to better grasp the mechanisms of regional development that are driven by institutional factors and circumstances.

In Chapter 3 Robert Huggins and Piers Thompson push the theoretical inquiries a step further by scrutinizing the role of human behaviour in shaping regional economic trajectories. Emerging theories of economic development and growth differences across regions and cities are moving toward a (re)turn to addressing the role of individual and collective behaviour in determining regional development outcomes. The chapter seeks to propose a behavioural theory of how such places evolve and develop. To achieve this, the key constructs and principles relating to this behavioural theory of urban and regional development are defined. It is argued that the roots of behavioural differences across cities and regions are co-determined by two key factors, namely: culture and personality psychology. In essence, it is the interaction of these two factors in the form of a psychocultural profile that generates the human agency of individuals. Along with developing a new perspective on the factors underlying human agency and its role in explaining the growth of cities and regions, the chapter further explores this for a number of case study cities. Evidence is provided illustrating the role played by key individuals in ensuring urban and regional development through innovation. This provides insights into the policies that can be embraced to encourage the psychocultural conditions that promote the types of human agency boosting development and avoiding lock-in.

Innovations in research design and methodology

In this volume's Part II, the demonstration of how collaboration can lead to methodological innovation and therefore new insights is done through chapters about three distinctly different uses of innovation in research design and methodology: interdisciplinary composition of the research team, use of new data sets and advancement of comparative methods applied to studies of regions.

Chapter 4 is written by Polish scholars Justyna Kościńska and Mikołaj Herbst, both at the University of Warsaw. They describe how they applied an interdisciplinary approach in examining the impact of historical institutions on present-day educational achievements in Poland. They make use of a distinct feature with relation to the history of education in Poland; during the time at which the Polish education system was formed in the 19th century, Poland was not an independent country but was partitioned between the three empires of Russia, the Kingdom of Prussia, and the Habsburg-ruled dual monarchy of Austria-Hungary. The project team included representatives from different fields, such as economics, sociology, geography, mathematics and history, and combined different methods including quantitative techniques, qualitative tools and elements of spatial analysis resulting in the use of new variables. Using this varied methodology, they found that the institutions shaped during the period of the territorial division of Poland had a significant effect on average achievements in contemporary schools.

In Chapter 5, economic historians Kerstin Enflo and Anna Missiaia show the importance of coming up with new and innovative ways to enable long-time analysis of phenomena that are core to current regional development debates such as the source of inequality. Both national and regional GDP are relatively recent economic indicators: they have been systematically produced by statistical offices only well after the end of the Second World War. For earlier periods, GDP at any geographical level can only be reconstructed using data that were not gathered to this end. The estimation of historical regional GDP relies on even thinner evidence compared to the national one. This chapter provides an overview of the existing literature devoted to estimating historical regional GDP and discusses the methodological challenges faced by scholars. The potential yields of long-term regional time-series is shown through an illustrative case study of the Swedish NUTS-3 regions for which regional GDP estimates in selected benchmark years are available from 1571 to today. These estimates provide the longest series of regional GDP to date for any given country, giving a unique perspective of regional inequality from pre-industrial to present times.

The historian Martin Åberg and political scientist Thomas Denk pose the question in Chapter 6 of how social science and historical approaches can be combined in order to enrich the regional studies theme. Their chapter focuses on designs for small-N comparative research, specifically the problem of how to apply systematically structured synchronic *and* diachronic comparisons as a means to analyse interdependence. They hold that comparative sequence design (CSD) poses an important methodological option in that perspective. In contrast to standard research designs, such as cross-sectional design and development design ("historical case studies"), CSD allows for both systematic (1) cross-unit and cross-case comparisons as well as (2) within-unit analyses. It (3) opens up for the use of process-oriented models with a focus on explaining developmental outcomes among sub-national level units, and thereby (4) facilitates analysis of both spatial, temporal and temporal-spatial interdependence among sub-national level units (regions). CSD provides a tool for examining, for instance, policy-making and policy diffusion as dynamic, historically contingent processes; and, from the perspective of the historical disciplines, allows analysts to move beyond the limits of traditional case studies of regions and localities.

Empirical case studies

Part III invites the reader to look at long-term empirical studies based on regional development from Latin America (Brazil), North America and Europe, as well as Asia (China). Chapter 7, written by Tomàs Fernández-de-Sevilla and Armando J. dalla Costa, uses a common narrative approach in historical analyses. The chapter seeks to discover the role played by factors such as the presence of external (or Marshallian) economies, local institutions, industrial policy and big companies in the formation and expansion of the São Paulo automotive industry cluster. The evidence presented shows how the clustering of the automotive industry around São Paulo in the 1940s to the detriment of other Brazilian regions is explained by the presence of external economies generated in the 1920s. However, the expansion of the cluster was only possible with the application of strategic policies to protect the nascent industry in the 1950s. It was precisely the associations of local manufacturers which campaigned for the application of this type of policy, that had a bearing on the establishment of strict requirements for national content. The closing of the market forced the establishment of the big brands in the sector which, from the 1960s, acted as hub companies and hierarchized the cluster. In this phase, the role of the associations of local manufacturers consisted of providing advice and training for the autoparts industry.

In Chapter 8, Kevin Cox focuses explicitly on traditions of regional economic policies in modern, industrialized nations. In his comparison between the United States and Western Europe, he uncovers essential differences. Urban and regional development policy emerged as a clear government focus after the Second World War. Legitimated by the earlier emergence of city and regional planning, it based itself on a new mobility of firms and people in the space economy, albeit mediated by a newly-emergent property capital. It would assume very different forms in the countries of Western Europe and the USA. In the former, central states would play an important role, facilitating the movement of employment to backward areas and those of high unemployment. New towns were constructed to take the pressure off major metropolitan centres. In the US, the emphasis would be bottom-up. Local governments competed for inward investment in a market for locations. Immediate reasons for this difference include contrasting state structures, particularly in their territorial aspects. These structures, though, are one aspect of more fundamental variations in social formations having to do with the fact that in Western Europe capitalism emerged from pre-capitalist social relations, accompanied by the absolutist state. In the US this was not the case. These archetypes of policy traditions help to characterize regional economic policies in a general way.

Meimei Wang and Bas van Leeuwen provide the last empirical chapter (9), in which they examine economic dynamics by looking at urban centres in China as cores of educational development and modernization. As economic historians, Wang and Van Leeuwen combine various disciplines like political science and sociology and history, and discuss systematically the relation between urbanization and education in multiple political periods. Their findings are, first, that academic fragmentation on this topic has persisted over time, with the exception of the 1949–1978 period when research was dominated by political scientists. Second, the chapter demonstrates how different statistical definitions of urbanity and urbanites have been translated into policies of essential relevance for the schooling opportunities of children, but also how the effects of this (urban versus rural schooling) must be seen in relation to other long-term factors.

Finally, Marijn Molema draws together the picture as based on the different contributions in the volume, and sketches the way ahead for the field. It delineates a field of research in which regional historians exchange knowledge with colleagues from the social sciences, such as geographers, economists, political scientists and sociologists. The field, programmatically described as "New Regional History", is demarcated by four points of departure or "corner flags". The first corner flag argues that every multidisciplinary exchange should start from a *societal* problem or challenge. The second corner flag stands for the idea that history and regional studies should together increase our understanding of how regions were constructed, by whom and on the basis of what kind of arguments. The third corner flag introduces multidisciplinary exchanges between regional and historical studies as a rule of conduct, and the fourth commands a comparative approach and a preference for analyzing the transfer of people, ideas and commodities between regions.

Time to look forward, and time to look back

No social science consists solely of events that are static in time. Yet the relation to time in social science has often been an uneasy one, since both quantitative and qualitative methods struggle with well-known and often-discussed difficulties. Examples of these constraints are the difficulty to assess the direction of causality, or the (often faulty) memories of interviewees. Short time-frames and attention spans of policy-makers, which increasingly ask for quick and directly applicable research results, does not favour a more evolutionary approach either. However, we hope that the edited volume will help set a research agenda in which regional development will also be studied from a historical perspective.

Part I

Disciplinary and theoretical explorations

2 Regional development, history and the institutional lens

Marijn Molema and John Tomaney

Introduction

What is the role of history and historians in understanding patterns of regional economic development? Most politicians, policy-makers, entrepreneurs, and indeed, scholars are forward-looking. But there is also a growing awareness that history matters in understanding patterns of regional change. Scholars of regional development frequently sketch historical contexts of economic and/or political processes in their work. In this chapter we explore this increased historical awareness, especially with regard to the study of economic development in regions. Understanding the role of history is part of a broader trend in the social sciences, to which the interdisciplinary field of regional studies belongs. Viewing the development of cities and regions as embedded in frameworks of institutions favours a longer-time horizon for the study of regions. As such, the recent past offers a laboratory in which all kinds of concepts and theories can be tested and refined.

Conversely, concepts such as "resilience", that originate in the social sciences, are closely related to historical studies, because they analyze long- or medium term processes which have dimensions of continuity and change (Martin and Sunley, 2015). Simultaneously, historians make use of concepts borrowed from the social sciences. For example, historians have operationalized concepts such as "institutions", "industrial districts" and "clusters" (Molema, Segers and Karel, 2016). But research which aims to be policy relevant often lacks signs of multidisciplinary exchange between historical and regional studies. The gap has its origins in methodological differences between historians and social scientists, in which, broadly, the former apply a narrative approach while the latter search for general theories.

Seen from the perspective of the research object, however, historical and regional studies may overlap. Both scientific domains study phenomena that are situated in a (regional) *society*. The societal basis of both sciences makes it possible to find a middle way between atheoretical histories on the one hand and ahistorical social science on the other. A search for this middle way needs some understanding of how the traditions within historical and regional studies have evolved. Disciplinary traditions include customary practices about the incorporation of research themes, theories and methodologies. These have travelled from the social sciences in to history, and vice versa. This chapter will begin with an overview of the dynamic relationship between history and the social sciences between 1890 and 1980. Next, we will examine the institutional turn in the social sciences during the last quarter of the 20th century, and its repercussion for historical studies. We propose that institutional analysis can function as the binding agent for multidisciplinary connections between regional and historical studies. Finally, we explore the relevance of these themes for the study of regional economic development. The chapter shows how the institutional turn impacts on regional perspectives in both the social sciences and the study of history. We conclude by discussing why it is important to engage historians in current debates on regional development.

History and social sciences: A dynamic relationship

The connections between history and the social sciences are of crucial importance for those who are interested in historiography, theory and methodology. During the 19th century, history and the social sciences became professionalized and established themselves within universities as new academic disciplines. As such, they sought to define their research objects and demarcate themselves in the wider academic landscape, resulting in a series of intellectual conflicts.

Divergence (1890–1945)

At the end of the 19th century, history and the social sciences met at a crossroads. The methodological and theoretical differentiation was most visible in the German academic dispute about the correct form of historiography and the difference between history and the social sciences. The narrative approach was prescribed by the influential historian Leopold von Ranke (1795–1886). It was the task of historians to gain insight into the growth and development of the state. This insight was necessary for an understanding of the present and the achievement of good governance. As the master of a ship has to know the difference "between a warship and a cargo ship", the politician has to grasp "not only the nature of the sea in which he is to sail, but, above all, the complete recognition and grasping of the nature of his state" (Ranke, 1925, p. 43). History served politicians and policymakers, and good history had to show, on the basis of primary sources, "how it actually has been". The link between history, criticism of the sources and politics meant that historiography was strongly focused on individuals and their role in political processes, such as the contribution of important statesmen and their role in the great events of the national past.

By the end of the 19th century, the Rankean view on history was being criticized (Iggers, 1984). One of the challengers was Karl Lamprecht (1856–1915), who pursued two goals in his writing of history. First, Lamprecht contended that the field of historical science had to move its centre of attention to the social and cultural aspects of history. Second, he stressed the value of analytical frameworks and comparative approaches to ensure that history was scientifically based. Lamprecht criticized the lack of clear theories and methodologies of the (Neo)-Rankeans, and pleaded for the exploration of causal laws. Lamprecht's attempt to modernize the historical sciences itself attracted opposition. The debate in German historiography between 1891 and 1899 is known as the "Methodenstreit" and set the tone for academic debates around the world. Lamprecht was accused of neglecting peculiarity and variation in history. The search for causality did not belong in history.

In the debate about methods, two different approaches emerged which can be called "nomothetic" and "ideographic" (Windelband, 1915). The ideographical approach centres on individual and collective experiences and particularities. The nomothetic method, on the other hand, aims to generalize, categorize and find general laws. Scientists use the nomothetic method to *explain*, and the ideographical method to *understand*. The controversy inspired a distinction between history and the social sciences in the first half of the 20th century. The "ideographic" method was accepted by the historians and theoretically deepened by hermeneutic philosophers such as Gadamer (1960). Although the "nomothetic" procedure also found adherents among historians, the search for generalizations and regularities was assigned to social sciences such as sociology, economics and political science. Between historiography and the social sciences, two different (prototypical) methods emerged. The historians worked narratively, focusing on context peculiarities and tried to present a synthetic account of temporal change. Social scientists focused on the general, investigated structures and processes with a theoretical reference and tried to analyze social structures and regularities.

There were important exceptions to the broad categorization we have made so far. Combinations of nomothetic and ideographic approaches can be found during the whole first half of the 20th century as well. One of these strands in the historiography consists of works inspired by the Marxist materialist conception of history. This conception rested on a clear theory about the development of the society, driven by the accumulation of capital and class-based forms of exploitation and attendant conflicts. The Industrial Revolution and the concomitant formation of class consciousness became a central theme for historians such as John and Barbara Hammond (1920). The French Annales School of History eschewed teleological views on the historical process, focusing on the long-run development of social structures to explain historical change (Burke, 1990). Continuing on the path laid by Lamprecht, historians in the Annales tradition emphasized the importance of social and economic processes in history, opening the possibility of multidisciplinary cooperation with cognate disciplines such as sociology, demography and anthropology, among others (Febvre and Bloch, 1929).

Convergence (1945–1980)

Marxist history (Thompson, 1963) as well as the Annales School (Braudel, 2009) remained influential after the Second World War. At the same time however, historians searched for connections with the social sciences on a much broader scale. Social science, as Iggers (2006, p. 238) reminds us, "gained momentum in the three decades immediately following World War II", which had implications for the discipline of history. Historians sought to place the discipline on more scientific foundations, paying special attention to questions of method (Stone, 1977). In this view, every historical project should start with a clearly-defined problem, derived from rigorously determined concepts that direct the research process. Awareness that history is not just a collection of facts derived from the past, and that historical narrations are mediated by assumptions of the historian, required explication of their intentions and expectations. Such new basic rules were inspired and influenced by the social sciences. The impact of neighbouring disciplines such as sociology and economics was undeniable in another way as well. In their attempt to make reflections on the past more scientific, historians embraced comparative and quantitative techniques. The adaptation of these methodological aspects was closely connected with a reassessment of theories. Historical reasoning moved toward the use of hypotheses that could be tested and refined theories about societal development as a consequence. As such, historians learned to work with explanatory models, as well as classifications and typologies, so that general processes and structures from the past could be revealed (Tosh, 1999, p. 134).

The methodological and theoretical transformations led to new historical movements in various countries. Among Anglo-American historians for example, "social history" emerged which dedicated itself to research on the development on the capitalist, industrial society and the rise of national states (Tilly, 2002). Anglo-American social history was inspired by an international comparative study about long-term political development, with social and economic structures as important variables that explained differences in political regimes of 20th century America, Asia, Europe and Russia (Moore, 1966). Strong influence of the social sciences, together with multi-case comparisons, became paradigmatic for an approach that has been labelled as "social science history" (Monkkonen, 1994). The Nordic and the Low Countries, among others, also contributed to this movement. Scholars in West Germany modified the quest for innovation in history into a "historical social science" or *Historische Sozialwissenschaft* (Nolte, 2002). This approach was programmatic in the sense that it sought a new narrative of Germany's past in which societal processes and structures, instead of political events, were revealed and analyzed as the drivers of history. Compared to the social science history that was produced in other countries, the German historical social science was less characterized by international comparisons. The national focus was in line with the historians' engagement: reconstructions of the past could contribute to democratic developments in Germany. We underscore this feature, because it links to our own aspirations regarding a stronger role of historians in current debates about regional development.

As a result of the new, interdisciplinary orientation among historians and their references to socio-economic structures and processes, history and social science converged in the third quarter of the 20th century. While historians discovered the value of scientific methods, comparative research and the development of hypotheses, social scientists, in turn, stretched their research objects to incorporate a concern with the past leading to the emergence of disciplines such as historical sociology and historical geography. Sociologists dealing with "big issues in social theory" acknowledged the value of looking into the past for understanding present-day life. The rapid transition from an agrarian to an industrial society called for an interpretation which included historical perspectives and led to the establishment of "historical sociology" as a sub-discipline (Calhoun, 2003). Historical geographers developed a focus on the changing relationship between people and the environment over time (Baker, 2003).

The institutional turn

The multidisciplinary connections between the social sciences and history were strengthened, during the third quarter of the 20th century, by an overlap in research objects as well as methodological and theoretical approaches. During the fourth quarter of the 20th century, we suggest, institutional analysis acted as another binding agent between both scientific domains. The concept of institutions originated and survives in the study of sociology (Schelsky, 1970). From a sociological point of view, institutions can be broadly defined (Acham, 1992). First, the concept refers to a normative behavioural structure or a system of social rules. This behavioural structure can be general or specific. For example, a religion influences the general behavioural structure and Catholicism influences specific behaviour. Second, organized associations can be seen as institutions. Organizations have formal characteristics and are typified by explicitly formulated goals, rules and practices. This regulates the behaviour of their members. Power and hierarchical structures determine the distribution of areas of competence and the responsibility for making decisions. An example of an organization is the convent. The members of the convent are nuns who have specific tasks, such as praying and working. Third, specific forms of knowledge can be analyzed as an institution. These forms of knowledge ensure a conscious standardization of action through an explicit formulation of values and norms, in relation to beliefs, such as religion, ideology, philosophical or scientific convictions. In addition to the canonization of behavioural structures, specific forms of knowledge justify and legitimize human action. An example is theology.

Institutions and the economy

"Institutions" refers to a wide range of phenomena, but in Douglass North's classic definition consist of, "the humanly devised constraints that structure political, economic and social interaction. They consist of both informal constraints (sanctions, taboos, customs, traditions, and codes of conduct), and formal rules (constitutions, laws, property rights)" (North, 1991, p. 97). Within contemporary economics, the definitions presented by the sub-discipline of the "new institutional economics" include: "(…) a rule or system of rules, a contract or system of contracts (including their enforcement mechanisms) through which the behaviour of individuals is channelled" (Erlei, Leschke and Sauerland, 1999, p. 23). The neoclassical approach to economics that emerged at the end of the 19th century incorporated a strong methodological individualism and largely eschewed a concern with the institutional foundations of economic life. Although periodically modified, neoclassical approaches remain mainstream within the discipline, which has taken on an increasingly mathematical character, focused on the building of increasingly complex models. The neoclassical approach eclipsed alternative theorizations, which existed in the 19th century and afterwards. For instance, in Germany from 1830 to about 1880, the "Historical School" focused less on building models and more on historical data; it did not only rely on mathematics, but attended also to social-cultural interactions between agents as a development factor (Drukker, 2006). The institutional approach was used to explain how markets were ordered, and how ownership relationships developed as well as the evolution of economic standards such as measurement and monetary systems. Other alternative theorizations of the economy such as those proposed by Henry George were also marginalized in this period (Ryan-Collins, Lloyd and MacFarlane, 2017). Although marginalized, these alternative ways of viewing the economy did not disappear. Later, economists such as Polanyi (1944) stressed the role of institutions as providing the framework within which markets and economic development processes operated.

"New institutional economics", as a term, was introduced by Williamson (1975), simultaneously invoking and distinguishing the old institutional approach represented by the Historical School and others. The new institutional economics remained embedded in a neoclassical framework, accepting the underlying rules that theory determined the economic process, regarding institutional theories as complementary to (or a development of) the orthodoxy. The new institutional economics paid particular attention to the role of phenomena such as property rights, transaction costs and principal-agent theories (Hazeu, 2007, p. 86). Although highly influential, this approach was not revolutionary and was seen by its protagonists as amounting to a loosening of some of the strictures of neoclassical orthodoxy rather than their displacement.

These developments impacted upon economic history. North identified a science of "cliometrics", which used the "building blocks" of neoclassical economics (North, 1984). Such approaches developed the use of quantitative approaches to examine the evolution of economies, such as the reconstruction of historical national accounts (Bolt and Van Zanden, 2014) or the role of infrastructural development on economic growth (Fogel, 1964). New institutional economics encouraged economic historians to go a step further and draw the social context in which economic relationships originate into the centre of academic attention. Institutions originate in the society; insight and knowledge of societal development offered the key for understanding how, why and when institutions that favoured (or hampered) economic growth came into being in the first place. Instead of excluding institutions from explanatory models by taking them as given, economic historians tried to take institutional development as the starting point of grasping economic development. An important purpose of economic history became, in the words of North (1991, p. 98) "to account for the evolution of political and economic institutions that create an economic environment that induces increasing productivity".

Institutions and the political

The institutional turn was not limited to the economic realm. Political scientists focused their attention on the formation of political institutions from the 1980s. This led to new approaches, summarized under the term "new institutionalism" (March and Olsen, 2008). Among the different kinds of institutionalism (Hall and Taylor, 1996) the approach of the new Historical Institutionalism is most relevant in our context, which focuses on the influence of informal procedures, routines, norms and conventions of an organizational structure or certain political policy (Skocpol and Pierson, 2002). The focus of historical institutionalists was on longer periods, with particular reference to context and political variation. Institutions provided a normative framework for interpretation.

The concern for institutional development in political science, economics and economic history also impacted on historical studies. The rise of the new social and economic history during the second half of the 20th century aroused criticism from some American scholars in the 1980s. Skocpol's (1985) call to "bring the state back in" signalled a concern to reemphasize the importance of the *political* in explaining longer-term patterns of change. On the one hand, the state was regarded as an actor: state organizations impacted on society in general and events of public policy in particular. On the other hand, it was emphasized that the state with its arrangement and patterns of action influenced political cultures. So, the formation of groups, agendas and the way in which political groups drew attention to their claims became important research topics. This novel approach stimulated comparative studies which, while remaining concerned with the impact of socio-economic structures, focused on the evolution of the political structure of society.

The rediscovery of the political, and renewed concern with the structures of the state, was the backdrop to the emergence of "territorial politics" (Keating, 2008). Although sub-national politics is always present, the degree to which it attracts the attention of scholars varies over time. An underlying teleological assumption of the post-war period was that territorial differences would be eroded by processes of national integration and, more broadly, the march of modernity. The "political sciences" contributed to the neglect of the local and regional in its pursuit of universal laws of development. The persistence of local political claims was conceived theoretically as "revolts against modernity" (Lipset, 1985). The focus on territorial politics emerged in response to the neglect of sub-national geography in political studies. The rise of "small nationalisms", the claims of stateless nations and the emergence of regionalist movements attracted the attention of political scientists from the 1970s. Decentralization of political authority to local and regional government was often the response to these developments. New theories sought to explain these developments through the prism of centre/periphery relationships, by problematizing assumptions about the formation of nation states and by rediscovering the importance of regional political economy. Bulpitt (2008, p. 59) defined territorial politics as:

> (...) that arena of political activity concerned with the relations between the central political institutions in the capital city and those interests, communities, political organisations and governmental bodies outside the central institutional complex, but within the accepted boundaries of the state, which possess, or are commonly perceived to possess, a significant geographical or local/regional character.

Political scientists typically made great use of historical evidence in order to make sense of the new terrain.

Institutional analysis and development in space

The preceding review of the evolution of the relationship between history and the social sciences is a necessary prelude to our main task which is to apply these insights to the relationship between history and regional studies. In particular, we have identified the "institutional turn" as fertile ground for an explanation of the development of more historically informed understanding of regional development.

Regional development in the social sciences

Region is a key concept in human geography. A concern with the region is bound up with the beginnings of the discipline in the modern era. Regional geographers placed the study of areal delineation at the heart of the discipline. Regional geography in different forms became influential in many countries by the turn of the 20th century but, in essence, concerned the interrelationship of landscape and life. The "chorographical tradition" provides rich historically informed accounts of the development of the region but was left marginalized by the social scientific revolution. The growth of regional science after the Second World War drew on and reflected the growing importance of economics as a discipline in itself and in the policy world, as well as the growth of computational forms of analysis and, more broadly, the pervasive influence of logical positivism. In addition, it spoke to the needs of rapidly-growing industrial economies in the post-war period providing data to aid planning. A concern with the region did not vanish as a result of the quantitative revolution and the rise of regional science, but the problem was reformulated. Defining the region became a special type of classification problem. While classification of populations into mutually exclusive categories is a vital element of quantitative techniques in social science, the need to define contiguous areas meant that they were not necessarily as homogeneous as other classified groups. Thus, the development of complex mathematical models and theories became central to the definition of regions (Tomaney, 2009).

Political and economic crises in the 1970s and 1980s brought into question regional science approaches that looked for statistical regularities, when what was required was more attention to the qualitative factors that shape different patterns of development. In an era of increasing global integration geographers argued that regions were being reshaped by accelerating material and discursive flows that, simultaneously, were undermining the political authority of the nation-state. New research showed that the region remained an important cultural, political, and ecological category in countries across the world, albeit with great diversity in their formation and transformation. There is no unfolding logic of regionalization.

On the other hand, according to some geographers, the intensification of global flows is undermining the notion of territorial political identities. In these accounts, regions are understood as open and discontinuous spaces, constituted by social relationships and material, discursive, and symbolic forms stretched across and through regions, founded on a topological rather than topographical approach to space that ultimately rejects the notion that regions are territorially fixed, bounded or closed. "Regions" are defined by their place in networks and by their relationship within and beyond predefined territorial boundaries. Regions are "unbound". Ideas of stable and clearly demarcated hierarchies of scale are eschewed in this perspective. Indeed, the notion of the region is replaced by the idea of a "regional assemblage" or, a multi-actor, multi-scalar topological geometry. This relational view draws attention to the way in which (post-)modern life is embedded in socially-constituted and spatially stretched networks. But, in this perspective, there is a danger in overlooking the persistence of territoriality and the reproduction of boundary setting and the enduring presence of scales as expressions of social practice, discourse and power (Tomaney, 2009).

Attention to the fate of regions has been central to the emergence of "evolutionary economic geography". This sub-discipline emerged in the 1980s under the influence of institutional and evolutionary economics. The Schumpeterian view on economic renewal, so influential among evolutionary economists, was now applied to specific regions and territories. The basic concern of this sub-discipline is the "processes by which the economic landscape – the spatial organization of economic production, distribution and consumption – is transformed over time" (Boschma and Martin, 2007, p. 539). Key concepts deployed in evolutionary economic geography include regional "path dependency", "lock-in" and "resilience", each of which are historical formations (Martin and Sunley, 2011). Moreover, the institutional conditions in which regional economies are embedded are critical to the shaping of patterns of development and to the extent of resilience in the face of economic shocks (Pike et al., 2010). While influenced by the social-cultural approach of the institutionalists, the emerging evolutionary perspective focused on Schumpeterian processes of economic change and renewal. With his emphasis on creative destruction and new combinations of economic resources, Schumpeter offered a theoretical direction to study the process of innovation and provided the foundations for another sub-discipline: evolutionary economic geography. Evolutionary economists focused on the dynamics within an economic process and studied "the generation and impact of *novelty* as the ultimate source of self-transformation" (Boschma and Martin, 2007, p. 537). However, the evolutionary economic geographers combined the evolutionary angle with a spatial view on the economic process. They studied the relationship between regional concentration and economic renewal. As such, evolutionary economic geographers introduced research themes that attracted the attention of economic and business historians, who embraced concepts like path dependency (Valdaliso et al., 2014) and clusters (Popp and Wilson, 2007; Molema, Segers and Karel, 2016).

Regional development in history

Regional economic development has been an important theme in (economic) history, albeit at the periphery of the discipline. Mainstream history is more inclined to study *national* economic development – and more recently *global* differences between, for example, Europe and Asia. Recently, some historians have sought to explain differences in national patterns of development with reference to the historical evolution of institutions. Notably, Acemoglu and Robinson (2012) stress the inclusiveness of economic and political institutions as the determining factor in the prosperity of nation states. Since the late 1970s, historians have paid attention to the uneven geography of economic growth between and within states. Work by Fremdling and Tilly (1979, Pollard (1981) and Kiesewetter (2004), among others, showed how economic processes are inscribed geographically. Against the dominant national frame of reference, they stressed the role of regional business concentrations within economic and social history. Their programmatic goal was to complement the historical view on the Industrial Revolution with its important regional dimensions. These kinds of studies of regional development, with a combination of quantitative and qualitative approaches, largely fell out of fashion. However, the last couple of decades have seen progress in the quantification of regional growth. Like the reconstruction of national accounts, economic historians have worked on the quantification of historical regional development throughout Europe (Wolf and Rosés, 2018; Enflo and Missiaia, this volume).

Another, more continuous line of inquiry is the field of urban history. Cities are obviously the critical unit of analysis within this historical sub-field, which took root from the beginning of the 20th century. There are two reasons why urban history is of relevance in the search for the overlap between regional and historical studies. First, urban historians cultivated a deep concern with the categorization and conceptualization of space and place on the sub-national level.

They developed a rich typological framework (Ewen, 2016) which is helpful for regional research as well. For instance, cities are topologized by virtue of their *scale* (e.g. megacities, metropoles); political-economic *function* (e.g. port city, capital city); and/or thematic *categories* (e.g. "manufacturing" cities). Such typologies serve the comparative approach and help urban historians to grasp the development of specific places in their wider, global contexts.

This brings us to the second reason why urban history is instructive in our multidisciplinary search for connections between historical and regional studies. Urban history has been a multidisciplinary field of study from its outset, and was highly influenced by the social sciences. Especially in the last quarter of the 20th century, inspired by sociological studies of urbanization and its accompanying societal challenges, urban histories employed empirical studies inspired by theoretical models. Another characteristic of urban history which brings the sub-field close to regional studies is its preoccupation with planning. Modern cities and city-regions are, for a great part, the result of human intervention in urban structures and networks. The intellectual history of planning measures is an important theme for urban historians and overlaps with the field of planning history, to which urban historians contribute as well (Hein, 2018).

Conclusion: A new engagement for regional history

Let us return to the initial position of this essay, in which we questioned the absence of historians in debates about the development of European regions (see Applegate, 1999 for an exception to this statement). A possible explanation might be that contributors to this debate (academics, politicians, policymakers, etc.) are not interested in the past at all. But this argument is not valid: impactful social scientists include historical arguments in their analysis as well. A more plausible reason seems to be the national- and global-centred view of mainstream history, and the subsequent marginalization of regional history. Regional history has typically been associated with provincial themes, with *Heimat,* and traditionally seen as the field of the amateur or antiquarian. The programmatic goals of the historians who worked on a regionalized view on industrial development did not inspire a new generation of historians, and, with notable exceptions, historians who engage with regional perspectives do not connect to current debates about how to deal with key policy questions such as the fates of hi-tech clusters, the emergence of economically vulnerable regions and the evolution of spatial inequalities more generally – they leave this to regional studies.

Fundamental to this problem are the methodological and theoretical differences between historical and regional studies. Against the background of a disciplinary overview, we have argued that this gap has been narrowed thanks to the institutional turn in political science, economics and geography; indeed, that the institutional approaches bind history and regional studies together. Acham's (1992) threefold, sociological definition of institutions (1) as a system of social rules, (2) as organized associations and, (3) as forms of knowledge, connects to the holistic view of historians. Within the social sciences, the conviction that institutions are the result of an evolutionary process has taken root. These evolutionary convictions suggest links with historians' engagement with processes of continuity and change. When historians are willing to embrace the concept of institutions and give it a central position in their research designs, a practical bridge between the historical and the social sciences is constructed. For sure, this bridge should be strengthened by greater theoretical, methodological and conceptual clarification.

What historians can learn from social scientists is, first of all, to become engaged with current problems such as regional economic development. Regional inequality is part of history just as other phenomena such as nationalism or global connections. Regional inequality is an important theme for policymakers on the European level, as well as in individual countries and many regions suffer from economic vulnerability. Indeed, the salience of regional questions has risen in the age of Brexit, Trump and European populism (Rodrìguez-Pose, 2018). Social scientific research tries to understand how regional inequality evolves, and what kind of human action helps vulnerable regions. For example, political scientists study power structures, and evolutionary economic geographers explore the capacity of regions to innovate. They use historical perspectives in their research approaches, but do not interact with the historical sciences systematically. Such interaction has the potential to be highly profitable. Social scientists run the risk of oversimplifying the past. Since most social scientists tend towards the nomothetic approach, the warning as formulated in the *Methodenstreit* comes into play once again: do social scientists properly respect peculiarities, contexts and variations in history?

The added value of historians lies in their empirical strength and holistic approach. Most historians eschew highly specified models and schemes, because it hinders the exploration of the contingent factors that shape processes or big events. Contingency refers to the more or less coincidental circumstances which drive (regional) developments. The narrative skills of the historian help not only to understand *how*, but also *why* things happened: by analyzing the interplay between different circumstances and factors they help to grasp the phenomenon of regional development (Popp and Wilson, 2007). As such, they are well equipped to signify and understand processes of continuity and change. However, an extremist stance on the ideographical approach has its own limits. A historian's claim that every process or event is singular and incomparable gives ammunition to the idea that "history is just one damned thing after another" (Toynbee, 1954, p. 195). At the same time, there is a need to go further than understanding these mechanisms in singular cases. A multidisciplinary research agenda should, inspired by earlier traditions such as historical sociology, be comparative in nature. The discrepancy between atheoretical history and ahistorical theory might be bridged by a shared interest in institutions. As such, the research approaches of historians and social scientists can cross disciplinary divides and become complementary to each other. There is potential for these domains to cooperate in order to better grasp the mechanisms of regional development that are driven by institutional factors and circumstances.

References

Acemoglu, D. and Robinson, J., 2012. *Why nations fail: The origins of power, prosperity, and poverty*. London: Profile Books.

Acham, K., 1992. Struktur, funktion und genese von institutionen aus sozialwissenschaftlicher sicht. In: G. Melville, ed. *Institutionen und geschichte. Theoretische aspekte und mittelalterliche befunde*. Cologne: Böhlau. Pp. 25–71.

Applegate, C., 1999. A Europe of regions: Reflections on the historiography of sub-national places in modern times. *American Historical Review*, 104(4), pp. 1157–1182. https://doi.org/10.2307/2649565

Baker, A. R. H., 2003. *Geography and history: Bridging the divide*. Cambridge: Cambridge University Press.

Bolt, J. and Van Zanden, J. L., 2014. The Maddison Project: Collaborative research on historical national accounts. *The Economic History Review*, 67(3), pp. 627–651. https://doi.org/10.1111/1468-0289.12032

Boschma, R. and Martin, R., 2007. Editorial: Constructing an Evolutionary Economic Geography. *Journal of Economic Geography*, 7(5), pp. 537–548. https://doi.org/10.1093/jeg/lbm021

Braudel, F., 2009. History and the social sciences: The longue durée. *Review (Fernand Braudel Center)*, 32(2), pp. 171–203.

Bulpitt, J., 2008. *Territory and power in the United Kingdom: An interpretation*. Manchester: Manchester University Press.

Burke, P., 1990. *The French historical revolution: The Annales School, 1929–89*. Cambridge: Polity Press.

Calhoun, C., 2003. Why historical sociology? In: G. Delanty and E. Isin, eds. *Handbook of historical sociology*. London, Thousand Oaks and New Delhi: Sage. Pp. 383–393.

Drukker, J. W., 2006. *The revolution that bit its own tail: How economic history changed our ideas on economic growth*. Amsterdam: Aksant.

Enflo, K. and Missiaia, A., 2019. Regional GDP before GDP: A methodological survey of historical regional accounts. In: M. Molema and S. Svensson, eds. *Regional economic development and history*. London: Routledge. Pp. 82–97.

Erlei, M., Leschke, M. and Sauerland, D., 1999. *Neue institutionenökonomie*. Stuttgart: Schäffer-Poeschel Verlag.

Ewen, S., 2016. *What is urban history?* Cambridge: Polity.

Febvre, L. and Bloch, M., 1929. À nos lecteurs. *Annales d'histoire économique et sociale*, 1(1), pp. 1–2.

Fogel, R. W., 1964. *Railroads and American economic growth: Essays in econometric history*. Baltimore: John Hopkins Press.

Fremdling, R. and Tilly, R. H., 1979. *Industrialisierung und raum: Studien zur regionalen differenzierung im Deutschland des 19. Jahrhunderts*. Stuttgart: Klett-Cotta.

Gadamer, H.-G., 1960. *Wahrheit und methode: Grundzüge einer philosophischen hermeneutik*. Tübingen: J. C. B. Mohr.

Hall, P. A. and Taylor, R. A., 1996. Political science and the new institutionalism. *Political Studies*, 44, pp. 936–957. https://doi.org/10.1111/j.1467–9248.1996.tb00343.x

Hammond, J. L. and Hammond, B., 1920. *The skilled labourer 1760–1832*. London: Longmans, Green and Co.

Hazeu, C.A., 2007. *Institutionele economie: Een optiek op organisatie – en sturingsvraagstukken*. Bussum: Coutinho.

Hein, C., 2018. The what, why, and how of planning history. In: C. Hein, ed. *The Routledge handbook of planning history*. London: Routledge. Pp. 1–10. https://doi.org/10.4324/9781315718996

Iggers, G. G., 1984. The "Methodenstreit" in international perspective. The reorientation of historical studies at the turn from the nineteenth to the twentieth century. *Storia Della Storiografia*, 6, pp. 21–32.

Iggers, G. G., 2006. The professionalization of historical studies and the guiding assumptions of modern historical thought. In: L. Kramer and S. Maza, eds. *A companion to western historical thought*. Malden, Massachusetts: Blackwell. Pp. 225–242. https://doi.org/10.1002/9780470998748

Keating, M., 2008. Thirty years of territorial politics. *West European Politics*, 31(1–2), 60–81. https://doi.org/10.1080/01402380701833723

Kiesewetter, H., 2004. *Industrielle revolution in Deutschland. Regionen als Wachstumsmotoren*. Stuttgart: Franz Steiner Verlag.

Lipset, S. M., 1985. The revolt against modernity. In: S. M. Lipset, ed. *Consensus and conflict. Essays in political sociology*. New Brunswick, NJ: Transaction. Pp. 253–294.

March, J. G. and Olsen, J. P., 2008. Elaborating the "New Institutionalism". In: R. A. W. Rhodes, S. Binder, and A. B. Rockman, eds. *The Oxford handbook of political institutions*. Oxford: Oxford University Press. Pp. 3–20. https://doi.org/10.1093/oxfordhb/9780199548460.001.0001

Martin, R. and Sunley, P., 2011. Conceptualizing cluster evolution: Beyond the life cycle model? *Regional Studies*, 45(10), pp. 1299–1318. https://doi.org/10.1080/00343404.2011.622263

Martin, R. and Sunley, P., 2015. On the notion of regional economic resilience: Conceptualization and explanation. *Journal of Economic Geography*, 15(1), pp. 1–42. https://doi.org/10.1093/jeg/lbu015

Molema, M., Segers, Y. and Karel, E., 2016. Introduction: Agribusiness clusters in Europe, 19th and 20th centuries. *The Low Countries Journal of Social and Economic History*, 13(4), pp. 1–16. http://doi.org/10.18352/tseg.894

Monkkonen, E. H., 1994. *Engaging the past: The uses of history across the social sciences*. Durham: Duke University Press.

Moore Jr., B., 1966. *Social origins of dictatorship and democracy: Lord and peasant in the making of the modern world*. Boston: Beacon Press.

Nolte, P., 2002. Historische sozialwissenschaft. In: J. Eibach and G. Lottes, eds. *Kompass der geschichtswissenschaft: Ein handbuch*. Göttingen: Vandenhoeck & Ruprecht. Pp. 53–68.

North, D. C., 1984. Transaction costs, institutions and economic history. *Zeitschrift für die Gesamte Staatwissenschaft*, 140(1), pp. 7–17.

North, D. C., 1991. Institutions. *Journal of Economic Perspectives*, 5(1), pp. 97–112. http://doi.org/10.1257/jep.5.1.97

Pike, A., Dawley, S. and Tomaney J., 2010. Resilience, adaptation and adaptability. *Cambridge Journal of Regions, Economy and Society*, 3(1), pp. 59–70. https://doi.org/10.1093/cjres/rsq001

Polanyi, K., 1944. *The great transformation. The political and economic origins of our time*. Boston, MA: Beacon Press.

Pollard, S., 1981. *Peaceful conquest. The industrialization of Europe 1760–1970*. Oxford: Oxford University Press.

Popp, A. and Wilson, J. F., 2007. Life cycles, contingency, and agency: Growth, development, and change in English industrial districts and clusters. *Environment and Planning A*, 39, pp. 2975–2992. https://doi.org/10.1068/a38403

Rodrìguez-Pose, A., 2018. The revenge of the places that don't matter (and what to do about it). *Cambridge Journal of Regions, Economy and Society*, 11(1), pp. 189–209. https://doi.org/10.1093/cjres/rsx024

Ryan-Collins, J., Lloyd, T. and MacFarlane, L., 2017. *Rethinking the economics of land and housing*. London: Zed Books.

Schelsky, H., 1970. Zur soziologischen Theorie der Institution. In: H. Schelsky ed. *Zur Theorie der Institution*. Dusseldorf: Bertelsmann Universitätsverlag. Pp. 9–26.

Skocpol, T., 1985. Bringing the state back in: Strategies of analysis in current research. In: P. B. Evans, D. Rueschmeyer and T. Skocpol, eds. *Bringing the state back in*. Cambridge: Cambridge University Press. Pp. 3–35.

Skocpol, T. and Pierson, P., 2002. Historical institutionalism in contemporary political science. In: I. Katznelson and H.V. Milne, eds. *Political science: State of the discipline*. New York: W.W. Norton. Pp. 693–721.

Stone, L., 1977. History and the social sciences in the twentieth century. In: C. F. Delzel, ed. *The future of history: Essays in the Vanderbilt University centennial*. Nashville: Vanderbilt University Press. Pp. 3–43.

Thompson, E. P., 1963. *The making of the English working class*. London: Victor Gollancz.

Tilly, C., 2002. Neue angloamerikanische Sozialgeschichte. In: J. Eibach and G. Lottes, eds., *Kompass der Geschichtswissenschaft: Ein Handbuch*. Göttingen: Vandenhoeck & Ruprecht.

Tomaney, J., 2009. Region. In: R. Kitchin and N. Thrift, eds. *International encyclopedia of human geography*, vol. 9. Oxford: Elsevier. Pp. 136–150.

Tosh, J., 1999. *The pursuit of history*. Harlow: Longman.

Toynbee, A., 1954. *A study of history*, vol. 9. London: Oxford University Press.

Valdaliso, J. M., Magro, E., Navarro, M., Aranguren, M. J. and Wilson, J. R., 2014. Path dependence in policies supporting smart specialisation strategies: Insights from the Basque case. *European Journal of Innovation Management*, 17(4), pp. 390–408. https://doi.org/10.1108/EJIM-12-2013-0136

von Ranke, L., 1925. *Das politische Gespräch und andere Schriftchen zur Wissenschaftslehre, Philosophie und Geisteswissenschaften; Bd. 2; Philosophie und Geisteswissenschaften*. Halle: M. Niemeyer.

Williamson, O. E., 1975. *Markets and hierarchies: Analysis and antitrust implications (a study in the economics of internal organization)*. New York: Free Press.

Windelband, W., 1915. *Präludien: Aufsätze und Reden zur Einleitung in die Philosophie und ihrer Geschichte*. Tübingen: Mohr.

Wolf, N. and Rosés, J. R. eds., 2018. *The economic development of Europe's regions: A quantitative history since 1900*. New York: Routledge.

3 Behavioural economic geography and regional history

Explaining uneven development from a human perspective

Robert Huggins and Piers Thompson

Introduction

Explanations of economic development and growth differences across regions are generally rooted in factors based on the structure, dynamics and organization of firms, industries and capital. Emerging theories, however, are moving toward a (re)turn to addressing the role of individual and collective behaviour in determining regional development outcomes (Obschonka et al., 2013). Contemporaneously, a greater focus has been given to the behaviour of those associated with the political economy of cities and regions as a form of agency that determines the future of these places (Beer and Clower, 2014). Indeed, leading scholars such as Chang (2013) and Piketty (2014), for example, highlight the role of political leadership in determining economic outcomes. More generally, a number of concepts relating to the behaviour of individuals and groups of individuals have taken an increasingly central role in shaping an understanding of why some places are better able to generate higher rates of development and growth, and avoid the low-road development trajectories and associated higher rates of inequality found in weaker regions (Huggins and Thompson, 2019; Huggins et al., 2018; Tabellini, 2010; Tubadji, 2013).

A behavioural approach is not strictly "new" in either comparative economics or economic geography. Myrdal (1968), for instance, takes a behavioural and cultural approach to understanding economic development across Asian economies, in particular the role of religious and social (caste) systems. From the 1960s there was also an emerging school of behavioural geography largely concerned with identifying the cognitive processes that led to individuals and communities codifying, reacting to, and recreating their environments. Pred (1967), in particular, argued that economic geographic and locational distribution patterns are a consequence of the aggregate manifestation of decisional acts made at the individual, group and/or firm level.

Given a range of theoretical developments in recent years, it would appear appropriate to examine behavioural explanations of regional growth and development. Based on thinking from behavioural economics, some scholars suggest that individual decision-making results from local influences experienced through situations. Such "situations" equate to the dominant cultural traits embedded within the local communities where these "influences" are formed (Storper, 2013). Behavioural economics generally concerns the integration of psychological theories of behaviour as a means of explaining economic action (Cartwright, 2014). Such theories have increasingly shown the limits of rational-choice theories in explaining economic as well as social action and the underlying decision-making processes of individuals in determining such action (Hodgson, 2013).

The aim of this chapter is to propose a behavioural theory of how such cities and regions evolve and develop. The chapter outlines the key constructs and principles relating to this behavioural theory of urban and regional development, and argues that the roots of behavioural differences across cities and regions are co-determined by two key factors, namely: culture and personality psychology. In essence, it is the interaction of these two factors that form the human agency of individuals. Based on a historic perspective and building on institutional theory, the chapter proposes that research needs to pay more attention to the "pyschocultural life" of cities and regions when seeking to understand differing types of behaviour and their relationship with economic development outcomes. In summary, the fundamental objective is to argue that in order to explain why economic development is more advanced in some places than others, it is necessary to move beyond the known factors and mechanisms of such development, and to analyze deeper and more fundamental and historically entrenched causes of uneven development.

Human behaviour and regional development

Drawing on Simon's (1982) notion of "bounded rationality", behavioural economics suggests that the minds of individuals are required to be understood in terms of the environmental context in which they have evolved, resulting in restrictions to human information processing, due to limits in knowledge and computational capacity (Kahneman, 2003). Similarly, the rise in importance given to cultural values in regional development theory has led to the emergence of a "new sociology of development" that entwines the role of geography with factors relating to individual and collective behaviour (Sachs, 2000; Hadjimichalis, 2006; Spigel, 2013). As Clark (2015) argues, human behaviour is fundamental to the social sciences in terms of understanding what people do, where and why they do it, and the costs and benefits of this behaviour. In order to understand the "aggregate" differences in socio-economic activities and performance there is a need to explore how these differences stem from the experiences and actions of individual actors (Ariely, 2008; Storper, 2013).

The issue of how cultural factors impact on urban and regional development, in innovation and entrepreneurial-led development (Spigel, 2013), has been increasingly debated in recent years (Tubadji and Nijkamp, 2015). In particular, recent work on socio-spatial culture and the spatial nature of personality psychology has sought to address knowledge gaps relating to the role of context and environment in shaping behaviour (Beugelsdijk, 2009; Obschonka et al.,

2013). The fact that concepts such as "tolerance" are found to be associated with the form and trajectory of urban and regional development is an indication of the apparent importance of psychological and behavioural dimensions in determining these trajectories (Florida, 2002; Storper, 2013). From this psychological perspective, Obschonka et al. (2015), for example, draw from the "five-factor theory of personality – the big five traits", which is the predominant personality model in contemporary psychological science – to explain such differences in behaviour across places. Rentfrow et al. (2013) have identified three psychological profiles of regions – friendly and conventional, relaxed and creative, temperamental and uninhibited – covering the US states. They find that in terms of economic prosperity a positive link exists with openness and extraversion, while conscientiousness displays a negative association. Taken together, it can be suggested that culture and personality psychology form the psycho-cultural behaviour of a city.

These psychocultural behaviours have the potential to be persistent and deeply rooted in previously dominant economic activities, so that their influence is felt many decades later. For example, a historically high level of mining is found to be associated with lower entrepreneurial activity (Glaeser et al., 2015), positive attitudes to collective behaviour in the form of unionism (Holmes, 2006), and preferences against redistribution (Couttenier and Sangier, 2015). Therefore, there are strong reasons to suggest that the concentration of large-scale coal-based industries in mature regions, for example, leave a lasting psychological imprint on local culture of the old industrial regions, with selective outmigration resulting in more optimistic and resilient individuals with positive and agentic mindsets seeking new environments that offer new economic opportunities, resulting in an indigenous population in the home region lacking in "entrepreneurial spirit" (Stuetzer et al., 2016; Obschonka et al., 2018). Others suggest that these regions now suffer from a case of "social haunting", whereby there is a kind of "ghosted" affective atmosphere that has endured long after the traditional industries associated with these regions have disappeared (Gordon, 1997; Bright, 2016).

In general, an acknowledgement of these cultural and psychological factors has given rise to calls to examine the role of behavioural traits in promoting or hindering regional renewal, resilience and transformation (Martin and Sunley, 2015). In recent years, scholars have also increasingly highlighted the role of agency and associated institutions in fostering urban and regional development, particularly through the welfare effects it generates within and through communities (Bristow and Healy, 2014). A growing literature also suggests that the development of cities and regions is linked to the types of key agents within these places (Storper, 2013; Savini, 2016). Others note the role of agency in hindering urban and regional development, with rent-seeking behaviour being an example of the potentially negative development outcomes resulting from, for example, political agency (Ayres, 2014).

As indicated above, studies have frequently found a role for personality traits, culture and institutions in determining economic growth, but equally it should be noted that there are important differences between each of these factors.

In fundamental terms, these factors work at different levels of aggregation. Whilst personality traits are individually held, community culture concerns the shared values, beliefs and expectations of a group (Van Maanen and Schein, 1979). Hofstede (1980) refers to culture as systems of meaning within and across ascribed and acquired social groups, and the collective programming of the mind. Institutions, on the other hand, have been described as the rules of the game (Hwang and Powell, 2005). In the literature stemming from economic and political science, in particular, institutions act through rules, procedures and agreements (North, 1990; 2005). The following sections analyze the role of institutions, culture, personality psychology and agency in further detail.

Institutions and culture

Effective institutions have a key role in shaping the success of cities and regions (Storper, 2010). In this sense, formal institutions are not necessarily restricted to being the rules of the game, but also include regulatory aspects such as the monitoring and enforcement of these rules (Scott, 2008). Institutions, therefore, can promote, hold back or even shape particular economic activities that facilitate urban and regional competitiveness and development, such as entrepreneurship and innovation (Peng et al., 2010; Stenholm et al., 2013). Although enforcement and monitoring may vary across the cities and regions of nations, informal institutions in the form of socially accepted norms within professional and organizational interaction, as well as the cognitive dimensions of institutions are also likely to vary across cities and regions (Scott, 2008). This means that alongside the role of more formal institutions, it is becoming increasingly recognized that the individual actions leading to places being better positioned to take higher economic development roads are encouraged or limited by local and regional influences, whereby these influences are formed by the dominant cultural traits embedded in local communities (Storper, 2013). Furthermore, the role of institutions in development has been acknowledged, and it is, therefore, a fairly reasonable assumption to extend this to cultural influences. As well as the incentives and constraints that institutions and culture provide, they are themselves also reflective of human agency (Bristow and Healy, 2014). As such, a growing number of studies have considered the link between community culture and economic activities, and resultant rates of economic development (Huggins and Thompson, 2014; Tubadji and Nijkamp, 2015).

One of the most commonly analyzed aspects of culture is social cohesion, which reflects the complexity of the cultural-economic growth relationship. Whilst studies such as Easterly et al. (2006) have found social cohesion, as captured by the lack of ethnic fractionalization, to be positively associated with economic growth, greater social cohesion is thought to reduce transaction costs and improve cooperation and information flows (Beugelsdijk and van Schaik, 2005; Kwon and Adler, 2014; Putnam et al., 1993). This is achieved through the generation of greater trust from the development of social capital (Dasgupta, 2011).

Institutions associated with publically-funded education may have a key role in developing the common social norms that benefit society (Gradstein and Justman, 2000). Such cooperation and collaboration are considered to be key components of the innovative activities required to achieve lasting economic growth (Rutten and Boekema, 2007). It is no surprise, therefore, that where deep divisions exist within communities these are often associated with poorer economic performance (Aghion et al., 2004). However, social cohesion may also have a downside when it leads to rent-seeking behaviour by dominant groups and produces insider–outsider problems (Rodríguez-Pose and Storper, 2006).

As well as the role of social cohesion, another group of studies inspired by Florida (2002) have found that open tolerant societies grow faster, reflecting the attraction of both conventional human capital and a greater presence of the creative class (Florida et al., 2008). This may allow access to more ideas, but can also help exploit the knowledge held and developed within an area as more diverse sets of skills become available. Studies also suggest that migrants may be better placed to see the opportunities available by providing a fresh pair of eyes and drawing on international and extra-local networks (Levie, 2007). For example, Rodríguez-Pose and Hardy (2015) examine the link between diversity and entrepreneurial activity and find that place of birth diversity, rather than ethnic background, has the strongest relationship with entrepreneurship.

Given these counteracting forces, it is no surprise that empirical studies have provided mixed evidence in terms of the association between economic growth and social cohesion with both significant positive (Guiso et al., 2004; Knack and Keefer, 1997; Zak and Knack, 2001), and insignificant results found (Rodríguez-Pose, 2001). A further group of studies find evidence of a relationship between social capital and improved performance at the level of individual firms, but there is less evidence of this when considering a region or locality as a whole (Cooke et al., 2005). Conflicts may also arise from the need to distinguish between bonding and bridging social capital (Putnam, 2000). Whereas bridging social capital may reduce rent-seeking behaviour and provide access to knowledge, bonding social capital may promote the achievement of non-materialistic objectives, sometimes at the expense of economic growth (Beugelsdijk and Smulders, 2003). In a similar vein, Bjørnskov (2006) finds that only social trust is related to outcomes such as improved governance and life satisfaction. On the other hand, some studies find that associational activity, and the weak ties this generates, is of particular importance for economic activity related to innovation (Hauser et al., 2007). Furthermore, the form of social capital and associated policy interventions may also vary depending on the type of innovation sought, for example traditional, hidden or social (Murphy et al., 2016). The complexities of the association between cultural measures and economic performance measures are further compounded by studies that find links between economic growth and individualism and a lack of collectivism and more "masculine" cultures (Gorodnichenko and Roland, 2016; Huggins and Thompson, 2016).

A further direction for investigation returned to in more detail below is that it is not always appropriate to study cultural dimensions purely in terms of one aspect, but rather through specific combinations. For example, social cohesion may have positive effects when combined with an openness to ideas, but equally could form a further barrier when combined with a limited acceptance of ideas from outside a community (Adler and Kwon, 2000). Similarly, Stephan and Uhlaner (2010) use seven of House et al.'s (2004) nine dimensions of descriptive norms to create measures reflecting performance-based culture (rewarding individual accomplishment rather than collective membership, family relationships), and socially supportive culture (promoting support and cooperation). They find that the norms combining to generate a performance-based culture are associated with demand for entrepreneurial activities, whilst the norms generating socially supportive culture with close links to social capital increase the supply of entrepreneurs.

Psychology and personality science

In parallel with theoretical and empirical developments concerning the influence of culture on economic growth, another stream of literature has considered how individual behaviour may have an impact at the aggregate and spatial level (Obschonka et al., 2013; Stuetzer et al., 2016). There have long been studies within psychology and personality science with regard to the different personality traits possessed by individuals (Cattell, 1943). As indicated above, one of the most commonly utilized approaches is that associated with the Big Five framework, which consists of the identification and measurement of the following concepts: extraversion, agreeableness, conscientiousness, neuroticism and openness (Costa and McCrae, 1992). Studies have found that more extravert individuals tend to exhibit higher levels of sociability and energy, whilst prosocial behaviour as captured by the notion of agreeableness is found to be linked to factors such as social capital and reduced crime (Rentfrow, 2010; Rentfrow et al., 2008). Conscientiousness is associated with individual levels of organization and self-discipline, with neuroticism reflecting differences in anxiety and depression. The concept of openness is associated with individual differences in curiosity and liberal values. Whilst such measures have traditionally been used to examine how particular personalities may lead to particular behaviour and outcomes at the individual level (Judge et al., 1999), the use of large surveys has allowed much bigger databases that compare personality traits across nations to be established (Schmitt et al., 2007). The size of these surveys has allowed an examination of the distribution of personality traits across different areas of countries such as the United States (Rentfrow, 2010; Rentfrow et al., 2009) and the United Kingdom (Rentfrow et al., 2015).

Unlike cultural norms, which are formed at the group level, these personality traits are based on the individual, but where a place has a relatively larger proportion of individuals with particular types of personality, this may affect local or regional factors such as economic or other quality of life outcomes (Obschonka et al., 2013). There is a recognition that activities such as innovation and entrepreneurship are likely to be promoted by certain cultural characteristics or the presence of particular personality traits (Wyrwich, 2015). Rentfrow et al. (2015) find a positive link between economic prosperity and openness and extraversion, whilst conscientiousness displays a negative association. This is interesting as Lee (2017) finds that conscientiousness in England and Wales is positively associated with innovation as captured by patenting activity.

As with community culture, the majority of psychological research has examined the impact of particular individual personality traits on a variety of outcomes in isolation. However, in order to move beyond these single variable perspectives at the local and regional level, there is a need for a more holistic conceptualization of these factors (Rentfrow et al., 2013), especially as certain configurations of traits have been found to be good predictors of developmental outcomes such as: achievement at school (Hart et al., 2003); the development of social support networks (Caspi, 2000); older age health issues such as the prevalence of strokes and heart disease (Chapman and Goldberg, 2011); and the likelihood of having spells in unemployment (Caspi, 2000). Understandably, where such configurations are more prevalent in a locality or region it would be expected that community outcomes will differ. Rentfrow et al.'s (2013) study introduced a spatially-oriented perspective on personality psychology by finding and examining three spatial clusters across the United States described as: friendly and conventional; relaxed and creative; and temperamental and uninhibited. This study is one of the first to develop a holistic spatially-oriented psychological perspective, and found numerous associations between the geographic clustering of personality types and economic outcomes. However, it does not account for the role of local cultural aspects when examining these relationships.

The psychocultural profile of cities and regions

When examining the culture and personality traits present within a city or region, studies have frequently noted that the two are likely to be closely linked, without explicitly examining this link. For example, in their study of voting patterns Rentfrow et al. (2009) suggest a bi-directional relationship between culture and the presence of particular personality traits. This is understandable given research suggesting that in the long-term the genetic and cultural evolution of humans is interactive, that is cultural-genetic co-evolution (Van den Bergh and Stagl, 2003). This co-evolution can be related to theories of "generation" and "collective memory", or as "generational units" of meaningful collectives that move through time with high degrees of self-awareness (Lippmann and Aldrich, 2016). Given the above, it can be proposed that it is this interactive and co-evolving psychocultural behaviour, rather than an individual trait or aspect of community culture that is most likely to be important for economic growth. In order to understand this co-evolution, it is necessary to examine the mechanisms that have been suggested by previous studies linking the development of one to the other. First, those links stemming from culture and influencing personality are examined, followed by those running in the opposite direction.

Initially, it should be recognized that personality traits are usually found to be stable or slowly evolving at the individual level (Cobb-Clark and Schurer, 2012). Rentfrow et al. (2015) highlight three routes that may result in differences in personality developing within countries or regions. These three mechanisms act through: traditions and social norms; physical environment; and selective migration. With regard to the first of these, community culture provides the social norms that may influence an individual's attitude and behaviour (Hofstede and McCrae, 2004). This can include a pressure to conform and fit with the prevailing culture; for example exposure to a more diverse and tolerant population is found to be positively associated with greater acceptance and openness (Pettigrew and Tropp, 2006). Similarly, a prevailing culture that adheres to social rules is strongly linked to an individual's habits and perceptions of others (Bourgeois and Bowen, 2001).

The second mechanism, physical environment, is less likely to be directly linked to community culture but can influence personality traits (van de Vliert, 2009) and the underpinning culture present (Huggins and Thompson, 2016). For example, agreeableness and conscientiousness may develop as a coping mechanism in challenging environments (Steel et al., 2008; Jokela et al., 2015). The third mechanism, selective migration, may also be linked to community culture, whereby migrant individuals base their choice of location on community cultures that provide a good psychological fit with their own personality traits. Indeed, Jokela et al.'s (2015) finding that those with high openness seek out communities with similar traits is consistent with this proposition.

As well as community culture influencing the personalities of those residing in these communities, it is just as plausible that personality at an individual level will affect the development of community culture through its influence on social norms and attitudes. Although a particular community culture may attract or dissuade the inward migration of certain personalities, once within a locality such personality traits may influence community culture evolution. This may be a slow process, but where, for example, a less socially cohesive community culture attracts individuals of a more extravert and less agreeable nature, such individuals are likely to reinforce the reproduction of existing social norms associated with such a local community culture. The potential for a reinforcing pattern to behavioural development is captured by studies such as Florida (2002), which suggests that the presence of bohemians attracts other high-skilled individuals. This presumably operates through those pursuing a bohemian lifestyle helping to generate a tolerant community culture that does not exclude outsiders, particularly more extravert individuals who are willing to explore new ideas. At the other end of the spectrum, where agreeableness is higher it is suggested that outward migration is reduced (Boneva et al., 1998; Jokela et al., 2008). This helps to generate a more socially cohesive society, potentially to such an extent that outsiders are excluded (Rodríguez-Pose and Storper, 2006). Societies with more bonding social capital have been found to place greater weight on non-materialistic outcomes and a higher value on family life (Beugelsdijk and Smulders, 2003), which may become engrained in the social norms of the community culture present.

In an attempt to empirically measure differences in psychocultural behaviour across cities, regions and localities, Huggins et al. (2018) undertook a study of the UK that identified measures for three different forms of psychocultural behaviour at the local level, namely: *Inclusive Amenability, Individual Commitment* and *Diverse Extraversion*. These three forms of psychocultural behaviour integrate both cultural and personality traits, with inclusive amenability referring to places that are high in agreeableness, social cohesion, feminine and caring activities and adherence to social rules, but low in openness. Individual Commitment consists of places high in conscientiousness, engagement with education and adherence to social rules but with low levels of collective activity. Diverse Extraversion concerns places where there are high levels of extraversion and openness, as well as low levels of neuroticism. With regard to psychocultural behaviour that can be regarded as inclusively amenable, localities in more geographically peripheral parts of Britain tend to display higher levels of such behaviour, as shown by Figure 3.1.

At the regional level, Wales, Scotland and North East England have the highest rates of inclusive amenability, with London having by far the lowest rate. At the local level, there is found to be a significant negative relationship between rates of inclusive amenability and economic competitiveness. This suggests that places portraying behaviour that tends to be agreeable and cohesive do not generally generate the highest rates of competitiveness and economic performance. In other words, whilst such culture and psychology may have significant positive attributes with regard to social development, such attributes do not always appear to be the "right" ingredients for stimulating economic growth and development (Huggins and Thompson, 2017).

Behaviour based on individual commitment shows strong geographical differences across Britain. Localities situated in South East England, the East of England, South West England and the East Midlands have the highest concentration of this behavioural form. Although parts of London appear to have above average concentrations of these individuals, the region as a whole has, perhaps a lower density of these types of individuals to that which might be expected. The regions where this behaviour is least prevalent are Wales, Scotland, North East England and North West England.

As shown by Figure 3.1, diverse extravert behaviour is most commonly clustered in London and parts of South East England. Whilst London, South East England and South West England have the highest rates of diverse extraversion, the least diverse extravert behaviour is found in the regions of West Midlands, East Midlands and Yorkshire and Humber. A positive relationship is found between diverse extraversion and economic competitiveness at the local level (Huggins and Thompson, 2017). This suggests that cosmopolitanism and outwardly-facing behaviour tends to foster greater economic strength and competitiveness, and hint at the possibility that some regions and localities possess the "wrong" type of behaviour when it comes to catalyzing economic development.

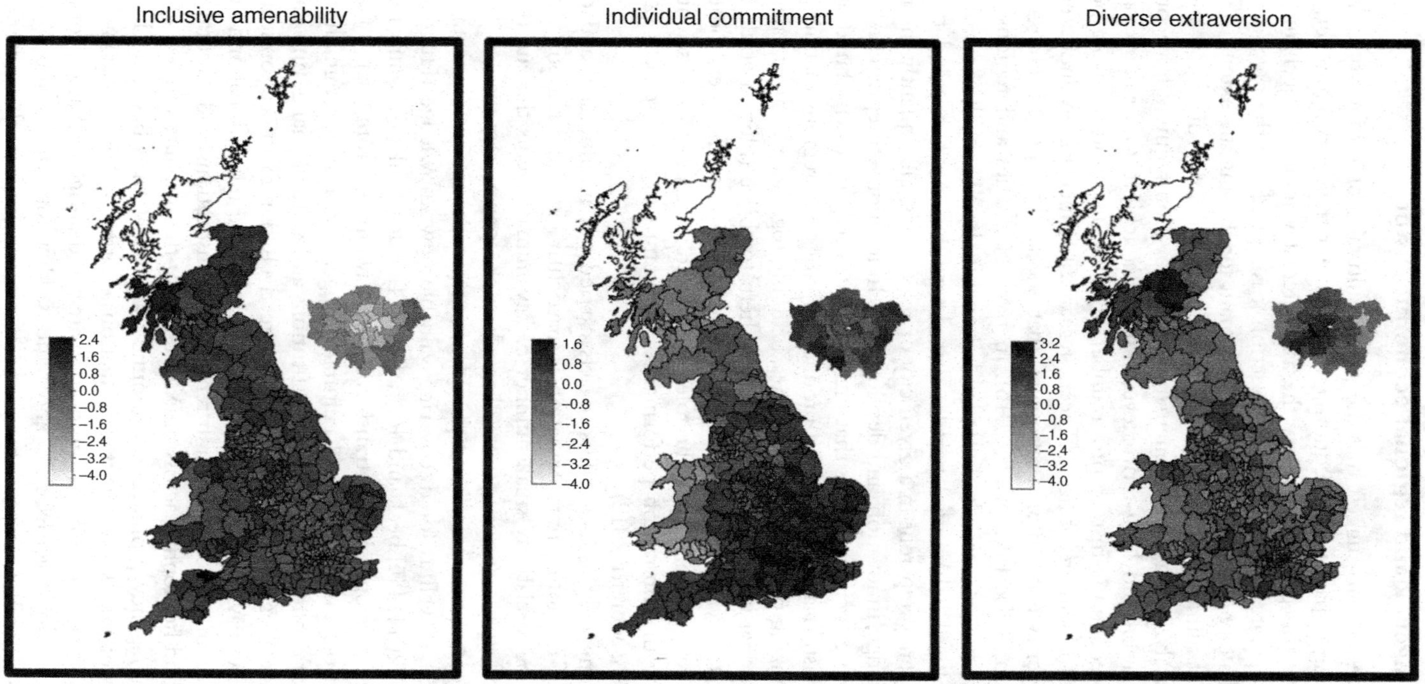

Figure 3.1 Psychocultural behavioural profiles

Human agency and regional economic history

The above sections suggest that the pyschocultural profile of a city or region has a strong impact on its economic development trajectory. However, it says little about this process and how the associated development mechanisms are likely to operate in practice. In this section it is argued that the psychocultural profile of a city or region is a key determinant for shaping the extent to which a sufficient number of the types of human agents in a city or region are capable of catalyzing the entrepreneurship and innovation required for economic transformation and long-term development. To achieve this, some examples from the economic history of a number of cities and regions during periods of transformation are utilized. Recent research has increasingly indicated that human agency is based on a rationality that is spatially bounded (Huggins and Thompson, 2019; Pike et al., 2016). In particular, cities and regions themselves produce a spatially bounded rationality based on their underlying psychocultural behavioural profiles that determines the forms and types of human agency apparent in a given city or region, and subsequently the nature of knowledge, innovation, and development. Innovation, entrepreneurship and creativity are social processes that involve groups of people who build off one another historically, and are the products of cities and regions that act as the key organizing unit for these activities, bringing together the firms, talent and other regional institutions necessary for them to thrive (Florida et al., 2017). Similarly, the symbiotic relationship between key agents and their location is found in research relating to the role of a limited number of "star" scientists in promoting the innovation performance of certain cities and regions (Zucker et al., 1998; Moretti, 2012).

Fundamentally, agency refers to acts carried out intentionally, and during periods of economic transformation in particular cities and regions there are likely to be a relatively small number of key human agents that are the core drivers of such transformation. Through such agency, regions can become "incubators of new ideas" and provide opportunities for entrepreneurship to take place, as well as for discovering valuable new knowledge (Huggins and Williams, 2011; Hülsbeck and Pickavé, 2014). Successful urban and regional economic development and transformation may emerge from forms of agency that promote institutional and cultural change, especially through the introduction of economically efficient institutions and cultural change and diversity across time. Regions that are unable to effectively transform economically and industrially may be marked by agents that promote institutional and cultural persistence, in particular through rent-seeking institutions, and cultural reproduction and homophily across time. In terms of the spatiality of these changes, whilst the agency promoting economic transformation is based on localized networks of agents, broader transformations relating to "ideas" that often precede industrial and economic innovation are based on agents that are connected through networks across cities and regions. Therefore, the notion of human agency is a useful concept with regard to integrating industrial, structural, institutional and evolutionary explanations of urban and regional development and transformation, as it represents a fundamental building block of the mechanisms and processes underpinning economic change.

A compelling analysis of the role of human agency in propelling economic transformation is provided by Mokyr (2017) who argues that from 1500 to 1700, parts of European society – largely the educated elite – developed a set of cultural traits and accompanying institutions that were highly attuned to fostering the forms of intellectual innovation and knowledge that ultimately propelled the Industrial Revolution. Specifically, Mokyr (2017) suggests that key cultural changes relating to the increased value placed on innovation and ideas occurred during this period, and through the formation of a market for ideas, a relatively small number of cultural entrepreneurs across Europe were responsible for driving this cultural change. Mokyr (2017) describes how these entrepreneurs stimulated (directly and indirectly) economic evolution on an unprecedented scale, with the interaction of cultural evolution and evolutionary biology resulting in the emergence of adaptive agents who chose whether to adopt new ideas from a series of cultural menus that led to intellectual innovation.

Following in the footsteps of Mokyr (2017), it is of interest to examine whether his key agent thesis of development at a pan-European level holds up when regional and city territories are analyzed. Although a full analysis would require extensive new data collection, one useful and bounded source of information is Peter Hall's (1998) *Cities in Civilization*. In this book, which consists of more than 1,000 pages, Hall describes the evolution of 18 cities and regions at the height of their innovative and transformative prowess on a chapter-by-chapter basis. Although Hall's own analysis may be partial in terms of its coverage, it does give a good indication of the protagonists at the heart of the regional transformation process. Therefore, it is of value to undertake a content analysis of Hall's text in order to identify the extent of key agents and their role in catalyzing transformation.

As part of the results of the content analysis, Table 3.1 presents a summary of the key agents and the time of their most important agentic activity highlighted by Hall (1998) in nine of the leading cities and regions he describes, ranging from the emergence of Silicon Valley and the Bay Area of San Francisco between 1950 and 1990 to as far back the Roman Empire from 50 BC to AD 100. Many of the agents will be familiar to those with a historic knowledge of these cities, and what is marked is that in the majority of cases approximately 20–30 agents are considered to have been the major catalysts that fuelled the urban and regional innovation and development that took place. This begins to suggest that much like Mokyr's (2017) arguments regarding the role of an elite group of entrepreneurial agents in triggering the role of the Industrial Revolution, as well as research on the role of star scientists in underpinning regional innovation success (Zucker et al., 1998; Moretti, 2012), a more historic analysis of urban and regional transformation is likely to pinpoint a relatively small number of agents as being central catalyzing forces propelling the evolution of their respective urban and regional ecosystems.

In order to consider the process of transformative regional evolution a little more closely, Tables 3.2 and 3.3 present more detailed findings from the content

Table 3.1 Agents of innovation, transformation and development for a cross section of cities and regions at key points in their evolution

City (time period)	*Key agents*
Silicon Valley/ Bay Area (1950–1990)	Alexander M. Poniatoff (1944–1956); Bill Gates (1981); Charles Litton (1932); Cy Elwell (1909); Ed Roberts, Leslie Solomon, Roger Melen (1974); Frederick Terman (1951); Gary Kildall (1973); Harold Lindsay (1947–1956); Lee De Forest (1906); Robert Noyce (1956); Stephen Wozniak and Steven Jobs (1976); William Weber, Sigurd Varian and Russell Varian (1939).
Los Angeles (1910–1945)	Adolph Zukor (1903–06); Alexander Black (1893–1994); Thomas Armat and Charles Francis Jenkins (1895–1896); Carl Laemmle (1912); David W. Griffith (1915); Harry Cohn (1920); Horace Henderson Wilcox (1883); John P. Harris and Harry Davis (1905); Louis B. Mayer (1924); Thomas Alva Edison (1887–1889); Harry, Albert, Sam and Jack Warner (1918); William Fox (1903).
New York (1880–1940)	Alexander G. Bell (1876); Clifford M. Holland (1919–1927); John B. Dunlop (1888); Thomas Alva Edison (1879); Frank Julian (1887); John Augustus (1844); John Francis Hylan (Red Mike) (1920s); Fiorello La Guardia (1934–1940); Ottmar Mergenthaler (1885); Othmar Hermann Ammann (1931); Robert Fulton (1807); George Westinghouse (1868); William J. Wilgus (1903–1913).
Berlin (1840–1930)	Emil Rathenau (1889–1890); Frank J. Sprague (late 1880s); Friedrich Wilhelm Anton von Heynitz (1778–1799); Sir Humphry Davy (1808); John Gibbs and Lucien Gaulard (1880); Nikola Tesla (1887); Samuel Morse (1837); Werner von Siemens (1879).
Detroit (1890–1915)	Charles E. Duryea and J. Frank Duryea (1893); Gottlieb Daimler and Karl Benz (1885); Etienne Lenoir (1860); Henry Ford, Ransom E. Olds and Charles B. King (1870s–1890s); Oliver Evans (1875); Nicolaus A. Otto (1876); Ransom E. Olds (1899); Alfred P. Sloan (1918 onwards); Wilhelm Maybach (1893).
London (1825–1900)	Jeremy Bentham (1784); Sir Edwin Chadwick (1839–1942); Dr. John Snow (1849); Henry Fielding (1750); John Howard, Sir William Blackstone and William Eden (1778); John Nash (1820s); Lord John S. Eldon (1819); Lord Charles Grey (1830); Lord John Russell (1839); Messrs Haden of Trowbridge (1842); Prince of Wales (1865); Colonel Sir Charles Rowan and Sir Richard Mayne; William Allen (1817); William Farr (1841).
Glasgow (1770–1890)	James Beaumont (1828); Henry Bell (1812); William Denny (1818); John Elder and Alexander C. Kirk (1854); John Golborne (1775); Samuel Hall (1834); Patrick Miller and William Symington (1788); David Mushet (1801); David Napier (1819 and 1822); James Napier (1830); J. C. Perier (1775); John Robertson (1812); John Roebuck (1760); Sir John Biles; William Symington (1801); Tod and MacGregor (1836 and 1850); James Watt (1769); John Wilkinson (1787); Thomas Wingate (1838).
Manchester (1760–1830)	John Aikin (1795); Richard Arkwright (1771); Edmund Cartwright (1786); Peter Clare (1778); Samuel Crompton (1779); Abraham Darby (1709); Edward III (1400); William Galloway (1790); Grimshaw of Gorton (1790); James Hargreaves (1765); John Kay (1733); William Lee (1589); Thomas Lombe (1721); Robert Peel; Richard Roberts (1825); Andrew Ure (1835); John Wyatt and Lewis Paul (1741).
Rome (50BC–AD100)	Augustus Caesar (22BC); Julius Caesar (1BC); Claudius (52AD); Domitian; Sextus Julius Frontinus (96AD); Marcus Vipsanius Agrippa (20BC–12BC); Marcus Vitruvius Pollio (30BC–15BC).

Source: Based on the authors' analysis of Hall (1998)

Table 3.2 Agents of innovation, transformation and development in Manchester 1760–1830

Agent	*Occupation*	*Year (Time)*	*Key contribution to economic development*
Edward III	Monarch	1400	Brought Flemish weavers to settle in various places in the north of England including Manchester, Rossendale and Pendle in 14th century (latterly the Weaver's Act 1558 freed the weaving industry from medieval regulations, and thus Lancashire enjoyed a rare degree of economic freedom)
William Lee	Clergyman	1589	Invented stocking frame, creating complex domestic production
Abraham Darby	Ironmaster and Quaker	1709	Smelted iron with coal
Thomas Lombe	Silk-thrower	1721	Built first recognizable factory
John Kay	Innovator and Iindustrialist	1733	Innovated flying shuttle which increased the efficiency of weaving two-fold. This eventually created pressure on the supply of weft needed for weave
John Wyatt and Lewis Paul	Carpenter and innovator	1741	Innovated and applied the system of spinning cotton by rollers
James Hargreaves	Weaver, carpenter	1765	Invented the spinning jenny which reduced the labour required to produce yarn
Peter Clare	Clockmaker	1778	Proposed to establish philosophical school emphasizing mechanics and similar subjects
Samuel Crompton	Biographer, industrialist	1779	Invented the mule machine, which was cheap, compact, light and could be hand-operated in an ordinary house
Edmund Cartwright	Professor of Poetry	1786	Improved weaving machine model which stopped if the thread was accidentally broken
Robert Peel	Industrialist	1787	Improved the factory system. In 1787 he built an integrated spinning, weaving and printing factory
William Galloway	Mining engineer, professor, and industrialist	1790	Established firms to make water wheels
Richard Roberts	Millwright	1825	Developed self-acting mule in 1825 at the request of the manufacturers who were afflicted by the strikes of spinners.
Richard Arkwright	Economist, industrialist	1771	Arkwright did the most to make the spinning machine useful for production
Grimshaw of Gorton	Industrialist	1790	Developed power loom

Source: Based on the authors' analysis of Hall (1998)

Table 3.3 Agents of Innovation, Transformation and Development in Glasgow 1770–1890

Agent	*Occupation*	*Year (Time)*	*Key Contribution to Economic Development*
James Watt	Instrument maker	1769	Invented Watt Steam Engine
Sir John Biles	Professor		Devised new means of turbine efficiency
John Roebuck	Inventor and Industrialist	1760	Established first Scottish blast furnaces
John Golborne	Contactor, Navigation engineer	1775	Deepened the Clyde Channel
Robert Wilson	Founder of blast furnaces	1780	Set up a foundry with first furnace
John Wilkinson	Ironmaster	1787	Iron was first used in part-construction of a barrage called 'Trial'
Patrick Miller and William Symington	Banker and Engineer	1788	Sailed steamboat on Dalswinton Lake. The speed of the boat was about 5 miles per hour
David Mushet	Engineer	1801	Found that materials mined in the district abandoned as "wild coal" contained at least 30–50% iron when raw and up to 70% when calcined
William Symington	Engineer and Inventor	1801	Fitted a steamboat with a Watt engine
Henry Bell	Steamboat developer	1812	Started first commercial steamship services
John Robertson	Engineer	1812	The original 'Comet' engine was developed. He developed it mainly for land travel
William Denny	Ship builder	1818	Built 30 horsepower engines
David Napier	Marine engineer	1819 and 1822	Built the boiler for 'Comet' and engines for the Talbot. Also established the first commercial steamship line between Liverpool, Greenock and Glasgow
James Beaumont	Manager	1828	Discovered how to use hot instead of cold air in furnace blast
James Napier	Engineer and Inventor	1830	Invented the horizontal tubular boiler, giving 25–30 percent fuel saving
Samuel Hall	Engineer	1834	Patented a condenser
David Tod and John MacGregor	Engineers and Shipbuilders	1836 and 1850	Opened the first Clyde iron shipyard. Regular transatlantic passenger traffic by iron steamship
Thomas Wingate	Engineer	1838	Made the first Glasgow based transatlantic steam voyage in 1838, the 'British Queen'
John Elder and Alexander C. Kirk	Engineer	1854	Elder's compound engine of 1854 and Kirk's triple-expansion engine of 1886 offered price and speed advantages

Source: Based on the Authors' Analysis of Hall (1998)

analysis of Hall (1998) for the cases of the growth of the textile industry in Manchester between 1760 and 1830 and the shipping industry in Glasgow between 1770 and 1890. In both cases it is clear that a series of entrepreneurs, industrialists and intellectuals built on the success of their predecessors in each city through a process of knowledge accumulation and both radical and incremental innovation that typifies the regional evolutionary framework discussed above. Similarly, the establishment of economic scale and interdependence across a range of associated economic activities within each city echoes not only the Perroux-Hirschman theses of development, but are also markedly in line with analyses of the contemporary ecosystem of Silicon Valley (Perry Piscione, 2013). As with Silicon Valley, the initial triggers of the regional transformation can be much discussed and debated, and in the case of Manchester it is suggested by Hall (1998) that it can be partly traced to the migration of Flemish weavers to the north of England at the beginning of the 15th century, which indicates some of the temporal issues that need to be considered when looking at notions of economic evolution. Indeed, the ecosystems in both Glasgow and Manchester were ultimately to enter a period of demise. However, they are instructive in terms of highlighting the role of agency in fostering transformation within regional ecosystems.

Clearly, the source of long-term regional economic success and renewal is to create a behavioural environment that fosters positive lock-in allowing innovation to become psychoculturally embedded. As illustrated by Table 3.4, this would seem to require agents within regional economic systems that promote institutional and cultural change. In particular, such agents will be responsible for creating local economic institutions that are efficient in the sense that they incentivize innovation and help remove barriers to change, which can be seen in the case of both Glasgow and Manchester. Also, successful regions are those that are more likely to experience social and economic change and diversity across time, which again helps avoid an environment of stasis and instead stimulates one of vibrancy. The problem for mature regional economies is that they are likely to have suffered from negative lock-in, whereby the available agency has led to institutional and psychocultural persistence both economically and socially, resulting in an institutional environment within which rent-seeking behaviour becomes commonplace (Huggins and Pugh, 2015).

Table 3.4 Behavioural sources of positive and negative regional lock-in

	Positive lock-in regions	*Negative lock-in regions*
Agents	Agents promoting institutional and psychocultural change	Agents promoting institutional and psychocultural persistence
Culture	Psychocultural change and diversity across time	Psychocultural reproduction and homophily across time
Institutions	Economically efficient institutions	Rent-seeking institutions

Conclusions

This chapter has principally argued that the economic development histories and future trajectories of cities and regions are at least partly determined by their *behavioural life* in terms of the underlying and dominant cultural and psychological traits of individuals within these places. These traits determine the forms of human agency to be found in particular regions, and in terms of the mechanisms and processes through which the psychocultural profile of a place may impact upon development outcomes, it can be proposed that some psychocultural profiles may better facilitate the type of entrepreneurial and innovative agency that leads to economic development and growth (Hauser et al., 2007; Stuetzer et al., 2016; Wyrwich, 2015). Indeed, the type and nature of human agency existing within cities and regions at particular points in their development is a significant factor in explaining the capacity of these places to achieve economic transformation and continued upward development trajectories. In other words, human agency is likely to be one of the key rooted drivers associated with more traditional explanatory causes of economic development and transformation, and should be considered seriously when addressing the routes available to cities and regions in their bid to foster transformation.

It has been shown that complementary community cultures and personality traits reinforce one another to create quite distinct psychocultural behavioural profiles (Boneva et al., 1998; Hofstede and McCrae, 2004; Rentfrow et al., 2013). Three forms of psychocultural behavioural profile appear relevant. Whilst one, *Diverse Extraversion*, displays lower levels of social cohesion and neuroticism and higher levels of extraversion and openness, the other psychocultural profiles display higher levels of agreeableness, social cohesion and collective traits – defined as *Inclusive Amenability* – or independent and self-sufficient characteristics, defined as *Individual Commitment*. Therefore, although individual aspects of community culture and personality psychology traits have been linked to urban and regional economic development and growth (Huggins and Thompson, 2015; Obschonka et al., 2015; Stuetzer et al., 2016), it can be concluded that they may be even more strongly influenced by combinations that generate specific forms of a holistic psychocultural behavioural profile (Rentfrow et al., 2013). This is supported by emerging empirical evidence indicating that the psychocultural behaviour of cities, localities and regions helps to shape their long-term development trajectories. Regions that have relatively atomized behavioural environments with high levels of individual commitment tend to enjoy competitiveness and development benefits. Similarly, places with high rates of cultural diversity and extravert individuals also have relatively high levels of competitiveness.

On the other hand, more socially inclusive regions, with a significant number of people with amenable and agreeable personality traits, experience relatively low rates of competitiveness. To a large extent, the findings make intuitive sense with, for example, the individual commitment found in competitive localities and regions being a manifestation of a "personal competitiveness" that subsequently becomes visible at an aggregated spatial level. Clearly, however, the relationship between psychocultural human behaviour and urban and regional development and competitiveness is unlikely to be a direct one. It is more likely that behaviour initially impacts upon on other sources of competitiveness such as the form and efficiency of local agents and institutions. Positive urban and regional growth and development, therefore also requires high-quality institutions, in the form of growth-enabling rules and incentives, alongside the types of capital suggested by regional competitiveness theory. Whilst institutions can be considered to be the rules of the game governing growth processes, cultural and psychological traits encompass the extent to which such rules are adhered to, as well as the way in which they foster future institutional change.

In conclusion, it is suggested that within the field of urban and regional economic development research there is a need for further theoretical integration, particularly through the deployment of a behavioural conceptual lens that gives more consideration to historical context. Behavioural economic geography, encompassing culture, psychology and the agency of individuals, potentially provides new insights into the persistence of the long-term unevenness of development across regions. In particular, psychocultural behavioural patterns, and their evolution, provide a basis for understanding the type and nature of human agency that exists within cities and regions, and the institutions such agency generates. Furthermore, behavioural-based frameworks incorporating cultural and psychological aspects help us to understand why particular agents within a city or region may possess a proclivity towards fostering the forms of innovation that propel development and transformation. Finally, although the focus of urban and regional development narratives concerns explanations of economic outcomes, there is scope to consider further theoretical connections with wider development goals beyond economic growth, such as those related to social development, well-being and the sustainable development of cities and regions.

References

Adler, P. S. and Kwon, S. W., 2000. Social capital: The good, the bad, and the ugly. In: E. L. Lesser, ed. *Knowledge and social capital: Foundations and applications*. Boston, MA: Butterworth Heinemann. Pp. 89–115.

Aghion, P., Alesina, A. and Trebbi, F., 2004. Endogenous political institutions. *Quarterly Journal of Economics*, 119(2), pp. 565–612. https://doi.org/10.1162/0033553041382148

Ariely, D., 2008. *Predictably irrational: The hidden forces that shape our decisions*. New York, NY: Harper.

Ayres, S., 2014. Place-based leadership: Reflections on scale, agency and theory. *Regional Studies, Regional Science*, 1(1), pp. 21–24. https://doi.org/10.1080/21681376.2013.869424

Beer, A. and Clower, T., 2014. Mobilizing leadership in cities and regions. *Regional Studies, Regional Science*, 1(1), pp. 5–20. https://doi.org/10.1080/21681376.2013.869428

Beugelsdijk, S., 2009. Entrepreneurial culture, regional innovativeness and economic growth. In: A. Freytag and R. Thurik, eds. *Entrepreneurship and culture*. Heidelberg and New York, NY: Springer. Pp. 129–154.

Beugelsdijk, S. and Smulders, S., 2003. Bonding and bridging social capital: Which type is good for economic growth? In: W. Arts, L. Halman and J. Hagenaars, eds. *The cultural diversity of European unity: Findings, explanations and reflections from the European Values Study*. Boston, MA: Brill Leiden. Pp. 147–184.

Beugelsdijk, S. and van Schaik, T., 2005. Differences in social capital between 54 Western European regions. *Regional Studies*, 39(8), pp. 1053–1064. https://doi.org/10.1080/00343400500328040

Bjørnskov, C., 2006. The multiple facets of social capital. *European Journal of Political Economy*, 22(1), pp. 22–40. https://doi.org/10.1016/j.ejpoleco.2005.05.006

Boneva, B. S., Frieze, I. H., Ferligoj, A., Jaršová, E., Pauknerová, D. and Orgocka, A., 1998. Achievement, power, and affiliation motives as clues to emigration desires: A four-countries comparison. *European Psychologist*, 3(4), pp. 247–254. https://doi.org/10.1027/1016-9040.3.4.247

Bourgeois, M. J. and Bowen, A., 2001. Self-organization of alcohol-related attitudes and beliefs in a campus housing complex: An initial investigation. *Health Psychology*, 20(6), pp. 434–437. http://doi.org/10.1037/0278-6133.20.6.434

Bright, N. G., 2016. 'The lady is not returning!': Educational precarity and a social haunting in the UK coalfields. *Ethnography and Education*, 11(2), pp. 142–157. https://doi.org/10.1080/17457823.2015.1101381

Bristow, G. and Healy, A., 2014. Regional resilience: An agency perspective. *Regional Studies*, 48(5), pp. 923–935. https://doi.org/10.1080/00343404.2013.854879

Cartwright, E., 2014. *Behavioral economics*. 2nd ed. Abingdon and New York, NY: Routledge.

Caspi, A., 2000. The child is father of the man: Personality continuities from childhood to adulthood. *Journal of Personality and Social Psychology*, 78(1), pp. 158–172. https://doi.org/10.1037//0022-3514.78.1.158

Cattell, R. B., 1943. The description of personality: Basic traits resolved into clusters. *Journal of Abnormal and Social Psychology*, 38(4), pp. 476–506. http://dx.doi.org/10.1037/h0054116

Chang, H. J., 2013. Hamlet without the Prince of Denmark: How development has disappeared from today's 'development' discourse. In: D. Held and C. Roger, eds. *Global governance at risk*. Cambridge: Polity Press. Pp. 129–148.

Chapman, B. P. and Goldberg, L. R., 2011. Replicability and 40 year predictive power of childhood ARC types. *Journal of Personality and Social Psychology*, 101(3), pp. 593–606. http://dx.doi.org/10.1037/a0024289

Clark, G. L., 2015. *Behavior, cognition and context, mimeo*. Oxford: Smith School of Enterprise and the Environment, Oxford University.

Cobb-Clark, D. A. and Schurer, S., 2012. The stability of big-five personality traits. *Economic Letters*, 115(1), pp. 11–15. https://doi.org/10.1016/j.econlet.2011.11.015

Cooke, P., Clifton, N. and Oleaga, M., 2005. Social capital, firm embeddedness and regional development. *Regional Studies*, 39(8), pp. 1065–1077. https://doi.org/10.1080/00343400500328065

Costa Jr., P. T. and McCrae, R. R., 1992. *Revised NEO personality inventory (NEO-PI-R) and NEO five-factor inventory (NEO-FFI) professional manual*. Odessa, FL: Psychological Assessment Resources.

Couttenier, M. and Sangier, M., 2015. Living in the Garden of Eden: Mineral resources and preferences for redistribution. *Journal of Comparative Economics*, 43(2), pp. 243–256. https://doi.org/10.1016/j.jce.2015.01.008

Dasgupta, P., 2011. A matter of trust: Social capital and economic development. In: J. Y. Lin and B. Pleskovic, eds. *Annual Bank Conference on Development Economics (ABCDE) – Global 2010: Lessons from East Asia and the global financial crisis*. Washington, D.C: World Bank. Pp. 119–155.

Easterly, W., Ritzen, J. and Woolcock, M., 2006. Social cohesion, institutions, and growth. *Economics and Politics*, 18(2), pp. 103–120. https://doi.org/10.1111/j.1468-0343.2006.00165.x

Florida, R., 2002. *The rise of the creative class and how it's transforming work, life, community and everyday life*. New York, NY: Basic Books.

Florida, R., Adler, P. and Mellander, C., 2017. The city as innovation machine. *Regional Studies*, 51(1), pp. 86–96. https://doi.org/10.1080/00343404.2016.1255324

Florida, R., Mellander, C. and Stolarick, K., 2008. Inside the black box of regional development: Human capital, the creative class and tolerance. *Journal of Economic Geography*, 8(5), pp. 615–659. https://doi.org/10.1093/jeg/lbn023

Glaeser, E. L., Kerr, S. P. and Kerr, W. R., 2015. Entrepreneurship and urban growth: An empirical assessment with historical mines. *Review of Economics and Statistics*, 97(2), pp. 498–520. https://doi.org/10.1162/REST_a_00456

Gordon, A., 1997. *Ghostly matters: Haunting and the sociological imagination*. Minneapolis, MN: University of Minnesota Press.

Gorodnichenko, Y. and Roland, G., 2016. Culture, institutions and the wealth of nations. *Review of Economics and Statistics*, 99(3), pp. 402–416. https://doi.org/10.1162/REST_a_00599

Gradstein, M. and Justman, M., 2000. Human capital, social capital, and public schooling. *European Economic Review*, 44(4/6), pp. 879–889. https://doi.org/10.1016/S0014-2921(99)00044-6

Guiso, L., Sapienza, P. and Zingales, L., 2004. The role of social capital in financial development. *American Economic Review*, 94(3), pp. 526–556. https://doi.org/ 10.1257/0002828041464498

Hadjimichalis, C., 2006. Non-economic factors in Economic Geography and in 'new regionalism': A sympathetic critique. *International Journal of Urban and Regional Research*, 30(3), pp. 690–704. https://doi.org/10.1111/j.1468-2427.2006.00683.x

Hall, P., 1998. *Cities in civilization*. New York, NY: Pantheon Books.

Hart, D., Atkins, R. and Fegley, S., 2003. Personality and development in childhood: A person centred approach. *Monographs of the Society for Research in Child Development*, 68(1), pp. 1–122. http://dx.doi.org/10.1111/1540–5834.00231

Hauser, C., Tappeiner, G. and Walde, J., 2007. The learning region: The impact of social capital and weak ties on innovation. *Regional Studies*, 41(1), pp. 75–88. https://doi.org/10.1080/00343400600928368

Hodgson, G. M., 2013. *From pleasure machines to moral communities: An evolutionary economics without homo economicus*. Chicago, IL: University of Chicago Press.

Hofstede, G., 1980. *Culture's consequences: Internal differences in work related values*. Beverly Hills, CA: Sage.

Hofstede, G. and McCrae, R. R., 2004. Personality and culture revisited: Linking traits and dimensions of culture. *Cross-Cultural Research*, 38(1), pp. 52–88. https://doi.org/10.1177/1069397103259443

Holmes, T. J., 2006. Geographic spillover of unionism. *National Bureau of Economic Research working paper* no. 12025. https://doi.org/10.3386/w12025

House, R. J., Hanges, P. J., Javidan, M., Dorfman, P. W. and Gupta, V., 2004. *Culture, leadership and organizations: The GLOBE study of 62 societies*. Thousand Oaks, CA: Sage.

Huggins, R. and Pugh, R., 2015. Regional competitiveness and Schumpeterian development: Policy evolution in Wales. In: J. M. Valdaliso and J. R. Wilson, eds. *Strategies for shaping territorial competitiveness*. Abingdon: Routledge. Ch.8.

Huggins, R. and Thompson, P., 2014. Culture, entrepreneurship and uneven development: A spatial analysis. *Entrepreneurship and Regional Development*, 26(9/10), pp. 726–752. https://doi.org/10.1080/08985626.2014.985740

Huggins, R. and Thompson, P., 2015. Culture and place-based development: A socio-economic analysis. *Regional Studies*, 49(1), pp. 130–159. https://doi.org/10.1080/00343404.2014.889817

Huggins, R. and Thompson, P., 2016. Socio-spatial culture and entrepreneurship: Some theoretical and empirical observations. *Economic Geography*, 92(3), pp. 269–300. https://doi.org/10.1080/00130095.2016.1146075

Huggins, R. and Thompson, P., 2017. *Human behaviour and economic development: Culture, psychology and the competitiveness of Britain's regions and localities*. Cardiff: School of Geography and Planning, Cardiff University.

Huggins, R. and Thompson, P., 2019. The behavioural foundations of urban and regional development: Culture, psychology and agency. *Journal of Economic Geography* 19(1), pp. 121–146. https://doi.org/10.1093/jeg/lbx040

Huggins, R. and Williams, N., 2011. Entrepreneurship and regional competitiveness: The role and progression of policy. *Entrepreneurship and Regional Development*, 23(9/10), pp. 907–932. https://doi.org/10.1080/08985626.2011.577818

Huggins, R., Thompson, P. and Obschonka, M., 2018. Human behaviour and economic growth: A psychocultural perspective on local and regional development. *Environment and Planning A: Economy and Space*, 50(6), pp. 1269–1289. https://doi.org/10.1177/0308518X18778035

Hülsbeck, M. and Pickavé, E. N., 2014. Regional knowledge production as determinant of high-technology entrepreneurship: Empirical evidence for Germany. *International Entrepreneurship and Management Journal*, 10(1), pp. 121–138. https://doi.org/10.1007/s11365-011-0217-9

Hwang, H. and Powell, W. W., 2005. Institutions and entrepreneurship. In: S. A. Alvarez, R. Agarwal and O. Sorenson, eds. *Handbook of entrepreneurship research: Interdisciplinary perspectives*, New York, NY: Springer, pp. 201–232.

Jokela, M., Elovainio, M., Kivimäki, M. and Keltikangas-Järvinen, L., 2008. Temperament and migration patterns in Finland. *Psychological Science*, 19(9), pp. 831–837. https://doi.org/10.1111/j.1467-9280.2008.02164.x

Jokela, M., Bleidorn, W., Lamb, M. E., Gosling, S. D. and Rentfrow, P. J., 2015. Geographically varying associations between personality and life satisfaction in the London metropolitan area. *Proceedings of the National Academy of Sciences of United States of America*, 112(3), pp. 725–730. https://doi.org/10.1073/pnas.1415800112

Judge, T. A., Higgins, C. A., Thoresen, C. J. and Barrick, M. R., 1999. The big five personality traits, general mental ability, and career success across the life span. *Personnel Psychology*, 52(3), pp. 621–652. https://doi.org/10.1111/j.1744-6570.1999.tb00174.x

Kahneman, D., 2003. Maps of bounded rationality: Psychology for behavioral economics. *The American Economic Review*, 93(5), pp. 1449–1475. https://doi.org/10.1257/000282803322655392

Knack, S. and Keefer, P., 1997. Does social capital have an economic impact? A cross-country payoff. *Quarterly Journal of Economics*, 112(4), pp. 1251–1288. https://doi.org/10.1162/003355300555475

Kwon, S.W. and Adler, P. S., 2014. Social capital: Maturation of a field of research. *Academy of Management Review*, 39(4), pp. 412–422. https://doi.org/10.5465/amr.2014.0210

Lee, N. D., 2017. Psychology and the geography of innovation. *Economic Geography*, 93(2), pp. 106–130. https://doi.org/10.1080/00130095.2016.1249845

Levie, J., 2007. Immigration, in-migration, ethnicity and entrepreneurship in the United Kingdom. *Small Business Economics*, 28(2/3), pp. 143–170. https://doi.org/10.1007/s11187-006-9013-2

Lippmann, S. and Aldrich, H., 2016. A rolling stone gathers momentum: Generational units, collective memory, and entrepreneurship. *Academy of Management Review*, 41(4), pp. 658–675. https://doi.org/10.1007/s11187-006-9013-2

Martin, R. and Sunley, P., 2015. On the notion of regional economic resilience: Conceptualization and explanation. *Journal of Economic Geography*, 15(1), pp. 1–42. https://doi.org/10.1093/jeg/lbu015

Mokyr, J., 2017. *A culture of growth: The origins of the modern economy*. Princeton, NJ: Princeton University Press.

Moretti, E., 2012. *The new geography of jobs*. New York, NY: Houghton Mifflin and Harcourt.

Murphy, L., Huggins, R. and Thompson, P., 2016. Social capital and innovation: A comparative analysis of regional policies. *Environment and Planning C: Government and Policy*, 34(6), pp. 1025–1057. https://doi.org/10.1177/0263774X15597448

Myrdal, G., 1968. *Asian drama: An inquiry into the poverty of nations*. London: Allen Lane.

North, D. C., 1990. *Institutions, institutional change and economic performance*. Cambridge: Cambridge University Press.

North, D. C., 2005. *Understanding the process of economic change*. Princeton, NJ: Princeton University Press.

Obschonka, M., Schmitt-Rodermund, E., Gosling, S. D. and Silbereisen, R. K., 2013. The regional distribution and correlates of an entrepreneurship-prone personality profile in the United States, Germany, and the United Kingdom: A socioecological perspective. *Journal of Personality and Social Psychology*, 105(1), pp. 104–122. http://dx.doi.org/10.1037/a0032275

Obschonka, M., Stuetzer, M., Gosling, S. D., Rentfrow, P. J., Lamb, M. E., Potter, J. and Audretsch, D. B., 2015. Entrepreneurial regions: Do macro-psychological cultural characteristics of regions help solve the "knowledge paradox" of economics? *PloS One*, 10(6), e0129332. http://dx.doi.org/10.1037/a0032275

Obschonka, M., Stuetzer, M., Rentfrow, P. J., Shaw-Taylor, L., Satchell, M., Silbereisen, R. K., Potter, J. and Gosling, S. D., 2018. In the shadow of coal: How large-scale industries contributed to present-day regional differences in personality and well-being. *Journal of Personality and Social Psychology*, 115(5), pp. 903–927. https://doi.org/10.1037/pspp0000175

Peng, M. W., Yamakawa, Y. and Lee, S-H., 2010. Bankruptcy laws and entrepreneur-friendliness. *Entrepreneurship Theory and Practice*, 34(3), pp. 517–530. https://doi.org/10.1111/j.1540-6520.2009.00350.x

Perry Piscione, D., 2013. *Secrets of Silicon Valley: What everyone else can learn from the innovation capital of the world*. New York, NY: Palgrave Macmillan.

Pettigrew, T. F. and Tropp, L. R., 2006. A meta-analytical test of intergroup contact theory. *Journal of Personality and Social Psychology*, 90(5), pp. 751–783. https://doi.org/10.1037/0022-3514.90.5.751

Pike, A., MacKinnon, D., Cumbers A., Dawley, S. and McMaster, R., 2016. Doing evolution in Economic Geography? *Economic Geography*, 92(2), pp. 123–144. https://doi.org/10.1080/00130095.2015.1108830

Piketty, T., 2014. *Capital in the twenty-first century*. Cambridge: The Belknap Press of Harvard University Press.

Pred, A., 1967. *Behavior and location. Foundations for a geographic and dynamic location theory*. Lund: C.W. K Gleerup.

Putnam, R., 2000. *Bowling alone: The collapse and revival of American community*. New York, NY: Simon and Schuster.

Putnam, R. D., Leonardi, R. and Nanetti, R. Y., 1993. *Making democracy work: Civic traditions in modern Italy*. Princeton, NJ: Princeton University Press.

Rentfrow, P. J., 2010. Statewide differences in personality: Toward a psychological geography of the United States. *American Psychologist*, 65(6), pp. 548–558. http://dx.doi.org/10.1037/a0018194

Rentfrow, P. J., Gosling, S. D. and Potter, J., 2008. A theory of the emergence, persistence, and expression of geographical variation in psychological characteristics. *Perspectives on Psychological Science*, 3(5), pp. 339–369. https://doi.org/10.1111/j.1745-6924.2008.00084.x

Rentfrow, P. J., Jokela, M. and Lamb, M. E., 2015. Regional personality differences in Great Britain. *PloS One*, 10(3), e0122245. https://doi.org/10.1371/journal.pone.0122245

Rentfrow, P. J., Jost, J. T., Gosling, S. D. and Potter, J., 2009. Statewide differences in personality predict voting patterns in 1996–2004 U.S. presidential elections. In J. T. Jost, A. C. Kay and H. Thorisdottir, eds. *Social and psychological bases of ideology and system justification*. Oxford: Oxford University Press. Pp. 314–350.

Rentfrow, P. J., Gosling, S. D., Jokela, M., Stillwell, D. J., Kosinski, M. and Potter, J., 2013. Divided we stand: Three psychological regions of the United States and their political, economic, social and health correlates. *Journal of Personality and Social Psychology*, 105(6), pp. 996–1012. https://doi.org/10.1037/a0034434

Rodríguez-Pose, A., 2001. Local production systems and economic performance in Britain, France, Germany, and Italy. In: C. Crouch, P. Le Gales, C. Trigilia and H. Voelzkow, eds. *Local production systems in Europe. Rise or demise?* Oxford: Oxford University Press, pp. 25–45.

Rodríguez-Pose, A. and Hardy, D., 2015. Cultural diversity and entrepreneurship in England and Wales. *Environment and Planning A*, 47(2), pp. 392–411. https://doi.org/10.1068/a130146p

Rodríguez-Pose, A. and Storper, M., 2006. Better rules or stronger communities? On the social foundations of institutional change and its economic effects. *Economic Geography*, 82(1), pp. 1–25. https://doi.org/10.1111/j.1944–8287.2006.tb00286.x

Rutten, R. and Boekema, F., 2007. Regional social capital: Embeddedness, innovation networks and regional economic development. *Technological Forecasting and Social Change*, 74(9), pp. 1834–1846. https://doi.org/10.1016/j.techfore.2007.05.012

Sachs, J., 2000. Notes on a new sociology of economic development. In: L. E. Harrison and S. P. Huntington, eds. *Culture matters: How values shape human progress*. New York, NY: Basic Books. Pp. 29–43.

Savini, F., 2016. Self-organization and urban development. *International Journal of Urban and Regional Research*, 40(6), pp. 1152–1169. https://doi.org/10.1111/1468–2427.12469

Schmitt, D. P., Allik, J., McCrae, R. R. and Benet-Martinez, V. 2007. The geographic distribution of big five personality traits: Patterns and profiles of human self-description across 56 nations. *Journal of Cross-Cultural Psychology*, 38(2), pp. 173–212.

Scott, W. R., 2008. *Institutions and organizations: Ideas and interests*. 3rd ed. Thousand Oaks, CA: Sage.

Simon, H. A., 1982. *Models of bounded rationality*. Cambridge, MA: MIT Press.

Spigel, B., 2013. Bourdieuian approaches to the geography of entrepreneurial cultures. *Entrepreneurship and Regional Development*, 25(9/10), pp. 804–818. https://doi.org/10.1080/08985626.2013.862974

Steel, P., Schmidt, J. and Shultz, J., 2008. Refining the relationship between personality and subjective well-being. *Psychological Bulletin*, 134(1), pp. 138–161. https://doi.org/10.1037/0033-2909.134.1.138

Stenholm, P., Acs, Z. J. and Wuebker, R., 2013. Exploring country-level institutional arrangements on the rate and type of entrepreneurial activity. *Journal of Business Venturing*, 28(1), pp. 176–193. https://doi.org/10.1016/j.jbusvent.2011.11.002

Stephan, U. and Uhlaner, L. M., 2010. Performance-based vs socially supportive culture: A cross-national study of descriptive norms and entrepreneurship. *Journal of International Business Studies*, 41(8), pp. 1347–1364. https://doi.org/10.1057/jibs.2010.14

Storper, M., 2010. Why does a city grow? Specialisation, human capital or institutions? *Urban Studies*, 47(10), pp. 2027–2050. https://doi.org/10.1177/0042098009359957

Storper, M., 2013. *Keys to the City: How economics, institutions, social interaction and politics shape development*. Oxford and Princeton, NJ: Princeton University Press.

Stuetzer, M., Obschonka, M., Audretsch, D. B., Wyrwich, M., Rentfrow, P. J., Coombes, M., Shaw-Taylor, L. and Satchell, M., 2016. Industry structure, entrepreneurship, and culture: An empirical analysis using historical coalfields. *European Economic Review*, 86(1), pp. 52–72. https://doi.org/10.1016/j.euroecorev.2015.08.012

Tabellini, G., 2010. Culture and institutions: Economic development in the regions of Europe. *Journal of the European Economic Association*, 8(4), pp. 677–716. https://doi.org/10.1111/j.1542–4774.2010.tb00537.x

Tubadji, A., 2013. Culture-based development – culture and institutions: Economic development in the regions of Europe. *Society Systems Science*, 5(4), pp. 355–391. https://doi.org/10.1504/IJSSS.2013.058466

Tubadji, A. and Nijkamp, P., 2015. Cultural gravity effects among migrants: A comparative analysis of the EU15. *Economic Geography*, 91(3), pp. 343–380. https://doi.org/10.1111/ecge.12088

Van den Bergh, J. C. and Stagl, S., 2003. Coevolution of economic behaviour and institutions: Towards a theory of institutional change. *Journal of Evolutionary Economics*, 13(3), pp. 289-317. https://doi.org/10.1007/s00191-003-0158-8

Van de Vliert, E., 2009. *Climate, affluence, and culture*. Cambridge: Cambridge University Press.

Van Maanen, J. and Schein, E. H., 1979. Toward a theory of organizational socialization. *Research in Organizational Behavior*, 1(1), pp. 209–264.

Wyrwich, M., 2015. Entrepreneurship and the intergenerational transmission of values. *Small Business Economics*, 45(1), pp. 191–213. https://doi.org/10.1007/s11187-015-9649-x

Zak, P. and Knack, S., 2001. Trust and growth. *The Economic Journal*, 111(470), pp. 295–321. https://doi.org/10.1111/1468-0297.00609

Zucker, L. G., Darby, M. R. and Armstrong, J., 1998. Geographically localized knowledge: Spillovers or markets? *Economic Inquiry*, 36(1), pp. 65–86. https://doi.org/10.1111/j.1465–7295.1998.tb01696.x

Part II

Innovations in research design and methodology

4 An interdisciplinary approach to the persistent effects of Polish partitions on educational achievements[1]

Justyna Kościńska and Mikołaj Herbst

Introduction

An interdisciplinary approach is considered to be the key to innovatory and influential academic research. In some fields of study, cooperation between scholars from different disciplines seems to be essential. This is equally true in the case of research on the connections between history and regional development. For instance, despite many attempts, it seems to be impossible to explain observed differences in educational achievements between regions by using the concepts applied within one discipline. Working over traditional boundaries is also recommended by scholars studying the connections between the historical evolution of institutions and economic (North, 1990), social (Moore, 1966) and political development (historical institutionalists, e.g. Pierson and Skocpol, 2002; Hall and Soskice, 2001). Effective collaboration allows scholars to share not only their practical knowledge, but also different ideas and experiences. Social scientists can learn from historians that a longer-time perspective is crucial to understanding regional divisions. Meanwhile, historians can benefit from the theoretical background of social sciences. However, interdisciplinary work is often a challenge, as every discipline has its own perspective and distinctive methods.

In this chapter, we describe how we applied an interdisciplinary approach in examining the impact of historical institutions on present-day educational achievements in Poland. This work is based on a project conducted by seven researchers representing different academic fields, such as economics, sociology, geography, mathematics and history. The main objective of the research was to gain a better understanding of whether, and through what channels, historically rooted differences in institutional arrangements may exert a persistent influence on the outcomes of the education system. We expected that the institutions shaped during the period of the territorial division of Poland (1795–1918) will have had a significant effect on the average present-day school achievements.

Poland is a valuable case for research on the persistence of historical institutions. In the second half of the 18th century, as the result of a three-stage partitioning, the Polish-Lithuanian Commonwealth was carved up between its three neighbours: the Russian Empire, the Kingdom of Prussia and Habsburg in Austria.[2] As a result, Poland did not exist as a sovereign country until the end of the First World War in 1918. During that time, each partitioner[3] imposed different policies concerning various areas of life, including educational practice. Access to primary and secondary education varied significantly across the partitions (Herbst and Kaliszewska, 2017). After the Second World War, the boundaries of Poland were redefined once again. In our research we did not include the interwar period, the Polish People's Republic (1945–1989), or the democratic transition beginning in 1989. Since the reintegration of the country in 1918, political decisions concerning different sectors, including education, were aimed at the reintegration of the state (Trzebiatowski, 1970). However, recent studies show that the divisions between three former partitions are still visible (e.g. Bartkowski, 2003; Herbst, 2012; Wysokińska, 2011). Therefore, regional differences in Poland remain a very interesting subject for researchers. Due to the numerous border changes, the Polish case is well-suited for the theory of path dependency and longue durée. It also offers methodological lessons on how to design and implement such research.

This chapter is structured as follows: in the first section, we show examples of previously studied connections between history and educational achievements. In the second part, we introduce the methodology that we used. In the third section, we explain the results of the research. In this section we also present existing studies on the impact of Polish partitions on educational achievements. The last part is devoted to conclusions.

Why history matters

Institutional persistence and cumulative causation have been widely documented within various contexts. Many empirical studies show that institutional arrangements can have an impact on the functioning of societies long after the disappearance of the original processes. While studying connections between history and contemporary societies, we can distinguish two different effects: on the one hand, of formally established rules and arrangements, and on the other, of social norms and conventions. North (1990) proposes studying institutions as "any form of constraint that human beings devise to shape human interaction" (p. 4). Thus, present-day choices may be influenced by historical processes, including both informal norms and values shared in society and formal regulations imposed by the authorities. An analysis of the evolution of these institutions may be the key to understanding present-day differences between, as well as within, contemporary states.

History also matters for education. Scholars agree that the differences in educational outcomes between various regions cannot be fully explained by current trends, such as educational policy, the labour market, or present demographic conditions. Like many other aspects of social life, educational outcomes have been studied in the context of economic development. For example, in the United States, Parcel and Dufur (2009) highlighted the inequalities in educational achievements between the northern and southern states, and tried to explain them by regional variations in human and financial capital.

The sociologists stated that students in richer regions tend to have higher educational achievements, with family variables controlled (Parcel and Dufur, 2009). The authors referred mostly to demographic and socioeconomic differences, rather than to historical arguments.

The historical perspective was included by Lynn (2010) in his analysis of the projection of educational achievements in Italy, a country that was unified in the mid-19th century. Differences in living standards between the rich north and poor south of Italy persist to the present day (Putnam et al., 1993), with northern regions performing better than southern ones. The psychologist Lynn (2010) calculated the regional IQs from the Program for International Student Assessment (PISA) studies and compared them with average per capita income in euro. The study showed that academic achievement is much higher in the northern region of the country, and declines steadily into the South, in line with per capita income (Lynn, 2010). According to Lynn (2010) this situation results from the genetic differences between people living in the southern and northern regions of the country. The author refers to the processes of migration from North Africa and the Near East to Sicily and the southern Italian mainland that took place in the 8th century BC.

However, positive correlation between economic development and educational outcomes is not a universal rule. In Germany, students in the economically lagging eastern regions tend to have higher education achievements than students living in regions with a higher per capita income (Welt-Online, 2008). Differences between the historical eastern and western part of the country are tangible. Thus, the economic factor is not the only one explaining regional differences in academic achievements. Student efforts at school can also be affected by the social norms and attitudes towards education in a given region. It is most likely that regions with a prevalence of norms and attitudes such as motivation to study and the importance of education have higher educational achievements. Sociologist Chauvel (1999) distinguished three possible models of social structure in Europe with reference to the historical argument. The first is the German model, with its weak hierarchies and limited stratification. It is characterized by high economic development and a low market value of formal education. Meanwhile, in less developed Catholic countries such as Spain or Portugal, education is strongly connected with socio-economic status. The Latin model presents an intermediate structure. Consequently, the inhabitants of countries with lower economic development have stronger motivation to gain an education. In richer states, the schooling system is more closely linked to the labour market.

The relationship between history and present-day educational achievements can also be considered in the context of past political and administrative decisions. In Europe, the public schooling system was founded in the 19th century. It should be underlined that the development of public schooling depended on the economic position of the country. Using the example of the multiethnic Habsburg Empire, economists Cvrcek and Zajicek (2013) claimed that the politics of demand for schools was not motivated by economic return in terms of wage or employment prospects, but rather by the conflict between nationalities. Public schooling was supported by the local political elites, if taught in the "right" language of instruction. At the same time, the Austrian system was known for its tolerance and inclusiveness, along with its well-functioning administration. This may have translated into positive social attitudes towards education and, in consequence, higher academic achievements. Becker et al. (2016) conducted an analysis of attitudes among border area inhabitants of the former Habsburg Empire. The economists used a border specification and a two-dimensional geographic regression discontinuity based on a micro dataset of the 2006 Life in Transition Survey (LiTS). The results showed that historical Habsburg affiliation increases current trust toward local public services of any kind, including education.

While some studies analyze connections between educational achievements and different socio-economic factors (e.g. demography, per capita income), others include the historical perspective and institutional characteristics. In researching connections between history and present-day educational achievements, scholars use econometric tools such as regression discontinuity design, and conduct data analysis based on external sources (as PISA or LiTS). In studying the influence of history on educational outcomes there is still little research which combines both qualitative and quantitative techniques from different fields. Meanwhile, according to leading researchers from the domain of education, as well as historical institutionalists (e.g. Pierson and Skocpol, 2002; Hall and Soskice, 2001), studying path dependency requires crossing traditional boundaries between disciplines, and combining different approaches and research techniques. In this chapter we present a study which corresponds with these proposals.

Methodological explorations

In this chapter we attempt to explain the influence of historical processes on present-day educational outcomes by using extensive data from diverse sources. To reiterate, our project applied an interdisciplinary methodological approach, including historical analysis, quantitative techniques, qualitative tools and elements of spatial analysis. In this section, we show how different tools applied within various disciplines can be used in the analysis of path dependency. We begin with a description of our historical research. In the second part, we explain so-called quasi-experimental techniques and their application in economic studies. Next, we describe how we measured the effect of historical partitions on educational achievements in Poland by combining geographic and economic approaches. Finally, we show how sociological tools helped us in tracking history.

Historical insight

The existing research devoted to the persistent effect of former borders on the present geography of educational achievements in Poland is very much focused on measuring the gap in performance between different regions and on verifying its robustness in different diagnostic tests. When it comes to explaining channels and mechanisms, the literature is somewhat speculative, drawing different hypotheses, but not discussing them in depth. We realized that careful analysis of the foundations of educational systems in each of the three historical partitions, going back to the late 18th century, is necessary in order to proceed to the next step, and to provide a qualitative insight in the institutional differences behind the regional education systems, which would be complimentary to the economic and geographical approaches.

The research was based on a careful review of historical literature on the beginnings of public education in the territory of today's Poland. The analyzed material included monographs, articles in academic journals and daily press, legal acts and memorials. As the number of sources and the scope of the potential analysis exceeded the capability of our small research team, we decided to narrow the review to the institutional arrangements already mentioned in the existing literature. This led to us defining three major areas of interest: the introduction of compulsory schooling and school accessibility, formation of the teaching profession and common attitudes (norms) towards education. The results of our review were published in a standalone research article by Herbst and Kaliszewska (2017). However, the literature review was also used as input to design the quantitative part of our research including the parental questionnaire, and the scenario of the interview with educational leaders.

Quasi-experimental methods in economic research

Many economic studies tracking the impact of history on present differences in socio-economic development rely on so-called quasi-experimental techniques. This approach mimics the methods applied in evaluation studies, in which the effectiveness of implemented programs, policies or interventions is assessed. The quasi-experiment (or natural experiment) allows the researcher to compare, in terms of a certain measure of effectiveness, the performance of units covered by the program or intervention, with the performance of a properly selected control group. The terms "quasi" or "natural" indicate that the experiment was not designed by any research team, but happened unintentionally as a consequence of some policy implementation, historical event or by natural force.

To be effective as an evaluation tool, the experimental design requires the participation (or lack of participation) in the evaluated program to be the only factor that differentiates both groups. However, in quasi-experiments, in contrast to standard experiments, the division of the observed units into the treatment group and the control group is neither random, nor designed by the investigator. Therefore, some additional steps need to be taken in order to ensure the comparability of observations from both groups. One way to achieve this goal is to match observations from the two groups by analyzing the similarity of selected characteristics. The eventual comparisons are made only within small groups of observations sharing the same characteristics, but differing with respect to treatment status (where being "treated" means being subject to a certain policy or being affected by some event, as opposed to non-treated observations which belong to the control group). This method is called propensity score matching (Rosenbaum and Rubin, 1983). Another approach is to use instrumental variables in order to distinguish the effect of treatment from the impact of other factors that may differentiate the observations.

Public policy evaluators frequently apply the method called difference-in-difference which relies on assessing the performance of both the treated group and control group before and after the intervention. However, this approach is less useful in research on the consequences of historical events, policies or institutions, as it requires detailed data on the period preceding the intervention, which is rarely available. Instead, historically-oriented economic research sometimes uses a method called regression discontinuity design (Thistlethwaite and Campbell, 1960). This approach elicits the causal effects of interventions by assigning a cut-off or threshold, above or below which an intervention is assigned. By comparing observations lying closely on either side of the threshold, it is possible to estimate the average treatment effect in environments in which randomization is infeasible.

Combining geographic and economic approaches: A Geographical Regression Discontinuity Design

In order to estimate the effect of different historical experience on present achievements in education we used the historical administrative border as a factor determining regression discontinuity. In this kind of quasi-experimental approach, it is assumed that location (living, attending school) on one or the other side of this no-longer existing border is random. The "treatment" relies on the exposure of individuals to certain cultural and institutional arrangements due to their location on one side of the geographical boundary, while location on the other side of the border implies lack of treatment. The driving factor is the distance between the unit and the border. This approach is referred to in the literature as Geographic Regression Discontinuity (GRD) (e.g. Keele and Titiunik, 2015; 2016) or spatial regression discontinuity (e.g. Egger and Lassmann, 2015; Hidano et al., 2015).

Our assumption, based on the studies cited in the previous section, is that local communities living along the two sides of the border may have different norms and attitudes towards education because, back in the 19th century, they were exposed to different cultural, administrative and economic arrangements. However, we must take into account that the border of interest (between the Austro-Hungarian Empire and Russia) was abolished 100 years ago, when Poland regained its independence in 1918. It is obvious that populations from both sides of the border have been mixing since then, and thus so have their social norms. Instead of assuming the sharp cut-off effect of the border, we should associate living on one side of the historical border with a certain (high) probability of originating from the same region, and thus sharing the norms that are typical for that region.

We decided to define treatment as a continuous, rather than a discrete variable. We assigned each school with a certain probability of belonging to the treatment group. For obvious reasons, this probability depended on the side of the historical border where the school was located. However, it was also related to the distance between the school and the border. We assumed that in close proximity to the border, the percentage of crossovers (that is people originating from one partition, but living in another) would be higher, so the treatment variable would take a value between 0 and 1. Moving away from the border, we expected to observe a rapid increase in the probability of treatment for the schools on the "Austrian" side, and a decrease in the probability for those in the former Russian partition. In other words, we assumed that the further from the border a family lives today, the less likely it is that their ancestors migrated across the border in the past, and the higher their probability of having "consistent" norms towards education.

Because of the association with fuzzy experimental design[4] we have called our approach a quasi-fuzzy geographical Regression Discontinuity Design (RDD). The equation estimated within the RDD is:

$$Y_i = \beta_0 + \beta_1 D_i + \beta_2 dist_i + \beta_3 D_i dist_i + \sum_{j=4}^{p} \beta_j X_{ji} + \varepsilon_i$$

Where: i indexes observations, D_i is a treatment variable (discrete or continuous depending on specification), $dist_i$ is a distance from historical border and X_{ji} are additional control variables.

Sociological research

After conducting historical and econometric research, we decided to deepen our analysis by including sociological methods. This part of the research aimed at discovering social attitudes and the perception of educational systems, and consisted of field research and a questionnaire survey. In June 2017, we carried out individual in-depth interviews in three cities in regions of the former Russian, Austrian and Prussian partitions. The chosen cities had populations of between 25,000 and 50,000 people, and were located at least 60km from the nearest voivodeship capital city. We chose medium-sized towns, because we expected that agglomerations may no longer reflect the former partitions, as they have experienced shifts of migrants from different parts of the country. We tried to ensure comparability by choosing cities characterized by a similar level of: income per habitant, unemployment rate, percentage of the population aged less than 18 years, and availability of educational services.

Qualitative methods are aimed at gaining a broader understanding of the subject studied, and the reasons and motivations that underlie people's decisions and behaviours. By using the method of individual in-depth interviews, we wanted to discover people's attitudes towards history and the partitions, and identify local traditions in the field of education. For this reason, we decided to select respondents according to their occupation and profession. In each city studied we conducted about 12 interviews with local experts, each lasting from one to two hours. We conducted interviews with local journalists, school principals, history teachers, political leaders and members of non-governmental organizations from the field of history and education. During the field research we also carried out observations by visiting local schools and regional museums.

Since qualitative research helps to gain a better understanding of deeper motives and explain decisions made by people, quantitative research can show general trends in populations. In October and November 2017, a questionnaire survey was conducted using computer-assisted personal interviews. The study was conducted on a sample of 2,500 parents of students from the last two grades of secondary schools. The respondents were selected by quota sampling in two steps. First, schools in pre-war Germany that became part of the People's Republic of Poland after the Second World War and schools with fewer than ten students were excluded from the survey. Then, the sample was stratified according to the territory (formerly belonging to the Russian, Austrian or Prussian partition). Additionally, each layer was divided into categories according to town size. A total of 250 schools were selected for the survey with a probability proportional to the number of students attending the given school. In each school ten respondents filled out the survey. Thus, the chosen sample can be said to be representative of the population.

Results of the research

In this section we summarize the results of our interdisciplinary project. Our intention was to design the research in such a way that the different disciplinary approaches would be complimentary, and provide outcomes which could be presented as stand-alone results, but could also be used as input to further stages of the project. With such a design, the order of research steps is very important. We started by reviewing the existing empirical literature on the impact of partitions on educational achievements. We proceeded with a historical investigation focused on the education-related institutions in partitioned Poland in the early 19th century. We then conducted a careful cartographic analysis of recent educational achievements in Poland, followed by econometric modelling. Finally, we performed a survey among parents and in-depth interviews with local leaders in three towns, belonging historically to different partitions. We will preserve this order in presenting the major results of our research in the following sections.

Historical partitions and educational achievements in Poland – literature review

Since the first national examination in Polish primary schools in 2002, many studies have been conducted. They show that the territorial distribution of educational achievements clearly reflects historical partitions, with eastern and south-eastern regions performing better in school tests than the western part of the country (Herczyński and Herbst, 2002; Herbst, 2004). Eastern Poland outperforming the West is not a common finding in regional studies investigating the persistent effects of partitions on present-day Polish society. In other respects, the regions formerly under Prussian rule mostly outperform the former Austrian and Russian partitions. For example, authors show that the western parts of Poland governed by Prussia are better developed in terms of economy than the rest of the country (Herbst, 2012). This includes indicators such as: per capita income, urbanization level and infrastructure density (CPM, 2009). Moreover, former Prussian-controlled regions are characterized by a higher general trust indicator than former Russian territory (Wysokińska, 2011).

Scholars have tried to explain the fact that educational indicators do not follow patterns common in Polish society by proposing various hypotheses. Geographers Czapiewski and Śleszyński (2007) linked the differences in educational outcomes with the agricultural history of the territories formerly under Russian and Austrian rule. By referring to data derived from external nationwide surveys, they claimed that the inhabitants of eastern parts of the country are more devoted to their land and, accordingly, they feel more responsible for their families and the education of their children. The differences may also be connected with the fact that the inhabitants of territories which were formerly under Russian rule are conservative in their choices (Bartkowski, 2003). Furthermore, the authors highlight a second dimension of differentiation in educational outcomes, which is a division between urban and rural areas (Czapiewski and Śleszyński, 2007). Another possible explanation is the dependence of educational outcomes on the level of social capital in the region. Economists Herbst and Rivkin (2013) used data from the Polish Central Examination Board, Polish Central Statistical Office, and national census conducted in 2002 to elaborate on the possible role of social capital and uneven returns to education. In low economic performance areas higher academic achievements may be seen, according to the authors (Herbst and Rivkin, 2013), as generally more profitable. One possible reason is that economically lagging regions have low employment in the industrial sector, in which career opportunity is less dependent on academic credentials. They also tend to have a large share of jobs in the public sector, where education level matters. Finally, high academic achievements facilitate migration to more endowed regions (for further work-related studies), which increases the motivation to work hard at school.

More recently, Bukowski (2018) applied the regression discontinuity approach in a municipality-level analysis, and found a statistically significant difference between test results in post-Austrian and post-Russian territories. As mentioned above, the former Austrian regions perform better in school tests than the former Russian territories. The economist tried to explain the differences in educational achievements by referring to the general policy of former partitioners (Bukowski, 2018). For instance, in the Prussia-controlled territory, the public education system was oppressive. The Polish language was forbidden in schools and education was seen as a tool for spreading the state language and culture (Bukowski, 2018). Processes of Germanization and Russification may have resulted, according to Bukowski (2018), in negative social attitudes towards education. The author claims that higher educational achievements in territories which were formerly under Austrian rule result from its liberal and tolerant politics towards national minorities in the 19th century. The Austrian partitioner allowed Polish people to teach and learn in their mother tongue, which may have created a positive attitude to learning. They also had the opportunity to associate. This is also expressed in a higher level of satisfaction with received education in the former Austrian Partition and higher expectations regarding the schooling effort (Bukowski, 2018, p. 21).

Many authors have tried to explain the low educational achievements in the territories acquired from Germany after the Second World War (e.g. Bański, Kowalski and Śleszyński, 2004; Herczyński and Herbst, 2002; Herbst, 2004; Herbst and Rivkin, 2013). In 1945, Poland lost its eastern territories to the Soviet Union, and acquired parts of pre-war East and North East Germany. Borders shifts caused mass relocations of Polish, Russian and German citizens. The post-war Polish authorities used these newly-acquired territories to develop state-owned farms (PGR or State Agricultural Enterprises) and agricultural cooperatives. Most of them were closed after the beginning of economic transition in 1989. Herbst and Rivkin (2013) claim that mass migrations throughout the 20th century resulted in the absence of long-lasting social institutions, which may be the source of the educational failure. To this day, western and northern territories of Poland are struggling with high structural unemployment, slow economic growth and lack of infrastructure (Herczyński and Herbst, 2002; Bański, Kowalski and Śleszyński, 2004). Overall, there has been a lot of research on path dependence and differences in educational achievements between different partitions in analysis of regional development in Poland. However, most existing empirical studies which attempt to explain aforementioned differences use aggregated data for municipal level research. In contrast to these earlier studies, we base our work on school-level data obtained from questionnaire surveys. We also include qualitative data: individual in-depth interviews and observations.

Results of cartographic and econometric analysis[5]

The conclusions from the literature review are consistent with the pattern in Figure 4.1 showing the municipal averages of 9th-grade student test scores in mathematics (2016). The achievements in south-eastern Poland, which belonged to the Austro-Hungarian Empire until 1918, are high compared to other regions of Poland. The intervals shown on the map refer to the percentage maximum achievable score. For example, municipalities shaded in black (highest interval) had an average test score between 50.8 per cent and 74.6 per cent of the maximum score that could be achieved in this test. As one

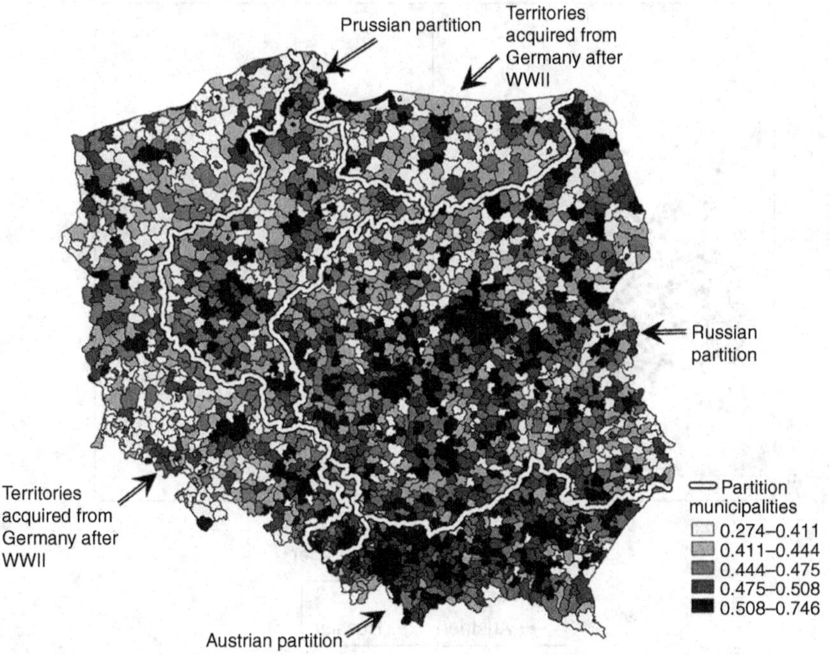

Figure 4.1 Municipal average scores on 9th-grade test in mathematics (2015) as a percent of maximum achievable score

can see, most of the municipalities in the former Austrian partition are ranked within the top two intervals.

More precise calculations were made by Herbst and Wójcik (2018), who used school level data weighted by the number of students. First, the actual scores were standardized so that the country average was 0 and standard deviation equalled 1. The average school score in the Austrian partition is higher than the country average by 0.18 standard deviations. The gap between the Austrian partition and the Prussian partition is even larger (0.25 standard deviations). The ex-Russian territory performs better than average, but still 0.13 standard deviations below the achievements in the ex-Austrian region. The worst score is observed in the territories acquired by Poland after the Second World War (from Germany). Students in this area perform 0.16 standard deviations below the country average, and 0.35 standard deviations below the mean score in the Austrian partition.

In the next step we applied a geographic regression discontinuity design (GRDD) to measure the effect of the partition in close proximity to the former border. We found that location in the former Austrian partition had a significant and positive effect on student performance in mathematics, as measured by the test score achieved by students graduating from middle schools. Even if

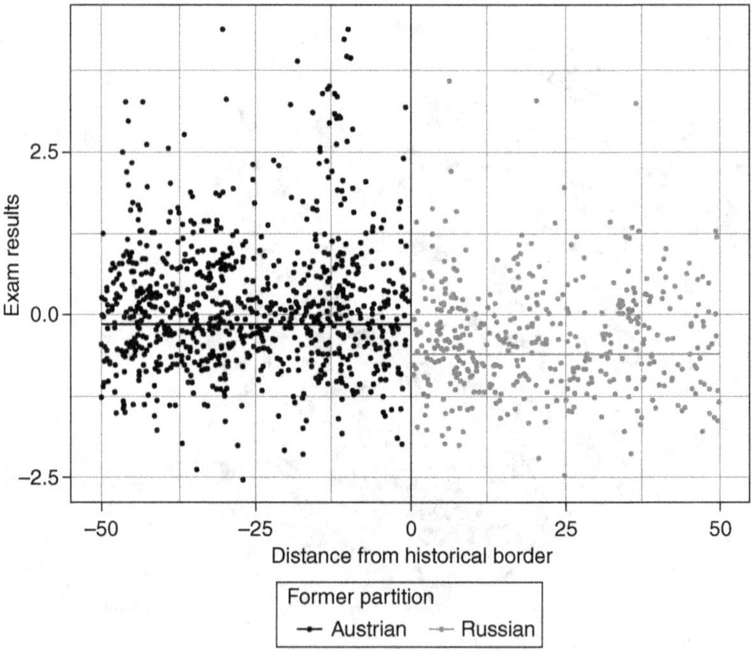

Figure 4.2 RDD plot with discontinuity at former border between the Austrian and Russian partitions

we controlled for school and municipal characteristics (including measures of poverty and educational attainment in the population) the magnitude of the effect was 0.4 standard deviations. Moreover, the effect remained significant in the value-added specification, when student achievements at an earlier stage of education were controlled, with the magnitude reduced to 0.15 standard deviations.

How does history matter? Sociological research based on historical insight

Our insight into the genesis of the education system in partitioned Poland, reaching back to the early 19th century, led to the conclusion that one fundamental difference between the early education system in Poland's territory under Austrian, Russian and Prussian rule may relate to the degree of social acceptance of school, teacher status and the role of education as a lever of social advancement. The former Austrian partition was superior to other regions with respect to all these factors (for details see Herbst and Kaliszewska, 2017). Another important difference between the partitions was how the state perceived the mission of public education: in terms of acquisition of practical skills, or rather in terms of personal development. In this respect, there was a clear dissimilarity between the former Austrian partition (which corresponds to the historical region of Galicia), where the curriculum was focused on the humanities, and other partitions (particularly Prussia), where schools were more closely linked to the economy.

In order to assess to what extent these historical differences may still affect the social norms towards education in Poland we conducted a research survey among parents. Using the methods of individual in-depth interviews, observation and a questionnaire survey (CAPI), we were searching for mechanisms which could have enabled the reproduction of historical institutions. In this section, we discuss two factors: the level of social capital in the region, and the norms and values prevailing in given territories.

Social capital and trust in the education system

Many authors have shown that there exists a significant relationship between social capital and educational achievements (Rogosic and Baranovic, 2016). "Social capital" refers to "connections among individuals – social networks and the norms of reciprocity and trustworthiness that arise from them" (Putnam, 2000, p. 19). Differences in educational outcomes can be explained by different levels of existing social capital, as it can support schooling in the form of appropriate values and motivation. While studying this phenomenon, it is important to analyze the level of trust in public institutions, including educational ones. It can be assumed that in regions with higher levels of social capital, respondents will declare a higher level of trust in the education system.

When asked about various public institutions (e.g. government, police, municipality) in the questionnaire survey, inhabitants of Galicia declared that they undoubtedly trust in them. In the questionnaire, 18.52 per cent of respondents from the former Galicia declared that they definitely trust the education system. In the former Prussian and Russian partitions, in turn, this percentage is 9.55 per cent and 9.30 per cent, respectively. Inhabitants of the former Austrian partition are also more satisfied with their jobs and family relations; they see good prospects for their future. They underline that they are satisfied with their child's school (25.93 per cent are very satisfied, in the Prussian partition 13.58 per cent; in the Russian 11.94 per cent). Of the respondents in the former Galicia, 43.15 per cent believe that their child's school is better than the country's average (in the Prussian partition 38.51 per cent, and in the Russian 26.12 per cent). To illustrate, during the individual in-depth interview, the principal of a primary school and local politician in the former Austrian partition said "when it comes to the value of education, it is certainly perceived as very, very high, and it must be admitted that it is important to people here in our region" (A1F, interviewed on 2017/06/06)[6]. Trust in education in Galicia can be summed up with the words of a local activist, who said "education is the issue number one" (A2M, interviewed on 2017/06/05). In contrast, the leader of a local group of scouts in the former Russian partition suspected that "if parents let children do what they want, they wouldn't even go to high school" (R3M, interviewed on

2017/06/08). These results confirm the thesis proposed by Becker and his team (2016) and by Bukowski (2018). In the 19th century, Austrian rule was liberal and tolerant. In contrast, in the Russian and Prussian partitions inhabitants experienced many forms of repression. We can assume that the more oppressive Russian and Prussian systems spawned reluctance towards formal education. By contrast, the liberal Austrian rule may have translated into positive attitudes towards education, and, as a result, higher educational achievements.

Social trust, as well as satisfaction from life and education may also result from the level of attachment to the region. Of the respondents from the former Austrian partition, 71.48 per cent were born in the town where they live right now. In contrast, in Prussian and Russian partitions this percentage is 60.75 per cent and 62.48 per cent, respectively. Accordingly, when asked about their relationship with the region, 26.30 per cent of inhabitants from the former region of Galicia declared a very strong attachment (in Prussian and Russian partition this was 19.25 per cent and 20.93 per cent, respectively). During our observations, we also discovered that in former Galicia local history is more often cultivated. Historical memory in the former Austrian partition is vivid. For example, when asked about the partitions, a history teacher answered: "from my perspective, and the perspective of this school, it was a very favourable time" (A4F, interviewed on 2017/06/06). In contrast, in a town studied in the Russian partition, neither schools nor streets have local patrons, and no writers or educational activists are commonly known. In former Galicia, inhabitants also express greater trust in the Church (both in the questionnaire survey and in individual in-depth interviews). It can be assumed that religion can strengthen social bonds, as it encourages people to meet each week and participate in parish life. In this dimension, religion can produce social capital, which can be later transferred to the other spheres of social life. To conclude, it can be stated that the high educational achievements in the former Galician region may result from the higher social capital and trust in educational institutions in these territories.

Formative versus applicative role of education

Prevailing social norms and educational motivation are other important channels for the persistence of institutions. Education can be recognized as having a formative or applicative role. Parents can believe that the role of the school is to shape a child's personality, or to teach directly applicable, practical skills. In the questionnaire, respondents were asked to prioritize the goals of school education by choosing three priorities from various options. Inhabitants of the former Austrian partition pointed more often to formative values such as patriotism or respect for the authorities. In contrast, residents of the former Prussian partition tended to select "utilitarian" goals such as self-reliance and knowledge about reality. Respondents were also asked to choose three factors which can help to "achieve success in life". In general, in first place most of the respondents chose "education". However, in further responses, differences between regions could be observed. In the former region of Galicia, emphasis was placed on resourcefulness, in the Prussian partition, on hard work, and in the Russian partition, on contacts.

Consequently, the interviewees in former Galicia agreed that school should provide general education and knowledge which will help students adapt to all possible conditions. To illustrate, a historian from the local high school in Galicia in the personal interview said that one of the main benefits of education is "understanding the world, first and foremost. The more you are closed in a specific niche and do not want to gain an education, expand your knowledge, the more difficult it will be for you to find your place in this contemporary world" (A4F, interviewed on 2017/06/06). Parents in Galicia share an opinion that schools should be teaching values such as justice, honour and patriotism, and should not be correlated with economic conditions. In contrast, inhabitants living in the former Prussian partition tend to declare that it is important to learn practical skills and have a concrete profession. For example, the leader of a local group of scouts in the former Prussian territories claimed that school should teach things that are needed in everyday life, "such as dealing with office work or writing letters" (P5M, interviewed on 2017/06/07). According to the principal of a primary school, students want "to have a concrete profession, which will bring them money, what does not necessarily have a lot in common with the knowledge" (P6F, interviewed on 2017/06/07).

In the questionnaire survey parents were also asked to choose three subjects they care about the most while monitoring their children's school achievements. In the Austrian partition parents tended to choose history, or artistic subjects (such as music or painting), while in the Prussian partition, they chose entrepreneurship and STEM subjects (i.e. science, technology, engineering and mathematics). Respondents in the former Russian partition also shared the opinion that it is more important to learn STEM subjects than the humanities. To illustrate, the principal of a local primary school said:

> Recently you can clearly see that there are some directions of education that are more likely to be valuable and useful later in life [...] if you finish a good technical university and good department there, well, life is completely different than after the humanities, which, not always [...] give you the possibility to choose a job.
>
> (R7M, interviewed on 2017/06/08)

Studying STEM subjects is seen as a key factor in finding a good job in the future. This may result from the more general norms shared in society about the market value of different disciplines as well as from present-day conditions in the local labour market.

In the former region of Galicia, belief that school should play a formative role may result from the historical events that took place in this territory in the 19th century. The Austrian partition was not well-developed in an economic sense. It was very difficult to pursue a career in technical professions. At the same time, the liberal Habsburg rule allowed minorities to associate and to have administrative and political representation. The education system was inclusive and open. As a result, careers were often pursued in official positions (Herbst and Kaliszewska, 2017). In contrast, in the Prussian partition, industries and agricultural technologies were well-developed, as these territories were meant to be an agricultural base for the Kingdom of Prussia. This generated a demand for workers with technical skills: in agriculture and in industry as well. Accordingly, available schooling in the Prussian partition offered vocational education in different trades. The Russian partition was the least advanced economically, although several industries existed in these territories. These institutional frameworks may have persisted in society as routines and customs.

The greater emphasis placed on the formative role of education may be an important factor in explaining the high educational achievements in former Galicia. More trust in personal development through education implies that the level of student effort is less dependent on the perceived material benefits from education, and on whether the achievement is measured using high stake examinations or just diagnostic tests. The observed regional differences in parental attitudes towards education may also suggest that the achievement gap between the Austrian partition and the other regions of Poland should be larger with respect to humanities (history, literature) than in mathematics or science. However, this last hypothesis was not confirmed in the quantitative analysis.

Conclusions

The aim of this chapter was to describe how an interdisciplinary approach can be applied in conducting research on the connections between history and regional development. We began our work with cartographic and econometric analysis. This showed that there exists a clear difference in educational achievements between regions which were governed by different partitioners in the 19th and early 20th centuries. However, by using econometric tools we could only measure the effect; we could not explain the mechanisms that underlie it. For this reason, we conducted a historical analysis which provided a qualitative insight into the regional differences of the education system. It helped us to designate main areas of interest, which later became the basis for sociological research. We used this to prepare scenarios for individual in-depth interviews and a questionnaire survey. During the sociological research we discovered that regional differences in educational outcomes can be explained with reference to two dimensions: the level of social capital, and the norms and values prevailing in the region. The complementarity of the perspectives offered by different fields was one of the greatest advantages of this interdisciplinary research.

Additionally, our research shows that the intergenerational transfer of long-inculcated norms may have a powerful impact on territorial patterns of socio-economic development, even if the administrative and political divisions that were at the foundation of these norms vanished a long time ago. This supports the earlier findings of Bisin and Verdier (2001), and Patacchini and Zenou (2011) on how parental effort combined with local social norms contributes to the petrification of regional differences in educational performance. With respect to educational policy, our results show that traditional measures of coping with inequalities that rely on redistribution of resources, providing extra teaching hours, or intensified evaluation of achievements may be ineffective if deeply rooted local norms towards education are not taken into account, and if policies fail to address different generations, and not just students at schools. Due to the interdisciplinary approach, we were able to analyze the mechanisms and channels of persistence. This kind of research could be applicable in other culturally diverse countries.

Notes

1 This work was supported by the National Science Centre (NCN), under the project "Persistent effects of historical partitions on educational achievements. An interdisciplinary approach" (2014/14/E/HS4/00089).
2 For a more detailed historical description of the partitions of Poland see Davies (1981).
3 The term "partitions" is commonly used in the international literature to describe the conquering of Poland's territory by the three superpowers between 1772 and 1795 (e.g. Davies, 1981; Encyclopaedia Britannica, 2018). We will therefore use this expression, as well the term "partitioners", to refer to the conquering countries.
4 Fuzzy Regression Discontinuity Design (Hahn et al., 2001) helps to assess the effect of treatment in the presence of crossovers. However, this method requires that we actually know the treatment status of each observation in the data. In our case however, we only know where students attend school now, but we can't be sure whether their families originate from the same region in which they live now, or from another partition. For this reason, on our analysis we replaced a dichotomous treatment variable (taking value 0 or 1) with the probability of treatment.
5 A more comprehensive discussion of results can be found in Herbst and Wójcik (2018).
6 All citations from interviewees are in the authors' possession. Chosen quotes are translated by the authors of the article. Quotes are described in the following way: A, R, or P (former Austrian, Russian, or Prussian partition), number of respondent, F or M (female or male), date of interview.

References

Bański, J., Kowalski, M. and Śleszyński, P., 2004. *Zarys problemów związanych z uwarunkowaniami zróżnicowań przestrzennych wyników sprawdzianu dla uczniów szkół podstawowych w 2002 r.* Warsaw: Polish Central Examination Board.

Bartkowski, J., 2003. *Tradycja i polityka. Wpływ tradycji kulturowych polskich regionów na współczesne zachowania społeczne i polityczne.* Warsaw: Żak.

Becker, S., Boeckh, K., Hainz, C. and Woessmann, L., 2016. The Empire is dead, long live the empire! Long-run persistence of trust and corruption in the bureaucracy. *The Economic Journal*, 126(590), pp. 40–74. https://doi.org/10.1111/ecoj.12220

Bisin, A. and Verdier, T., 2001. The economics of cultural transmission and the dynamics of preferences. *Journal of Economic Theory*, 97(2), pp. 298–319. https://doi.org/10.1006/jeth.2000.2678

Bukowski, P., (2018) How history matters for student performance: Lessons from the partitions of Poland. *Journal of Comparative Economics*. (Accepted for publication October 2018.) https://doi.org/10.1016/j.jce.2018.10.007

Chancellery of the Prime Minister (CPM), 2009. *Polska 2030. Wyzwania rozwojowe*. Warsaw: Chancellery of the Prime Minister.

Chauvel, L., 1999. Existe-t-il un modèle européen de structure sociale? *Revue de l'OFCE*, 71(1), pp. 281–298. https://doi.org/10.3406/ofce.1999.1562

Cvrcek, T. and Zajicek, M., 2013. *School, what is it good for? Useful human capital and the history of public education in central Europe*. Cambridge, MA: National Bureau of Economic Research. https://doi.org/10.3386/w19690

Czapiewski, K. and Śleszyński, P., 2007. Geografia zróżnicowania wyników egzaminów zewnętrznych. In: Polish Central Examination Board, 2007. *Egzamin. Biuletyn Badawczy Centralnej Komisji Egzaminacyjnej*. Warsaw: Polish Central Examination Board. Pp. 52–79.

Davies, N., 1981. *God's playground. A history of Poland: In two volumes*. New York, NY: Columbia University Press.

Encyclopedia Britannica, 2018. *Partitions of Poland*. Available online at: www.britannica.com/event/Partitions-of-Poland [Accessed 19 September 2018].

Egger, P. H. and Lassmann, A., 2015. The causal impact of common native language on international trade: Evidence from a spatial regression discontinuity design. *The Economic Journal*, 125(584), pp. 699–745. https://doi.org/10.1111/ecoj.12253

Hahn, J., Todd, P. and Klaauw, W. (2001). Identification and estimation of treatment effects with a regression-discontinuity design. *Econometrica*, 69(1), pp. 201–209. https://doi.org/10.1111/1468-0262.00183

Hall, P. A. and Soskice, D., eds. 2001. *Varieties of capitalism: The institutional foundations of comparative advantage*. Oxford: Oxford University Press.

Herbst, M., 2004. Human capital formation in Poland: Where does educational quality come from? *Studia Regionalne i Lokalne*, 17(3), pp. 89–104.

Herbst, M., 2012. *Edukacja jako czynnik i wynik rozwoju regionalnego: Doświadczenia Polski w perspektywie międzynarodowej*. Warsaw: Scholar.

Herbst, M. and Kaliszewska, A., 2017. The partitions and education: The beginnings of education establishments on the Polish territory in the context of today's differentiation of academic achievement. *Studia Regionalne i Lokalne*, 2(68), pp. 5–29.

Herbst, M. and Rivkin, S., 2013. Divergent historical experiences and inequality in academic achievement: The case of Poland. *Journal of Socio-Economics* (42), pp. 1–12. https://doi.org/10.1016/j.socec.2012.11.008

Herbst, M. and Wójcik, P., 2018. *The persistent legacy of the fallen empires: Assessing the effects of Poland's historical partitions on student achievement*. Warsaw: University of Warsaw EUROREG Working Paper.

Herczyński, J. and Herbst, M., 2002. *Pierwsza odsłona: Społeczne i terytorialne zróżnicowanie wyników sprawdzianu szóstoklasistów i egzaminu gimnazjalnego przeprowadzonych wiosną 2002 roku*. Warsaw: Friedrich Naumann Stiftung.

Hidano, N., Hoshino, T. and Sugiura, A., 2015. The effect of seismic hazard risk information on property prices: Evidence from a spatial regression discontinuity design. *Regional Science and Urban Economics*, 53, pp. 113–122. https://doi.org/10.1016/j.regsciurbeco.2015.05.005

Keele, L. J. and Titiunik, R., 2015. Geographic boundaries as regression discontinuities. *Political Analysis*, 23(1), pp. 127–155. https://doi.org/10.1017/psrm.2015.37

Keele, L. J. and Titiunik, R., 2016. Natural experiments based on geography: ERRATUM. *Political Science Research and Methods*, 4(2), p. 449. https://doi.org/DOI: 10.1017/psrm.2015.37

Lynn, R., 2010. In Italy, North–South differences in IQ predict differences in income, education, infant mortality, stature, and literacy. *Intelligence*, 38(1), pp. 93–100. https://doi.org/10.1016/j.intell.2009.07.004

Moore Jr., B., 1966. *Social origins of dictatorship and democracy: Lord and peasant in the making of the modern world.* Boston: Beacon Press.

North, D. C., 1990. *Institutions, institutional change and economic performance.* Cambridge, MA: Cambridge University Press.

Parcel, T. and Dufur, M., 2009. Family and school capital explaining regional variation in math and reading achievement. *Research in Social Stratification and Mobility*, 27(3), pp. 157–176. https://doi.org/10.1016/j.rssm.2009.04.003

Patacchini, E. and Zenou, Y., 2011. Neighbourhood effects and parental involvement in the intergenerational transmission of education. *Journal of Regional Science*, 51(5), pp. 987–1013. https://doi.org/10.1111/j.1467-9787.2011.00722.x

Pierson P. and Skocpol, T., 2002. Historical institutionalism in contemporary political science. In: I. Katznelson and H.V. Milner, eds. 2002. *Political science: State of the discipline.* New York, NY: W.W. Norton. Pp. 693–721.

Putnam, R. D., 2000. *Bowling alone: The collapse and revival of American community.* New York, NY: Simon & Schuster.

Putnam, R. D., Leonardi, R. and Nanetti, R. Y., 1993. *Making democracy work: Civic traditions in modern Italy.* Princeton, NJ: Princeton University Press.

Rogosic, S. and Baranovic, B., 2016. Social capital and educational achievements: Coleman vs. Bourdieu. *CEPS Journal*, 6(2), pp. 81–100.

Rosenbaum, P. R. and Rubin, D. B., 1983. The central role of the propensity score in observational studies for causal effects. *Biometrica*, 1(70), pp. 41–55.

Thistlethwaite, D. L. and Campbell, D. T., 1960. Regression-discontinuity analysis: An alternative to the ex post facto experiment. *Journal of Educational Psychology*, 51(6), pp. 309–317. https://doi.org/10.1037/h0044319

Trzebiatowski, K., 1970. *Szkolnictwo powszechne w Polsce w latach 1918–1932.* Wroclaw: Ossolineum.

Welt-Online, 2008. Pisa study results: East German education outperforms West. *Die Welt*, 19 Nov.

Wysokińska, A., 2011. *Invisible wall: Role of culture in long term development.* Florence: European University Institute.

5 Regional GDP before GDP

A methodological survey of historical regional accounts

Kerstin Enflo and Anna Missiaia★

Introduction

In a broad sense, economic inequality and ways of tackling it have for a long time been a focus in both academic research and policy-making. But different types of inequality are regarded as more or less relevant in different historical periods. In the aftermath of the financial crisis of 2008, the debate largely focused on the surge of interpersonal inequality (Piketty, 2014; Milanović, 2016). Growing interpersonal inequality has been proposed as a driver of political movements since the crisis. However, not all scholars agree that focusing on this particular type of inequality should be the priority. Rodríguez-Pose (2018) noted how the recent political turbulence originated not from people "that don't matter" but from places "that don't matter". The latter are the most depressed regions in both the US and Europe. As regards interpersonal inequality, the study of regional inequality prefers a long-term perspective to better understand its determinants. Rosés and Wolf (2018b) recently coordinated a collective effort by several economic historians to evaluate the regional GDP from 1900 to the present of several NUTS-2 European regions. The results are surprisingly similar to Piketty (2014) in terms of long-run aggregate tendency: regional inequality declined in Europe from an overall Gini of 0.55 in 1900 until the 1980s, when it reached 0.47; it then increased up to today. A similar U-shaped curve is observed for interpersonal inequality. Why then is regional inequality important? Rodríguez-Pose (2018) suggests that regional inequality cannot be neglected because its effects on voting behaviour are far stronger than those of interpersonal inequality. If political choices are driven by living in a poor region rather than living in a poor household, government policies should address regional inequality.

Historical research can provide a long-term view of the drivers of both types of inequality and their long-run evolution. Piketty (2014), in his study of historical interpersonal inequality suggested that the reduced inequality in the period following the Second World War was the exception rather than the rule, and warned that without the appropriate policies, inequality would by and large continue to increase. Similarly, Rosés and Wolf (2018a) suggest that the post-Second World War period, when regions experienced convergence, was an exception that should not be taken as a policy benchmark for our own times.

Reliable empirical evidence on both the outcome variable and the explanatory variables is essential for evaluating the extent of regional inequality and its causes and for eventually designing appropriate policies. For current regional inequality, there are extensive data from a range of geographical units that can be used for this purpose. The main measure used is the Gross Domestic Product (GDP), which is also the main measure for comparing countries. However, the level of precision and coverage that can be reached at the national level is not achievable at the regional one. For this reason, regional GDP is typically reconstructed using evidence at the industry rather than the household level and often neglects intra-regional imports and exports which would be too costly to record (Eurostat, 2013).

The evaluation of long-term regional inequality is even more complicated. Thus, the purpose of this chapter is to provide a methodological overview of existing approaches to measuring historical regional GDP. Even at national level, GDP is a late bloomer. Kuznets (1934) was a frontrunner of national accounts: he introduced the concept of national income in the 1930s, but with some differences from today's practice in what the measure included. The goal was primarily to measure economic growth. Standard GDP as we know it today was developed well after the end of the Second World War and is mostly based on a mix of direct information about production such as tax records and estimates for otherwise unrecorded production.

For estimates of national GDP before the mid-20th century, economic historians rely on both direct and indirect measures of production or income from sectors of the economy that are later aggregated into national series. One of the first to propose estimates of national accounts for various countries from a historical perspective was Gerschenkron (1962). Later, a massive effort to harmonize all the existing estimates worldwide over the very long run was made by the late Angus Maddison (Maddison, 2007). The Maddison dataset was constructed on the basis of two elements: the 1990 related income levels for all countries and the growth rates for each country, taken from the existing literature and with sometimes ad hoc adjustments decided by Maddison himself. Using these two, comparable estimates of GDP at a constant of 1990's international dollar rate were compiled. The efforts of Maddison are today continued by the members of the Maddison Project (Bolt et al., 2018).

For historical regional accounts, the challenges are even greater. Direct estimates of income or production similar to national ones are rarely achievable because of the lack of quantitative evidence at the regional level. In spite of the challenges, in the last 20 years scholars using various methods have been working towards the reconstruction of regional GDP series. Early attempts were based on the use of proxy variables. For instance, Good (1994) applied a method similar to that used at national level for the UK by Crafts (1983) to estimate the GDP per capita of the different regions of the Habsburg Empire. The method is based on various regional proxies that are plugged into a regression. The coefficients were then used to estimate the GDP for each of the regions. A similar attempt has been carried out by Esposto (1997) to estimate the regional GDP of the Italian regions after 1861. Another method, which is currently the most widely adopted by economic historians, is that proposed by Geary and Stark (2002). The Geary and Stark (G-S) method allocates the national series of the various sectors according to employment at regional and at sectoral level. Employment figures in benchmark years are often provided by population censuses. To correct for productivity differentials, regional wages are used. Quite frequently, scholars use a mix of direct estimates for sectors which are under a state monopoly (for instance, mining or tobacco), or find better direct evidence elsewhere. For the remaining sectors they employ the G-S method. Examples of these mixed estimates are Schulze (2007) on Austria-Hungary, Felice (2011) on Italy and Enflo and Missiaia (2018) on Sweden.

The period that can be covered varies from country to country and depends on the availability, quality and consistency of sources over time. Historical regional GDP can typically be estimated for the entire 20th century worldwide. Most European countries can rely on population censuses (or other sources) from the mid-19th century onwards. Before the mid-19th century, the regional GDP time series can be regarded as an exception. Two recent examples are the series from 1819 for Belgium (Buyst, 2018) and those from 1750 for Sweden (Enflo and Missiaia, 2018), along with the early benchmark of 1571. The Swedish case will be illustrated in detail below as a case study, where a mix of direct estimates for the mining sector and of G-S method estimates for the other sectors is used for the period 1750–1850. The 1571 benchmark was estimated using regional principles other than employment, providing a novel approach that may be adopted in other historical cases. The new Swedish series, jointly with those by Enflo, Henning and Schön (2014), represent a unique opportunity to consistently trace regional inequality in a European country from the pre-industrial period to the present day.

The structure of the chapter is as follows. Section 2 surveys the existing methodologies for estimating historical regional GDP and describes the types of source that have been employed for the task; Section 3 showcases a particular methodology through a case study of the NUTS-3 Swedish regions from 1571 to the present; Section 4 concludes with some reflections on future research.

Historical regional GDP: Methodological challenges

The estimation of regional GDP is for various reasons intimately connected to the effort to estimate national series. First, whenever possible, the regional series are calculated using the same methodology as the national ones. This is the case for bottom-up series seeking to estimate production directly, which represent the standard for most national GDP estimates but only a fraction of the corresponding regional ones.[1] National and regional series also share methodology in the case of the proxy-based approach. For instance, Crafts (1983) estimated the GDP of a group of European countries where the data were too poor to pursue a direct estimate of the production series (Spain, Switzerland, Austria-Hungary and the Netherlands). The estimates run from 1850 to 1910 and are based on a regression equation in which GDP per capita is a function of a number of proxy variables such as letters posted per capita, share of non-agricultural active population, coal consumed and infant mortality rates. As we will see in the next section, this methodology was also the one used for some early regional series. It should also be noted that regional GDP figures are often the result of a breakdown of the national ones according to some regional principle; therefore, the quality of the regional series depends on that of the national ones.

We have already observed that compiling regional GDP series for the present day that are up to the standards of the national is a challenge. This is due to conceptual issues that one encounters in trying to estimate GDP for sub-national units that are not sovereign and independent. According to Eurostat (2013), examples of conceptual problems are "the regional allocation of financial transactions of enterprises with establishments in several different regions or the regional allocation of the collective consumption of general government." The allocation of these transactions to one region rather than another is very problematic. Moreover, an estimation of regional GDP following the same conceptual guidelines as the national ones would require the quantification of imports and exports for every region. The administrative burden of this quantification for both firms and authorities would not be sustainable (Eurostat, 2013). Historical GDP estimations carry with them the same conceptual problems as the current estimations do, but face several additional data constraints. Under these constraints, suitable methodologies can be used to estimate regional GDP before the mid-20th century. This section illustrates the most widely used one.

Proxy-based approach for GDP

The estimation of regional GDP based on proxies was first introduced in the 1990s following the work by Crafts at the national level (1983). Good (1994) applied a similar strategy to that illustrated above to estimate the regional GDP for the Habsburg successor-state territories, consisting of 22 regions of the Habsburg Empire, with a ten-year benchmark from 1870 to 1910. The novelty of this approach at the time lay in using a regression equation to obtain coefficients that were used in the next step to weight the different proxies. This approach "let the data speak" in terms of the different weights for the proxies, rather than having to decide the weight of each one arbitrarily. This approach was, however, heavily criticized by Pammer (1997), who referred to the estimates by Good (1994) as "statistical artifacts." The criticism was mostly directed at the specification of the estimating equation and the application of the resulting coefficients to the most backward regions of the Empire. The first claim was demonstrated, for instance, by replacing the share of non-agricultural labour force with the agricultural one. This variable should have complemented the one used by Good (1994), but it led to dramatically different results. The reason suggested for this discrepancy was that GDP and the shares of workers in the labour force show a non-linear relationship because the latter (unlike GDP) are capped at 100 per cent. From a historical point of view, the use of the shares of employment as a proxy of GDP was challenged because of the different levels of development in the regions: the proxy was particularly poor for more backward regions, because the benchmark for the relationship over time was a sample from more advanced European countries. Similar points were brought forward regarding the other proxy variables used. The critique by Pammer (1997) led to a comprehensive revision of the series, published by Good (1999). Both the estimating procedure and the underlying data were revised: the share of agriculture in the active population in the latest series followed a logistic curve over time to accommodate the different rates of decline at different stages of industrialization. Finally, maximum likely estimation was used rather than ordinary least squares (OLS) and the other proxy variables relied on more disaggregated district-level data that helped to overcome measurement issues. The revised series showed a higher GDP level with lower growth rates and less regional inequality, which confirms that the previous estimates penalized the backward regions of the Empire too heavily. All in all, Austria-Hungary appears not to have lagged far behind the frontrunners of Europe. Another country for which the proxy variable approach to regional GDP was attempted in the 1990s was Italy. The first scholar to approach the estimation of regional GDP for post-unification Italy was Esposto (1997). His estimates largely relied on the method by Crafts (1983) that was also used by Good (1994; 1999). This work opened the door to the estimation of regional GDP for a country that presents one of the highest levels of regional inequality. The results showed a very wide GDP gap between north and south as early as 1861, which we will later see reduced by the estimates of Emanuele Felice using the G-S method (Felice, 2011; 2018).

Proxy-based approach for regional business cycles

Another approach to regional GDP should be mentioned; it is based on proxy variables, aiming at the more limited scope of studying regional business cycles. Two studies using such an approach focused on the historical cases of Italy and the Habsburg Empire. The first was by Ciccarelli, Fenoaltea and Proietti (2010), who used annual data on constructions to study the convergence of regional short-run business cycles in post-unification Italy. The underlying assumption here is that new constructions are a very sensitive measure of short-term fluctuations of the economy, and therefore of GDP.[2] The authors therefore employed some standard time-series techniques, such as the Hodrick and Prescott filter and the measurement of the inter-quantile range to assess the regional convergence or divergence of the cycles. Another study to mention among those using proxy variables is Ciccarelli and Missiaia (2018). The authors here made use of a composite annual series based on indirect taxes in order to assess the short-term movements of regional GDP in Imperial Austria from 1867 to 1913. The taxes were collected from official statistical yearbooks and cover all the 14 Austrian regions. The inclusion of specific taxes in the series was tied to the concept of aggregate demand (following which GDP is composed of consumption plus investment plus net exports). Each tax reflected one of these components: for consumption, they used consumption taxes, lotto, salt, tobacco; for investment, they used stamp duties and registration fees paid on business transactions; for net exports, they used import duties. The authors were of course aware that such a measure can provide only a sense of the co-movements of the regional series and that they reveal little on levels (either absolute or relative). For this reason, they took some measures to correct the proxy-based series with the information available on the ten-year benchmarks from Schulze (2007). In particular, they used only the tax-based series to fill the gaps between benchmark years, letting the superior series from Schulze (2007) set the level in the first and last year of each ten-year period. For this reason, the tax-based series are used only to indicate movements between two known levels. Since the series of taxes can be quite volatile from year to year, Ciccarelli and Missiaia (2018) also used a moving average to smooth out possible outlier years. Once the series were obtained, they were treated using standard filtering techniques to separate trend and cycles and a measure of dynamic correlation showed how the synchronization of the series evolved over time.

Regional employment-based method

The methodology introduced by Geary and Stark (2002) takes a step forward from the proxy variable approach. The "G-S method" is a short-cut method through which national value-added series are allocated to the regions according to their share of total employment. In doing so, the authors assumed that regional production depends on the number of workers employed in each region. The other assumption was that differences in regional wages in each of the main sectors of the economy reflect differences in productivity. Wages are therefore used to correct the allocation based on employment. Regional GDP Y in county i is defined in the following way:

$$Y_i = \sum^{j} y_j \beta_j \left(\frac{w_{ij}}{w_j} \right) \times L_{ij}$$

where y_{ij} is the average value added per worker in county i and sector j, and L_{ij} the number of workers in county i and industry j. β_j is a scalar reflecting regional relative differences, ensuring that regional totals add up to the national figure for each sector. The Geary-Stark method in essence allocates value added at the nation/sectoral level to the regions on the basis of their shares of the labour force corrected by wage differentials to take into account differences in labour productivity.

The G-S method has been widely used by economic historians for cases in which direct estimates of production were not viable but census data provide good enough information on employment and at least some evidence on wages was available. Geary and Stark (2002) used their method to estimate the

GDP of the four countries of the UK for the census years between 1861 and 1911. As a proof of concept, the authors also compared the estimates reached with this method with the direct ones for the year 1971, for which both were available. The results were close enough to consider the short-cut method valid. Since 2002, the G-S method has been widely applied to other historical cases and other periods in history. Examples of works using this method are Felice (2005a; 2005b) on Italy; Rosés, Martínez-Galarraga and Tirado (2010) on Spain; Buyst (2010) on Belgium; Enflo, Henning and Schön (2014) on Sweden; Enflo (2014) on Finland; and, recently Geary and Stark (2016) revising the series for the UK.[3]

The G-S method has several advantages. The procedure is fairly simple to implement, provided the necessary data are available. It is also a flexible procedure, in that it allows employment and wage series from different sources (and possibly of a different quality) to be used for different sectors. It is also flexible in the number of sectors that have to be used in order to estimate regional GDP. Conceptually, the minimum requirement is to be able to estimate separately the three main sectors of the economy (agriculture, industry and services); however, a finer breakdown of the economy is welcome and leads to more precise estimates because of the attribution of different average value added per worker in different sectors and the ad hoc correction of the productivity of each sector. This for instance is the case in the first generation series for Italy produced by Felice (2005a; 2005b), which made use of the detailed regional breakdown of employment from the population censuses already reclassified by Fenoaltea (2003). An example of flexibility in the various sources used comes from Enflo and Missiaia (2018), for which the series from 1750 to 1850 have been estimated using the G-S method (except for the mining sector). In their case, the evidence for agricultural wages was far richer than that for industrial wages: the G-S method allowed both sets of wages to be used in the same estimation.

Direct estimates, mixed and alternative method

The flexibility of the G-S method also allows the merging of sectors that have been reconstructed with different methods. Two cases can be conceptually distinguished here. The first is the one where direct evidence on production is available in some sectors but not all. In this case the rationale for not using a G-S approach is empirical in nature. Probably the most interesting of these cases occurs in the work by Emanuele Felice, who produced a first set of estimates in 2005 (Felice 2005a; 2005b) that was planned to use the G-S method for industry and later progressively replaced all the industrial series with those produced by Ciccarelli and Fenoaltea (2009; 2014) (see Felice, 2011 and the subsequent revisions).[4] The estimates of industrial value-added for the Italian regions represent an impressive and unprecedented effort because they contain bottom-up measures of production at the regional level. Their inclusion in the regional GDP estimates of Italy places these estimates among the most precise ever produced for any given country. Another example of mixed methods is the work of Schulze (2007) on Austria-Hungary. Here some series were reconstructed directly, some were a breakdown of the national figures according to employment and wages, and others were inferred using a proxy-based approach. In particular, the estimates for the Hungarian part of the Empire mirror the work by Good (1999), while direct estimates for the Austrian part were made possible by following the sources used also at the national level. Finally, manufacturing and construction were allocated according to employment and wages.

The second modification to the G-S method to be found in the literature is conceptual rather than being indicative of data availability. Crafts (2005) proposed a modified version of Geary and Stark (2002) that takes non-wage income into account, in order to calculate the regional GDP of the UK regions. This used the tax assessments for Great Britain in the period 1871–1911. According to Crafts, the G-S method based on employment and wages uses information on only half of the GDP (income from wages is estimated to be 50 per cent of the total). Geary and Stark (2016) in their reply to Crafts (2005) maintained that the joint use of wages, employment and tax data creates bias in the estimates and should be avoided. They justified their criticism on the grounds that wage and employment data provide an output perspective, while tax data provide an income perspective. The two should not be mixed to provide regional relative shares. Moreover, from an empirical point of view, they argued that their method was demonstrably robust by estimating the benchmark of 1971 and comparing it to direct estimates, an exercise that cannot be replicated for the estimates using the modification by Crafts (2005). The response by Geary and Stark (2016) is still relatively recent and the debate among scholars is still open. It is reassuring, however, that the overall long-term trend of regional inequality is similar in both methodologies, at least for the British regions. Finally, the set of regional estimates of personal income for the US between 1880 and 1910 by Klein (2009) is an important reference for readers interested in income calculated from the consumption side rather than that of production.[5]

It is beyond the scope of this chapter to survey all the sources and methodological issues encountered by the numerous scholars who have produced regional GDP estimates from the mid-19th century to the present. Nevertheless, in the next section we propose a more detailed discussion of one recent case study that gives a flavour of working with historical regional GDP estimates. This is the case of the Swedish regions in the period 1571–2010.

Swedish historical national accounts: Sources and methods

Swedish historical sources are well known for their exceptional quality. Swedish historical national accounts are no exception: the national series compiled by Schön and Krantz (2012; 2015) starting from the 16th century is just one example. The reason for such richness in the sources lies in the relative stability of Sweden as a unified country (in spite of the several wars it waged with its neighbours over the centuries). Moreover, after the Reformation, the overlap between the State and the Church allowed the King to rely on the religious institutions to collect taxes and record information on the population. In 1749, the first national population census based on parish-level data was released by the Royal Census Committee (Kungliga Kommissionen över Tabellverket), which can be considered one of the first statistical offices in the world. Censuses have since been undertaken every ten years without interruption to the present day. These population statistics constituted the backbone of our GDP estimates from 1750 onwards and allowed us to create the longest series of regional GDP for any given country (Enflo, Henning and Schön, 2014; Enflo and Missiaia, 2018) following the G-S method. The 1571 benchmark presented in Enflo and Missiaia (2018) is also a product of the extensive network of parishes controlled by the King. The main source for this benchmark was a special wealth tax called "Älvsborgs ransom" intended to regain control of the strategic castle of Älvsborg after a seven-year war against Denmark (1563–1570).

The availability of these exceptional sources allowed us to start a regular series of benchmark estimates about one hundred years earlier than generally possible for European countries. This brought a completely new contribution, in that it allowed regional inequality patterns to be observed well before modern industrial growth. It also posed more methodological challenges than 19th-century estimates did. A detailed account of all the sources and the methodological choices made in estimating all benchmarks is well beyond the scope of this chapter. We therefore focus in the sub-paragraph below, on the challenges that the 1750–1850 series posed, compared to those of 1860–2010. After that, in the sub-paragraph that follows, we give an account of the estimation of the 1571 benchmark as an interesting case study for scholars, in our view, which could promote access to similar sources for other countries.

Swedish regional accounts (1750–2010): The longest regional series

The ten-year benchmark series from 1750 to 2010 were produced by two different studies: Enflo and Missiaia (2018) for the period 1750–1850 and Enflo, Henning and Schön (2014) for 1860–2010. The two studies can be connected without further input; they both sum up to common national GDP estimates. In the case of Sweden, the longest and most detailed national series in terms of sectorial breakdown are the Swedish Historical National Accounts (SHNA) from 1560 onwards (Schön and Krantz 2012; 2015). The SHNA provide annual estimates for agriculture, manufacturing, building and construction, transportation and communication, private services, public services and services of dwelling.[6] The entire series of regional GDP relies on the regional labour force for each county and sector. For 1750–1850, they come from the *Tabellverket* provided by the CEDAR Umeå Demographic database. Here the number of individuals in each social group and the corresponding job titles are provided for each parish from its church registers. For the 1860–2010 benchmarks, various publications released by Statistics Sweden are used (for a detailed review, see Table 2 of Enflo, Henning and Schön, 2014).

Some methodological issues had to be solved with regard to the labour force figures. For instance, for the period 1750–1850, women were not included because of the difficult task of clearly defining their occupation. This is a frequent challenge when reconstructing historical labour force figures and it is often necessary to restrict the labour force to men. The second challenge related to the estimation of the labour force in services before 1860. The labour force figures for services as a whole in 1850 appear overestimated by some 10 per cent compared to those by Enflo et al. (2014) for 1860. Given that the share of GDP at national level from the SHNA is fairly stable over time, the share of workers in services was kept constant at the 1860 level in all years to avoid possible bias from misreporting by the Tabellverket. The excess workers were redistributed to the other sectors.

The G-S method also required using the wages for each sector to correct for regional productivity differentials. For the 1750–1850 series, agricultural wages were taken from the standard source, Jörberg (1972), which gives good coverage of all the 24 Swedish counties and was also one of the main sources for the 1860–2010 estimates. The industrial wages in the earlier series proved to be much harder to ascertain than in the 1860–2010 series, for which Lundh et al. (2004) is the main source. For the 1750–1850 period a series of builders for Stockholm from Söderberg (2010) and one for Malmö from Gary (2017) were used to compile a "Stockholm versus the rest" index. To reconstruct the wages for all counties, the wages of manufacturing workers in 1860 for all the 24 counties from Collin (2016) were extrapolated backwards in time using the Stockholm-Malmö ratio as a proxy of movements in time.[7]

A historical accident: The 1571 benchmark

The peace treaty of Stettin between Sweden and Denmark in 1570 stated that Sweden had to pay 150,000 silver coins after the war to regain the Älvsborgs castle, which was strategic for western access to the sea. This historical event represents a unique opportunity to gather parish-level data for 1571: in order to pay the ransom, a wealth tax comprising a tenth of all cattle, agricultural surplus and metal goods was imposed on the Swedish population. The tax collection was carried out and recorded by local priests under the supervision of regional bailiffs. These records were re-organized and aggregated at county level by Forsell (1869–1875; 1872–1883). Forsell remarks that the ransom can be seen as an enumeration of all that was considered of value in Swedish homes, seeing that chattels and smaller presses are often included. In this way, the source also gives an indication of the value of consumer goods in a pre-modern economy.

In order to move from a measure of wealth to a measure of the added value of production, however, a few adjustments had to be made. The material had to be made compatible with the industrial classification system in modern statistics, and the values of the input were estimated and deducted from the values of the output. For a pre-modern economy, this was in some ways less complicated since most goods were produced relatively low down the value-added chain. The pioneering efforts to construct national GDP from the wealth tax were made by Krantz (2004). He adapted the modern industrial classification system to the source material and derived value-added measures for all the sectors. Unsurprisingly, the results show that agriculture made up the largest share of the pre-modern GDP, although the value of production was not completely negligible in "industries" such as mining and metal goods, wood products and food and textiles.

Since employment figures and wages by county or industry do not exist for Sweden in 1571, Enflo and Missiaia (2018) could not opt for the usual Geary and Stark approach to regional GDP. Instead, the geographical scope of the wealth tax data was used for the regional disaggregation of industrial value-added. As an example, regional breakdowns of agricultural yields and various forms of cattle could be readily used to regionalize agricultural value-added while the existence of mines and metal works recorded in historical sources helped to regionally distribute the value of metal production. A full account of the guiding principles for the regionalization of industry value-added can be found in Enflo and Missiaia (2018). As far as possible, in the absence of regional wage data, the estimates were adjusted to take into account different levels of sectoral productivity between regions.

Although it is beyond the scope of this chapter to interpret the results of these estimations, a brief overview of the Swedish evolution of regional inequality can be provided by connecting the series by Enflo and Missiaia (2018) to those of Enflo, Henning and Schön (2014). Figure 5.1 shows the coefficients of variation for all the available benchmarks.

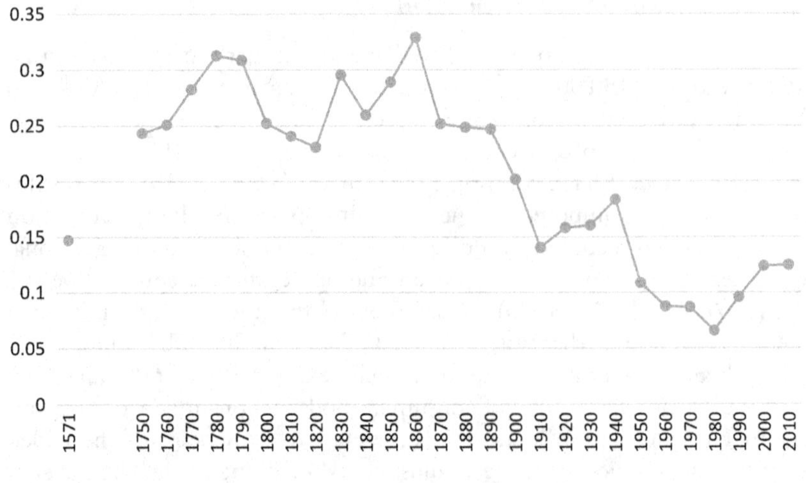

Figure 5.1 Coefficients of variation of Swedish regional GDP per capita.
Source: Enflo and Missiaia (2018).

For 1571, as expected for a highly agricultural and pre-industrial economy, regional inequality appears to be fairly low. What is surprising is the dramatic increase in the coefficient of variation in 1750, which pre-dates industrialization by some 100 years. Similarly, the decrease of regional inequality after 1850 corresponds to the industrialization of the country. The determinants of both pre-industrial inequality and of industrialization without regional inequality are discussed at length by Enflo and Missiaia (2017) and Enflo and Rosés (2015).

Conclusions and future research

Economic inequality can be considered in many dimensions. In the past few years, wealth and income inequality have been at the core of economic research because of the recent surge of interest in these themes. However, interpersonal inequality has not been the only type that has engaged scholars. Regional inequality within countries has also been increasing, with possible consequences for growth, welfare and political outcomes (Rodríguez-Pose, 2018). The study of regional inequality today is also intimately related to inequality in the past. This is because regional inequality is often rooted in imbalances that date back at least to the onset of modern industrialization in countries, if not earlier. Moreover, although regional inequality during the first industrialization has been studied in the past few years for a number of countries (Rosés and Wolf, 2018b), the assessment of pre-industrial inequality has proved to be exceptionally difficult to assess. This is because of data limitations that will require more effort to overcome. Until then, it will be hard to establish whether regional divergence is a phenomenon that predates modern economic growth or is observed only in connection with it.

This chapter is intended to provide a guide to existing empirical methods for estimating regional GDP in different historical periods. We have here introduced the most widely used methods, going from the proxy method approach for cases in which there is little evidence about regional employment and wages, to the popular Geary and Stark method of allocating national value-added according to employment and wages, finishing with the case of Sweden, where a mix of different methods, including direct estimation, can be employed. The challenges in estimating regional GDP before the mid-20th century are mostly empirical, since suitable series are hard to come by or are of poorer quality than current ones. Some of the challenges are also conceptual, in that the further back in time, the harder it is to divide economic activity into separate sectors without overlap. For the case of Sweden, we see that the correct assessment of women's employment presents researchers with a hard task. Moreover, the overlap between agriculture and private service employment makes it hard to correctly assess the size of these two sectors from original sources: the use of assumptions and proxies cannot be avoided. The Swedish series represent an exceptional effort to estimate pre-industrial regional inequality whether using the conventional Geary-Stark method for 1750–1850 or using a less conventional fiscal source for 1571.

Future research might do well to go in three directions. First, even for periods already covered by some estimates there is room for improvement through the collection of better data and further analysis of the existing material. For instance, a more targeted effort should be made to include women in the evidence from Sweden. Second, it is probable that the time-span in more countries could be expanded by using other sources, as is the case for Sweden in 1571. Some of these sources may be known but not yet employed for quantitative reconstructions. Finally, the amplification of the series from benchmark years to annual through short-cut methods could provide interesting insights into regional business fluctuations.

Notes

* The chapter was written thanks to the financial support of the Knut and Alice Wallenberg Foundation for the project 'The evolution of regional economies in the Nordic region – a long run approach' (ID: KAW2014.0138), Länsförsäkringars forskningsfond: and the Crafoord and Handelsbanken Foundations for the project 'Trade, market and regional development in pre-industrial Sweden (1750–1850)' (ID: 20160665 and ID: P2016-0247:1 respectively).

1 Most of the series included in the Maddison dataset, at least for the 20th century, are based on direct estimates of production following the framework of the historical national accounts; some regional GDP follow the same methodology for at least some sectors. One example comes from the second generation series used for the regional industrial value added by Ciccarelli and Fenoaltea (2009; 2014) that are incorporated in the most recent series of regional GDP for Italy by Felice (2018).

2 The authors cite the classic French expression "quand le bâtiment va, tout va" to evocate the economic relevance of the construction sector and its elasticity to short-term movements in the economy as a whole.

3 In this chapter we are going to discuss the sources used and the methodological challenges faced for the Swedish GDP series. For a more detailed and organic review of the existing series we refer the reader to Rosés and Wolf (2018b).

4 Daniele and Malanima (2007) also produce regional GDP estimates that have prompted much debate among Italian economic historians because of their surprising result that the North-South gap was not visible in 1861. The estimates have been criticized for the methodology adopted to allocate national production to regions, which is not based on the G-S methodology but makes use of the interpolation of regional quotas over time.

5 The alternative approach is common between national and regional estimates in the US and originates from different choices by the official statistical offices producing income estimates.

6 The exception is the period 1750–1850, for which mining is separated from the rest of the industrial sector and information at parish level from Olsson-Spjut (2007) is used to directly estimate the level of production.

7 Wages for services are not available for 1750–1850. Private services are proxied using the agricultural wages since it is assumed that a high level of substitution prevailed between agricultural workers and private services workers. Public services do not have a wage correction, given the assumption of homogeneity of the type of employment across counties.

References

Bolt, J., Inklaar, R., de Jong, H. and van Zanden, J. L., 2018. Rebasing 'Maddison': New income comparisons and the shape of long-run economic development. Maddison Project Working Paper 10.

Buyst, E., 2010. Reversal of fortune in a small, open economy: Regional GDP in Belgium, 1896–2000. *Rivista di Storia Economica* 26, pp. 75–92. https://doi.org/10.2139/ssrn.1586762

Buyst, E., 2018. Growth and regional imbalances during Belgium's classical Industrial Revolution. *Journal of Interdisciplinary History*, 49(1), pp. 71–92. https://doi.org/10.1162/jinh_a_01232

Centre for Demographic and Ageing Research (CEDAR). *The Demographic Data Base*. Umeå: Umeå University.

Ciccarelli, C. and Fenoaltea, S., 2009. *La produzione industriale delle regioni d'Italia, 1861–1913: Una ricostruzione quantitativa, 1. Le industrie non manifatturiere*. Roma: Banca d'Italia.

Ciccarelli, C. and Fenoaltea, S., 2014. *La produzione industriale delle regioni d'Italia, 1861–1913: Una ricostruzione quantitativa, 2. Le industrie manifatturiere*. Roma: Banca d'Italia.

Ciccarelli, C., and Missiaia, A., 2018. The fall and rise of business cycle co-movements in imperial Austria's regions. *Annals of Regional Science*, 60(1), pp. 171–193. https://doi.org/10.1007/s00168-017-0850-5

Ciccarelli, C., Fenoaltea, S., Proietti, T., 2010. The effects of unification: Markets, policy, and cyclical convergence in Italy, 1861–1913. *Cliometrica*, 4(3), pp. 269–292. https://doi.org/10.1007/s11698-009-0046-z

Collin, K., 2016. *Regional wages and labor market integration in Sweden, 1732–2009*. Gothenburg: Gothenburg University Dissertation.

Crafts, N. F. R., 1983. Gross national product in Europe: Some new estimates. *Explorations in Economic History*, 20, pp. 387–401. https://doi.org/10.1016/0014-4983(83)90026-8

Crafts, N. F. R., 2005. Regional GDP in Britain, 1871–1911: Some estimates. *Scottish Journal of Political Economy*, 52(1), pp. 54–64. https://doi.org/10.1111/j.0036-9292.2005.00334.x

Daniele, V. and Malanima, P., 2007. Il prodotto delle regioni e il divario Nord-Sud in Italia (1861–2004). *Rivista di Politica Economica*, 97, pp. 1–49.

Enflo, K., 2014. Finland's regional GDPs 1880–2010: Estimates, sources and interpretations. *Lund Papers in Economic History*, 135.

Enflo, K. and Missiaia, A., 2019. Between Malthus and the industrial take-off: Regional inequality in Sweden, 1571–1850. *Economic History Review*, forthcoming.

Enflo, K. and Missiaia, A., 2018. Regional GDP estimates for Sweden, 1571–1850. *Historical Methods*, 51(2), pp. 115–137.

Enflo, K. and Rosés, J. R., 2015. Coping with regional inequality in Sweden: Structural change, migrations and policy, 1860–2000. *Economic History Review*, 68(1), pp. 191–217.

Enflo, K., Henning, M., and Schön, L., 2014. Swedish regional GDP 1855–2000: Estimations and general trends in the Swedish regional system. *Research in Economic History*, 30, pp. 47–89.

Esposto, A. G. 1997. Estimating regional per capita income: Italy, 1861–1914. *Journal of European Economic History*, 26(3), pp. 585–604.

Eurostat, 2013. *Manual on regional account methods*. Luxemburg: Eurostat.

Felice, E., 2005a. Il reddito delle regioni italiane nel 1938 e nel 1951. Una stima basata sul costo del lavoro. *Rivista di Storia Economica*, 21, pp. 3–30.

Felice, E., 2005b. Il valore aggiunto regionale. Una stima per il 1891 e per il 1911 e alcune elaborazioni di lungo periodo (1891–1971). *Rivista di Storia Economica*, 2, pp. 273–314.

Felice, E., 2011. Regional value added in Italy, 1891–2001, and the foundation of a long-term picture. *Economic History Review*, 64(3), pp. 929–950.

Felice, E., 2018. The roots of a dual equilibrium: GDP, productivity, and structural change in the Italian regions in the long run (1871–2011). *European Review of Economic History*, forthcoming.

Fenoaltea, S., 2003. Peeking backward: Regional aspects of industrial growth in post-unification Italy. *Journal of Economic History*, 63, pp. 1059–102.

Forsell, H., 1869–1875. *Sveriges inre historia från Gustaf I, 1–2.* Stockholm: P.A. Norstedet & Söners Förlag.

Forsell, H., 1872–1883. *Sverige 1571. Försök till en administrativ-statisktisk beskrifning öfver det egentliga Sverige, utan Finland och Estland.* Stockholm: P. A. Norstedet & Söners Förlag.

Gary, K., 2017. Constructing equality? Women's wages for physical labor, 1550–1759. *Lund Papers in Economic History*, 158.

Geary, F. and Stark, T., 2002. Examining Ireland's post-famine economic growth performance. *Economic Journal*, 112(482), pp. 919–935.

Geary, F. and Stark, T. 2016. Regional GDP in the UK, 1861–1911: New estimates. *Economic History Review*, 68(1), pp. 123–144.

Gerschenkron, A. 1962. *Economic backwardness in historical perspective, a book of essays.* Cambridge, Massachusetts: Belknap Press of Harvard University Press.

Good, D. 1994. The economic lag of central and eastern Europe: Income estimates for the Habsburg successor states, 1870–1910. *Journal of Economic History*, 54(4), pp. 869–891.

Good, D. 1999. The economic growth of Central and Eastern Europe in comparative perspective, 1870–1989. *European Review of Economic History*, 3(2), pp. 103–137.

Jörberg, L. 1972. *A history of prices in Sweden 1732–1914. Part II.* Lund: CWK Gleerup.

Klein, A., 2009. Personal income of U.S. states: Estimates for the period 1880–1910. *Warwick Economic Research Papers*, 916.

Krantz, O., 2004. An estimate of Swedish GDP in 1571. In S. Heikkinen, and J. L. van Zanden, ed. 2004. *Exploring economic growth: Essays in measurement and analysis; a festschrift for Riita Hjerppe on her 60th birthday.* Amsterdam: Aksant. Pp. 105–130.

Kuznets, S. 1934. National income, 1929–1932. *National Bureau of Economic Research.*

Lundh, C., Olofsson, J., Schön, L., and Svensson, L., 2004. Wage formation, labor market institutions and economic transformation in Sweden 1860–2000. *Lund Studies in Economic History*, 32.

Maddison, A., 2007. *Contours of the world economy 1-2030 AD: Essays in macro-economic history.* Oxford: Oxford University Press.

Milanović, B., 2016. *Global inequality: A new approach for the age of globalization.* Cambridge, Massachusetts: Harvard University Press.

Olsson-Spjut, F., 2007. *Järnhanteringens dynamik: Produktion, lokalisering och agglomerationer i Bergslagen.* Umeå: Department of Economic History Dissertation.

Pammer, M. 1997. Proxy data and income estimates: The economic lag of central and eastern Europe. *Journal of Economic History*, 57(2), pp. 448–455.

Piketty, T., 2014. *Capital in the twenty-first century*. Cambridge, Massachusetts: Harvard University Press.

Rodríguez-Pose, A., 2018. The revenge of the places that don't matter (and what to do about it). *Cambridge Journal of Regions, Economy and Society*, 11(1).

Rosés, J. R. and Wolf, N., 2018a. Regional economic development in Europe, 1900–2010: A description of the patterns. *CEPR Discussion Paper* 12749.

Rosés, J. R. and Wolf, N., 2018b. *The economic development of Europe's regions: A quantitative history since 1900*. London: Routledge.

Rosés, J., Martínez-Galarraga, J. and Tirado, D., 2010. The upswing of regional income inequality in Spain (1860–1930). *Explorations in Economic History*, 47(2), pp. 244–257.

Schön, L. and Krantz, O., 2012. The Swedish economy in the early modern period: Constructing historical national accounts. *European Review of Economic History*, 16, pp. 529–549.

Schön, L., and Krantz, O., 2015. New Swedish historical national accounts since the 16th century in constant and current prices. *Lund Papers in Economic History*, 140.

Schulze, M. S., 2007. Regional income dispersion and market potential in the late nineteenth century Hapsburg Empire. *LSE Economic History Working Papers* 106/07.

Söderberg, J., 2010. *Long-term trends in real wages of labourers*. In: R. Edvinsson, T. Jacobsson, and D. Waldenström, ed. *Exchange rates, prices, and wages, 1277–2008*. Stockholm: Ekerlids Förlag & Sveriges RB. Pp. 453–478.

6 Comparative research designs

Interdependence as challenge and opportunity in regional studies

Martin Åberg and Thomas Denk

Introduction: Purpose, terminology, and layout of the chapter

Any combination of historical and social science approaches to regional development problems involves methodological challenges (cf. Capocci and Ziblatt, 2010; Møller, 2013). The application of comparative research designs is a case in point. On the one hand, the classic approach taken by historians, as well as by many historical sociologists, is intrinsically narrative, as illustrated by, among others, Bloch (1952 [1928]), Anderson (1974), Bendix (1964), and Sewell (1967 see also Kocka, 1999). On the other hand, social scientists typically tend towards systematically structured research designs for making comparisons, although often exclude the temporal dimension of societal and political change (Almond and Verba, 1963; Esping-Andersen, 1990; Lijphart, 1999). We argue that historical comparative research can be of great value for exploration of the subnational, regional level, but in order to enhance its explanatory potential this requires systematic application of structured research designs. In turn, this draws attention to a number of challenges involved with making comparisons.

Typically, regional-level studies involve only a limited number of units of analysis. In comparisons that involves the study of only a few regions, however, it is not possible to test several, alternative explanations, since the effects of these explanations cannot be isolated from each other. For example, we might formulate two competing hypotheses, each one claiming a specific condition as an explanation as to why two different regions are wealthy; yet, if the regions share the same two conditions, it is impossible to test which one explains regional wealth, or whether it is the combination of the two conditions that is important. In addition, comparisons of few units have limitations with respect to how far we may assume that the empirical observations represent general patterns. From both challenges it follows that the selection of units, but also the selection of cases and data, becomes a crucial task.

Finally, and importantly, a key premise of structured comparative research is the assumption that the units of comparison are *independent* of each other. This assumption, though, often proves incorrect. Rather than being independent of each other, the units are empirically *interdependent* and this, in turn, may lead the analyst to erroneous conclusions about causality. Arguably, therefore, interdependence represents the single most important challenge involved with making synchronic and diachronic comparisons of few regions.

Among historians the problem is often conceptualized in terms of how the units of analysis, such as regions or countries, share "entangled" histories, and how processes take colour from cultural and other types of "transfers" across political and administrative borders (Werner and Zimmermann, 2006; Ther, 2009; Christian, 2016, pp. 3–9). Among social scientists, the problem is, as indicated, analyzed in terms of how the units of comparisons are interdependent by force of spill-over effects, or by diffusion of traits between them. More to the point, interdependence are mutual connections between cases, such as regional-level industrial enterprises, or regional policy-makers. Interdependence – if not controlled for – creates uncertainty about the extent to which conditions (independent variables) relate causally to the observed outcome. To fail to identify correlations between cases, and not account for potential sources of interdependence consequently means that any explanation of outcomes will suffer from decreased reliability, whether the topic of analysis is industrial development or policy changes (Braun and Gilardi, 2006; Franzese and Hays, 2008; Naroll, 1965; Przeworski and Teune, 1970; Simmons, Dobbins and Garrett, 2006).

Whereas there have been considerable advancements in the study of interdependence within the framework of large-N ("large number") studies in the last decades, a similar development has not occurred considering small-N ("small number") comparative research designs. Regardless of whether the latter type of research designs draw on qualitative or quantitative methods, however, or on any combination of such methods, the main challenges involved with the study of interdependence remains the same. This holds for historical comparative research, too. Importantly, and on condition that other challenges, e.g. those mentioned in the above, are addressed by the research design, we also propose that interdependence is not just a methodological problem to small-N comparisons. Rather, the study of interdependence provides small-N comparative research with an opportunity as well.

Among others, Rokkan (1966) has questioned the assumption that nation-states are homogeneous units of analysis. More recently, Snyder (2001, p. 93) has suggested that "subnational comparisons can expand and strengthen the methodological repertoire available to social science researchers". Whereas Snyder does not pay attention to historical perspectives, we add to his observation that similar gains may be won by historians making comparisons. Adding systematic, comparative research designs within their methodological repertoire, provides historians with a powerful tool for moving beyond the limits of traditional case studies of regions and localities. Specifically, the study of interdependence and its temporal dimension has the potential to provide students of regional themes with more accurate explanations, for example with respect to problems such as regional resilience, and policy analysis (cf. e.g. Martin, Sunley and Tyler, 2015).

The topic of this chapter, then, are designs for comparative research involving small numbers of regions, and approaches for inclusion of synchronic as well as diachronic comparisons with these designs as a means to analyze interdependence. Since policy analysis and policy diffusion, among other regional themes, involves problems pertaining to values, culture, and "history", there is, indeed, a strong case for comparative, historical studies in the field. Yet, a clarification with respect to terminology is required before we proceed. As previously indicated with the help of the notion of "transfers", there are parallels between historians and social scientists when dealing with interdependence. However, historical transfer approaches lack of clarity with respect to key concepts and definitions (recently e.g. Ihalainen, 2017, pp. 23–30). For example, Werner and Zimmermann claim that "comparison favor[s] the implementation of a synchronic reasoning [in explanations], and [that] transfer studies tend toward an analysis of diachronic [sic] processes" (2006, p. 50). At the same time, e.g. Ther (2009, pp. 217–218), stresses that the definition of "cultural transfer" remains an open question.

At the same time, the study of interdependence and causality is a well-established topic among social scientists, notably among students of policy diffusion (Simmons and Elkins, 2004; Weyland, 2006; Shipan and Volden, 2008; Volden, Ting and Carpenter, 2008). In the following, we therefore use the terminology involved with this strand of research, but include, when deemed necessary, clarifications. Notions such as, e.g. "unit" and "case" have slightly different meaning and usage among different disciplines. In order to avoid any confusion in the following, we use a terminology that includes unit of analysis (e.g. regions), case (in order to describe units of observation, e.g. regional policies), factor, and variable in order to refer to condition (in terms of independent variable, or factor), and outcome (dependent variable or factor).

In the following sections, we first expatiate on the definition of interdependence. We identify three critically important dimensions of interdependence (spatial, temporal and temporal-spatial interdependence). In connection to this, we elaborate on our reasoning on interdependence, causality, and explanation. Second, we apply a simple typology in order to structure similarities and differences between three basic types of comparative research design. We demonstrate that they offer different options for dealing with the three dimensions of interdependence that we identify. Notably, approaches that combine synchronic and diachronic comparisons are particularly challenging – but also promising – with respect to the analysis of interdependence. In line with this, finally, we suggest Comparative Sequence Design (CSD) as a systematic means of facilitating controlled synchronic *and* diachronic comparisons. Application of CSD e.g. within policy analysis, a theme which traditionally tends towards synchronic and hence static comparisons, allows for the study of policy-making, policy diffusion and policy implementation as dynamic, historically contingent processes.

Interdependence: Spatial and temporal dimensions

Almost any number of approaches are possible with respect to the problem of explaining historical change, including the matter of whether there are societal and other regularities across time. Likewise, e.g. to Skocpol (1984, p. 385), though, we agree that history does involve certain patterns and regularities. Hence, too, the exploration and causality of such patterns and regularities is a valid, methodological concern, as demonstrated by systematically structured, comparative research designs. However, it is precisely in connection to this, that interdependence emerges as a challenge – and an opportunity.

As indicated, one chief source of interdependence is diffusion-processes. Conditions and outcomes spread among the spatial units of analysis (*spatial interdependence*). Let us by way of example consider a sample of ten administrative units (regions) from one country – chosen, let's say, to analyse how regional innovation policies are formulated and implemented. Let us for the sake of argument also assume that the administrative make-up of the ten regions is similar. Finally, let us also assume that, albeit each policy differs with respect to the specific challenges that they address, there are nevertheless substantial similarities between them, in terms of the overall strategies that the policies propose in order to promote innovation. Administrative similarities between the regions would lead the analyst to hypothesize that this condition explains the outcome, i.e. observed similarities in policy-making. This hypothesis cannot be verified, though, if we do not at the same time examine and rule out the possibility that the similarities are a result of diffusion between the ten regions, by way of learning or, perhaps, emulation. If the latter is indeed the case, diffusion of traits between regions means that ten supposedly independent cases of policy-making are, in fact, just one, single case. Interdependence caused by diffusion, then, provides a poignant illustration of the challenges involved with analysing causality with the help of controlled comparisons: it is necessary to separate correlations between factors on the *unit-level* from effects caused by factors in *other units*.[1]

Cross-border regions, i.e. regions that connect with other regions across nation-state borders, provide further illustrations to the problem. For example, cross-border regions are suitable for formulating and testing hypotheses about the malleability of administrative borders to various types of processes (e.g. Wolff, 2003; Laven and Baycrøft, 2008). Among other Askarov and Doucouliagos (2015), demonstrate that foreign aid spreads between countries not only through official channels but, importantly, also by informal channels, specifically through migration of guest workers. At the same time, this illustration also draws attention to an important distinction – that between direct and indirect interdependence.

Direct interdependence by diffusion (or "outcomes diffusion") means that outcome Y in region A also causes outcome Y in region B. In our first example in the above, a regional policy may emerge in region A, and then spread to region B, which explains why both regions come to share the same policy. Indirect interdependence, though, involves diffusion that causes effects on the independent variable(s). That is, condition X in region A, changes condition X in region B, thereby leading to outcome Y. In line with our second example, on foreign aid, diffusion of aid between regions in two countries may explain why the level of economic wealth increases in both countries, if we consider foreign aid in terms of condition (X) that spreads, and leads to a similar outcome (Y) in two different cases. Analyzing interdependence in this form too therefore opens up opportunities within the regional studies theme for the exploration of new problems involving causality and explanation.

In addition to the distinction between direct and indirect interdependence, there is also the difference between spatial interdependence and spatial autocorrelation to consider. Occasionally, these are confused with each other in research. However, the crucial difference is that spatial autocorrelation occurs when attributes (e.g. conditions or outcomes) cluster together spatially in countries or regions. This creates a strong correlation between location and attributes. Possible examples involve situations in which democratic regimes are concentrated in certain macro-regions, whereas non-democratic regimes tend to be more frequent in other macro-regions (O'Loughlin et al., 1998). Another example are situations, for instance, when an observed degree of institutional efficacy is larger in some sub-national regions, compared to other regions in the same country (Putnam, 1993).[2] By contrast, spatial interdependence refers to dependence between attributes not solely in terms of spatial co-location (note that the difference between autocorrelation and interdependence can also occur temporally).[3]

This brings us to what is at the heart of the historian's craft – temporality. First, change, such as by diffusion of traits, results from – in a wide sense – "historical" processes (Rogers, 1995; Strang, 1991; Elkins and Simmons, 2005). Second, causal explanations of change therefore necessarily involve an element of time and, consequently, must consider *temporal interdependence*. Temporal interdependence means that factors within the same spatial unit of analysis exercise effects on outcomes; but, importantly, these factors appear in the unit prior to outcomes and, hence, the effects extend across a shorter or longer period of time. Processes that illustrate this type of dynamics can include anything from regional diffusion and adoption of new crops in early modern society (Cipolla, 1972; Overton, 1985), to changes brought about by any type of technical innovation, business behaviour or policy in modern-day regions (Shipan and Volden, 2008; Balland, Boschma and Frenken, 2015; Boschma, Martin and Minondo, 2017). Some of these processes might occur with great strength and at relatively high speed, perhaps even more so in the era of globalization, such as indicated by studies of policy diffusion (Jahn, 2006; Franzese and Hays, 2008). To include temporal interdependence in the analysis offers regional studies with opportunities for the systematic incorporation of process-oriented models and approaches with the research design; but, importantly, with consideration for the limitations imposed by available, historical sources.

The above illustrations demonstrate that interdependence can involve both region-to-region and nation-to-region connections as well as global processes. Interdependence can be direct or indirect, synchronically as well as diachronically. Interdependence is also, in both these dimensions, distinct from autocorrelation. More important for the purpose of this chapter, however, is that sources of spatial and temporal interdependence can also *combine* into temporal-spatial interdependence, and thereby provide new challenges to the possibilities of formulating causal explanations (see below, Table 6.1; cf. Wellhofer, 1989).

In connection to this, it is important to note that the logic underpinning causal explanations, tested by the help of controlled comparisons, are the same, regardless of the type of interdependence involved, and regardless of disciplinary perspective. The logic of explanation by means of comparison harks back to John Stuart Mill (1875), who introduced the "method of agreement" and the "method of difference" and which, later, was developed by Przeworski and Teune (1970) into "most different systems design" (MDSD) and "most similar systems design" (MSSD).[4] Controlled comparisons aim systematically to eliminate all conditions that (by way of hypothesis) lack any effect on the observed outcome. For example, the method of agreement compares units in which the outcomes are similar to each other. The analysis excludes all conditions that make the units different from each other; potentially, these conditions cannot explain the outcome. Explanations of this type are therefore essentially similar to what McCullagh (2004, pp. 174–176) has termed "genetic explanations" in the historical disciplines. That is, when social scientists in comparative research define relevant independent variables and examine these, this is equivalent to when historians eliminate step-by-step less likely conditions from the analysis, and focus on those key conditions which, in all *probability*, caused a specific outcome (McCullagh, 2004, p. 176).[5]

Table 6.1 summarizes the three dimensions of interdependence in terms of the types of effects that they exercise with respect to causality.[6] The first type of effect occurs when factors – either a condition (X), or an outcome (Y) – in one unit (s_2) affect the outcome in *another* unit (s_1) simultaneously in time (t_1) ($Y_{t1,s2} => Y_{t1,s1}$; $X_{t1,s2} => Y_{t1,s1}$). Spatial interdependence has, by definition, no temporal dimension. However, since causality always involves an element of temporality (i.e. factors *lead* to an outcome), and since interdependence can be not only direct, but also indirect, it should again be stressed that Table 6.1 only indicates how spatial and temporal dimensions are normally dealt with in different research designs.

Table 6.1 Spatial and temporal dimensions of interdependence

Types of effects	*Spatial interdependence*	*Temporal interdependence*	*Form of causality*
Effects from spatial interdependence on $Y_{t1,s1}$	+	-	$Y_{t1,s2} => Y_{t1,s1}$ $X_{t1,s2} => Y_{t1,s1}$
Effects from temporal interdependence on $Y_{t1,s1}$	-	+	$Y_{t-n,s1} => Y_{t1,s1}$ $X_{t-n,s1} => Y_{t1,s1}$
Effects from temporal-spatial diffusion on $Y_{t1,s1}$	+	+	$Y_{t-n,s2} => Y_{t1,s1}$ $X_{t-n,s2} => Y_{t1,s1}$

The second type of effect are effects from factors on the outcome in the *same* unit, but factors that relate to an earlier stage in the development of the unit ($Y_{t-n,s1}$ => $Y_{t1,s1}$; $X_{t-n,s1}$ => $Y_{t1,s1}$). By definition, this type of effect has a temporal dimension but no spatial dimension, since the factors are endogenous to one unit. That is, the notion of temporal interdependence, first, underlines how the temporality of cause and outcome is a neglected problem in analyses that only account for spatial interdependence. Second though, and similar to spatial interdependence, temporality *is* at the same time indicated, since effects causing temporal interdependence, too, can be direct or indirect. For example, condition X in region A changes X in region B, which *eventually* leads to outcome Y in region B.

Temporal-spatial interdependence, finally, refers to situations when factors pertaining to preceding periods affects the outcome in *another* unit ($Y_{t-n,s2}$ => $Y_{t1,s1}$; $X_{t-n,s2}$ => $Y_{t1,s1}$). In research designs made to include this type of causality, the effects have temporal as well as spatial dimensions. As in our previous examples, interdependence in these cases can be direct but also indirect. Drawing on the logic outlined in Table 6.1, we will now review different comparative research designs with respect to how they deal with interdependence.

Comparative research designs and interdependence: A typology

Social scientists and historians use several different approaches to classification of comparative research designs. For example, Peters (2014) but also Landman and Carvalho (2016), define research designs in terms of case studies (of single units), comparative studies (involving few units), and statistical studies (involving many units). Similarly, historians have discussed how case study design relates to micro-history approaches in cases when the latter is applied to single units of analysis (Joyner, 1999; Alapuro, 2012). For our purpose, classifications such as these are misleading. Considering the combinations of spatial and temporal dimensions that interdependence may involve, it is the distinction between synchronic and diachronic comparisons, rather than the number of units, that is important to our classification, i.e. the potential for each research design to allow analysis of spatial, temporal and temporal-spatial interdependence.

Consequently, we suggest an alternative typology, one that focuses on how the synchronic and diachronic dimensions are dealt with in different research designs (Table 6.2). Typically, a comparative study will tend towards stressing either a synchronic (cross-sectional design) or a diachronic analysis (development design). Studies based on the principles of comparative sequence designs are an exception since they systematically incorporate both types of comparisons. CSD therefore has the potential to control for effects causing both spatial, temporal and spatial-temporal interdependence in small-N studies (note that we ignore case study design, i.e. static studies of a single region, since case studies neither involve controlled comparisons, nor include options for analyzing interdependence).[7] In addition, Table 6.2 includes references to a

Table 6.2 Synchronic and diachronic dimensions in comparative research designs

	No synchronic dimension	*Synchronic dimension*
No diachronic dimension	Case study design	Cross-sectional design (e.g. Kubicek, 2000; Doloreux, 2004; Reiser, Rademacher and Jaeck, 2008)
Diachronic dimension	Development design (e.g. Loughlin, 2007; Møller, 2017)	Comparative sequence design (e.g. Evenhuis, 2016, Basta, 2018)

few examples of studies that, albeit in different ways, involve regions as units of comparison, and which illustrate the logic of each research design.

In Table 6.2, the logic of cross-sectional design is illustrated by Kubicek's (2000) analysis of political behaviour in the L'viv and Donets'k *oblasts* (administrative regions) in Western and Eastern Ukraine; by Doloreux's (2004) study of entrepreneurship in the two, Canadian regions of Ottawa and Beauce; and by Reiser, Rademacher and Jaeck's (2008) study of independent local lists (ILLs) in different German *Länder.*[8] Development design, i.e. studies of a single unit across time, is demonstrated with the help of Møller's (2017) analysis of the formation of representative political institutions in medieval Aragon, and Loughlin's (2007) study on ethno-nationalism and policy-making in Northern Ireland, c.1880–1920. As illustrations to the logic of CSD, we draw on Basta (2018) and Evenhuis (2016). The first of these two studies focuses on the problem of territorial reform and political stability in Canada and Spain, whereas the latter is a multi-scalar analysis of economic change, policy and government in South Saarland and Teesside, c. 1960–1980. We will now proceed by focusing on cross-sectional design and in particular the challenge of spatial interdependence. After that, we devote one section to development design and temporal interdependence and, finally, comment on comparative sequence design and temporal-spatial interdependence.

Cross-sectional design and spatial interdependence

Cross-sectional design is a standard approach not only for comparisons of macro-level regions and nation-states, but also sub-national level units. Comparisons in the latter case, though, typically include only a small number of units (Kubicek, 2000; Doloreux, 2004; Table 6.2). Cross-sectional design is also the simplest illustration of the logic of explanation by comparison, although its stress on synchronic comparisons indicates some of the key problems involved with analysing interdependence.

Put simply, cross-sectional design is a means of structuring comparisons in order to avoid comparing "apples with pears". By way of illustration we may return to our two hypothetical cross-border regions – region A and region B – but we now include the assumption that these regions do not only share an observed similarity in terms of e.g. political behaviour, or regional development policy. We also assume that regions A and B are fundamentally different from each other with respect to a number of key conditions: region A might be highly industrialized, whereas region B is agricultural. Provided that political behaviour nevertheless tends to depend on one certain and *similar* key condition, consequently, the aim of the comparison of region A and region B is to determine, according to the logic of the "method of agreement", whether there is any such, so far undetected similarity, typical to both regions. The "method of difference" simply follows the opposite logic: a difference between units explain a difference in terms of outcomes (see previous section).

Importantly, though, comparisons made on the basis of cross-sectional design assume unit-homogeneity, i.e. that the units of analysis do not somehow relate to each other empirically. Consequently, diffusion of conditions or outcomes between regions A and B can, hypothetically speaking, exercise effects that lead to spatial interdependence (Table 6.1; Przeworski and Teune, 1970, p. 52). Still, there are also situations in which it is more or less unlikely that there are any such unit-to-unit effects on the observed outcome. For example, geographical distance between units, but also regional and nation-level institutional differences (in studies involving regions in different countries), suggests that unit-to-unit diffusion of policies is less likely to intervene as a factor in the analysis (Balland, Boschma and Frenken, 2015; Boschma, Marocců and Paci, 2016).

Presumably the first of these two conditions is relevant in Doloreux' (2004; Table 6.2) study of entrepreneurship in Ottawa and Beauce, at least to some extent. First, Doloreux describes the two Canadian regions as differentiated and highly specialized, i.e. features that perhaps make unit-to-unit effects leading to spatial interdependence less likely, even within the same nation-state context (Doloreux, 2004, pp. 489–490). Second, though, Doloreux at the same time notes that entrepreneurship in both regions actually draws a lot on "extra-regional networks" (2004, pp. 489–490).

By comparison, a situation that is more likely to involve spatial interdependence is illustrated by Kubicek's (2000; Table 6.2), analysis of West and East Ukrainian regions (L'viv and Donets'k). Whereas the two regions are mostly different from each other, notably in terms of political preferences among the voters (Kubicek, 2000), we could still be dealing with a case of spatial interdependence, caused by direct or indirect diffusion. Outcomes in terms of voting behaviour among citizens in L'viv may cause effects on the voting behaviour in Donets'k (or vice versa), since elections in the two regions are part of the same, nation-level institutional arrangements.

As already indicated, though, cross-sectional design does include options for controlling spatial interdependence. Within the framework of small-N cross-sectional studies, either the selection of units, or spatial-lagged variables,[9] can be used as means to control for spatial interdependence (Caramani, 2008). With respect to the first strategy, Doloreux's (2004) above-mentioned study is somewhat ambiguous, but the guiding principle is nevertheless to select regions that, beyond reasonable doubt, lack any connections whatsoever between them (real-world illustrations can include regional development policies in Australia and Sweden). According to the second strategy, the regional development policy e.g. in region A is included to control for diffusion effects on the development policy in region B.

But cross-sectional research design also suffers from methodological weaknesses. It can involve analysis of certain elements of temporality, as reflected in the use of temporal-lagged variables,[10] or by inclusion of the "historical backgrounds" of the units of analysis. Yet, cross-sectional comparisons of units from different, historical contexts are, by definition, problematic in this type of research design, since it is "unlikely that the same bases of [causal] inference are equally valid for all [social, political et al. types of] systems" (Przeworski and Tune, 1970, p. 113). Although cross-sectional design has inspired models for process-tracing, i.e. one of the methods often used in studies made according to development design (see next section), in its original form lacks options for specifying and analysing temporal and temporal-spatial interdependence (Table 6.1). The opportunities that analysts miss out because of this can be illustrated with the help of the last example listed in Table 6.2, that is, Reiser, Rademacher and Jaeck's (2008; Table 6.2) study of German independent local lists.

In a de-centralized, political system such as the *Bundesrepublik*, local political parties of this type have a potentially important role to play from a local and regional development perspective. However, their performance, including voter support, differs between regions and localities, and the purpose of Reiser, Rademacher and Jaeck's study is to explain these differences. Their conclusion is that the performance of ILLs is most likely tied to historically-transferred differences in "political culture" (2008, pp. 142–143). These variations, however, are analysed by studying cross-sectional differences in institutional design among the units (regions). Apart from the fact that behavioural and/or attitudinal data is more suitable as an indicator of political culture, the study, because of its cross-sectional design, overlooks the opportunity to investigate how historically-transferred differences in this relate causally to each other in the temporal dimension (Table 6.1).

Development design and temporal interdependence

Methodologically, the opposite of cross-sectional design is development design, since the latter does not include synchronic comparisons (and therefore, typically, no options for specification and analysis of spatial interdependence, although there are certain exceptions, see below). Rather, development design serves the purpose of making diachronic comparisons in analyses of one single unit. Studies made according to development design therefore face other types of challenges compared to cross-sectional design, but also open up opportunities for which the former type of study does not allow.

First, development design indicates the problem of causal lags in connection to diachronic comparisons. As previously pointed out, processes and, therefore, change always includes a temporal dimension. It takes *time* for the independent factor to cause effects in the dependent factor: how long does it take for a condition X in region A to cause an observed outcome with respect to outcome Y? Examples of outcomes can include features of regional policy or regional governance. That is, contrary to synchronic comparisons in which focus is on the causal relation between X and Y at a given, static moment in time, diachronic comparisons focus on changes between X and Y across time (Table 6.1).

Second, temporal interdependence also involves the contingency that the dependent factor might exercise effects on the independent factor, rather than the other way around. Causality is not necessary linear. Contrary to theoretical predictions in a study of region A, outcomes relating e.g. to regional policy, can involve a causality characterized by interaction, or feedback effects between conditions in the historical context of region A. The strategy to include temporal-lagged variables, or process-tracing models for the purpose of policy analysis (Beach and Pedersen, 2012), therefore helps to clarify the causal order between variables in studies made according to development design. Similar challenges, but also opportunities, face students who apply historical approaches to regional themes, but we will start by clarifying the logic of controlled diachronic comparisons with the help of Møller (2017; Table 6.2).

Møller's (2017) concern is the causality involved with formation of representative, political institutions (notably the *cortes*) from the 12th century onwards in Aragon, one of Europe's many principalities which were gradually emerging as sovereign states. The study stresses the role of discontinuity and specific events to change; it is, indeed, an analysis of a period in history during which distinguishable differences between institutional levels in society started to appear between local and (however primordial) state-levels of administration. Consequently, Møller starts by specifying possible sources of spatial interdependence, pertaining to the cases *within* the unit (Aragon), before considering temporal interdependence (labelled "historical diffusion" in the study). In so doing, he also devises a solution to the problem posed by the lack of extensive historical data. In the diachronic comparisons of Aragonese representative institutions, (scarce) historical narratives are systematically converted into within-case binary observations (2017, p. 2339). Binary categories are, according to Møller, easier to detect in the sources, compared to detailed information about institutions. Note therefore, that his approach is different to the manner in which historians apply source criticism as a tool to sift a limited number of sources in order to extract as much valid information as possible.

Yet, despite such disciplinary differences with respect to managing data, the explanatory logic on which development design studies draw, and the logic underpinning conventional historical case studies, remains the same. Provided that the data collected from the sources can confirm that similar outcomes in Aragon repeatedly relate to similar conditions in Aragon across time, these conditions and the observed outcomes are in all probability causally related. In analogy to Møller's (2017) study, historians can therefore exploit the advantages provided by detailed, in-depth analysis to examine generic processes (cf. Joyner, 1999). Consequently, the above-mentioned types of research design can potentially help explain developmental outcomes within single units.

In addition to shedding some light on the "root causes" of certain, generic phenomena, such as representative, political institutions, development design studies can however also highlight the historical specificity of particular cases. Loughlin's (2007; Table 6.2) study of Northern Ireland is a case in point. Since it is the relation between ethno-nationalism and policy-making, c. 1880–1920, that is the focus of the study, Loughlin involves processes that are typical to cross-border regions such as Northern Ireland, i.e. how identities are forced upon regions by their 'host states' (Wolff, 2003). Hence, the study, among other things, draws attention to travelogues as a means to construct a sense of Britishness in Northern Ireland, and, thereby, the creation of what Loughlin labels a "social and geographical fact" (Loughlin, 2007, p. 162).

At the same time, though, the above examples also point to the weaknesses of diachronic comparisons within the same unit. Although of theoretical and empirical value, studies made according to development design are less suitable for testing explanations of regularities and causality. Rather, for such purposes, proponents of quantitative research favour spatial-temporal lag models designed to capture both spatial as well as temporal interdependence in synchronic *and* diachronic comparisons (Darmofal, 2015). Spatial-temporal lag models require extensive access to historical data, and suffer from limited options for analysing causality between variables, but still allow considering interdependence in terms of an analytical opportunity. Comparative sequence design is a case in point.

Comparative sequence design and temporal-spatial interdependence

Falleti and Mahoney (2015) provide the best illustration to the logic underpinning CSD.[11] Being process-oriented, the purpose of this type of research design is comparisons of "events" ordered into historical "sequences". Events, then, are the basic unit of analysis in CSD. They are contextual in temporal and spatial terms, i.e. events occur in specific historical settings that infuse them with meaning and – depending on the sequence in which they occur, events relative to each other – causally decide their outcomes. Nevertheless, the analyst can still decide whether different events share enough commonalities to allow for comparisons. Following Falleti and Mahoney (2015, pp. 212–213), events are theoretically distinct from "occurrences", since the latter are singular and, thus, defy the logic of comparative analysis.

By the same logic, a sequence is a string of events that relate to a single, coherent mode of activity across time, such as democratization, decentralization, or mobilization. Also, sequences can be part of bigger, and more complex processes. Not surprisingly, Falleti and Mahoney (2015, p. 211) refer back to Barrington Moore's seminal (1966) study of democratization and dictatorship as a precursor, and in which study Moore compared sequences (of events) and societal processes in order to formulate conclusions about the determinants for political regimes (cf. also the analogy to Anderson, 1974, on the lineages of the Absolutist state).

First, according to the logic of CSD, e.g. process-tracing models are applied to order (inductively or deductively) the events temporally, and into at least two separate sequences for the purpose of diachronic and synchronic comparisons. The aim of the diachronic comparisons in CSD is to analyze causal links between different events, i.e. whether a temporal and/or causal order between the events can be determined. An important feature of this step is also to determine the extent to which the "speed" or duration of a specific event proves to be a causal condition for the observed outcome. This opens up the possibility for testing hypotheses about the causality of processes, and for the formulation of theoretical statements about case-specific modes of causality.

Second, CSD at the same time includes synchronic comparisons of sequences, according to the logic of cross-sectional comparisons previously described here (i.e. the methods of agreement and difference, but also qualitative comparative analysis). In this step of the analysis, the research design allows researchers to identify which types of sequences are sufficient or even necessary, to cause the observed outcome. That is, the inclusion of controlled, synchronic comparisons with the research design means that CSD meets the demands for observing the degree of regularity involved with causality among several spatial units, such as regions.

CSD therefore invites analysts to explore interdependence *between* the (spatial) units included in the analysis. An illustration to this is the opportunity to determine whether events in region A, such as the launching of a new development policy, connect to similar events in region B, or if events are part of independent processes in region A and region B. Furthermore, the diachronic dimension of CSD also allows inclusion of dynamic models focusing on explaining developmental outcomes and analysis of temporal interdependence. In technically more advanced models applicable to the research design, it is, as indicated, possible to identify the temporal order of events, and to analyse the temporal order of causality with respect to the dependent variable (outcome). This includes control for reverse effects, e.g. in terms of feedback-effects and time lags. Among others, the idea that *critical junctures* create path dependencies over time – and, hence, that historical "legacies" exercise effects on decision-making with respect to policy and governance (cf. Capocci and Ziblatt, 2010; Møller, 2013) – can be systematically tested in studies made according to CSD.

So far, however, actual examples of small-N regional-level studies, in which the analysis of both spatial, and temporal, as well as temporal-spatial interdependence is systematically included, are scarce. Yet, Basta's (2018; Table 6.2) study of territorial reform in Canada and Spain during two time periods is one possible illustration. Basta's focus lies on the reinforcing effects exercised by sequences of accommodation and reactiveness respectively on political stability (in terms of demands for regional independence). Basta's aim is to test the hypothesis that territorial reform, through policy substance, produces effects on political stability. Canadian and Spanish sequences of accommodation and reaction are first identified (two sequences in each country, but under different periods). Basta then compares the sequences in two pair-comparisons. The conclusion is that a combination of decentralization and symbolic recognition of minority nationhood, rather than political and economic divisions between governmental levels, better explains political stability (Basta, 2018, pp. 66–67). Finally, Evenhuis' (2016; Table 6.2) multi-scalar analysis of economic change, policy and government in two industrial regions, South Saarland and Teesside, c. 1960–1980, should be mentioned as an illustration to the logic of comparative sequence design. Although described by the author as a "comparative case study", the methodology, in fact, draws on a combination of cross-sectional design and path-dependency analysis for the study of resilience and adaptation across time in the two regions (Evenhuis, 2016, pp. 65, 80–85).

Unlike cross-sectional design and development design, CSD provides guiding principles for how to analyse *combinations* of spatial and temporal interdependence (temporal-spatial interdependence, Table 6.1). For instance, provided that a particular policy initiative (X) was implemented in region A, in 2000, and region B chose to introduce the same policy 15 years later – does this indicate that policy X has, indeed, travelled across time, from region A to region B? CSD opens up for an exploration of precisely how events of this kind in one unit affect later events in yet other units, for example, by force of diffusion.

Conclusions

We have demonstrated the methodological challenges, but also the opportunities involved with the analysis of interdependence in comparative research. Different types of comparative research designs, however, offer different options for specifying and analyzing spatial, temporal and temporal-spatial interdependence (summarized in Table 6.3). We conclude that above all, comparative sequence design poses an important methodological option, ripe for further exploration within the framework of small-N comparative research on regions.

CSD invites the researcher to combine controlled synchronic *and* diachronic comparisons. In relation to other types of research design, it offers the

Table 6.3 Spatial and temporal dimensions of interdependence

Type of research design	*Spatial interdependence*	*Temporal interdependence*	*Dimension of interdependence*
Cross-sectional design	+	-	Spatial interdependence
Development design	-	+	Temporal interdependence
Comparative sequence design	+	+	Spatial independence Temporal interdependence Temporal-spatial interdependence

most extensive toolbox for specifying and analysing interdependence and its role in causal explanations: CSD allows for both (i) cross-unit and cross-case comparisons as well as (ii) within-unit analyses. It (iii) allows the researcher to use dynamic (process-oriented) models with a focus on explaining developmental outcomes among sub-national level units. Thus, allowing analysis of the temporal and spatial order of causality, including a control for reverse effects, and time and spatial lags, CSD (iv) enhances the opportunities to analyse spatial, temporal and temporal-spatial interdependence among sub-national level units. Regional themes that can profit from this historically-oriented *and* methodologically versatile research design include policy-making, policy diffusion, and policy implementation as dynamic, historically contingent processes.

Notes

1 Originally, the challenges involved with interdependence were addressed by Francis Galton (1889) in a comment on a study by Edward Taylor (1889) on social complexity, marriage and descent (hence the reason why interdependence is also known as "Galton's problem"). Galton questioned Taylor's conclusion about a strong correlation between degree of social complexity and the degree of modernity of marriage institutions, simply by pointing out that these institutions often diffuse between societies. It should also be noted that diffusion-processes, in addition to learning and emulation, can also involve coercion, competition, migration and also commonality of cultural norms and symbolic imitation, only to mention some of the most commonly researched mechanisms: Braun and Gilardi (2006); Franzese and Hays (2008); Simmons, Dobbins and Garrett (2006).

2 Sample size is an important parameter for estimating the strength of spatial autocorrelation, but this is not necessarily always a problem in small-N comparative studies, since small-N studies can involve large samples of empirical observations.

3 This happens when attributes cluster closely together diachronically. Let us consider democratization of political regimes, and a situation in which the degree of democracy in one year correlates strongly with the degree of democracy in the previous year. In such cases, the duration of *conditions* favouring democratization must also be included in the analysis in order to decide whether we are dealing with temporal autocorrelation, or temporal interdependence, see Coppedge (2015).

4 For the purpose of this chapter, we find that commenting any further e.g. on the "method of concomitant variation" is superfluous.

5 We have added probability to McCullagh's definition, since quantitative and qualitative approaches in social sciences and historical research alike always, to some extent, involves interpretation and, because of this, a certain amount of (theoretically informed) probability-reasoning. Note also that we refer to societal et al. regularities, similarly to McCullagh's reasoning about explanations of structural phenomena.

6 Note that Table 6.1 does not include effects appearing as contemporaneous effects of factors *within* the unit on the observed outcome, since this effect includes neither spatial nor temporal dimensions. This type of effect involves the relation between factors in the same time-period and unit ($X_{t1,s1} => Y_{t1,s1}$), and it causes no interdependence *between* units. Spatial autocorrelation, as mentioned above in the text, is one illustration to this type of effect.

7 It should however be noted that studies made according to case study design normally include references e.g. to the nation-state "context" of a specific region, or offer "parallels", or "analogies" or anything such to yet other regions; "context" indicates a spatial dimension but, importantly, not controlled (synchronic or diachronic) comparisons. Similarly, if we consider studies made according to development design, we can note that these are fundamentally similar to historical case studies. However, whereas development design includes the potential for specifying and analysing temporal interdependence, it lacks options for controlling spatial interdependence.

8 ILLs are local political parties that organize and compete for votes locally, and are independent from the national party system.

9 A spatial-lagged variable refers to a condition or outcome in another unit than the unit of the dependent variable.

10 Temporal-lagged variables are included in order to define the temporal location of the compared cases. This strategy challenges the notion of cross-sectional design, since this design focuses exclusively on synchronic comparisons. Note also that comparative analyses use the time dimension as a response to the classic problem of "too-many-variables-too-few-cases"; see Lijphart (1971). That is, in order to avoid overloading the analyses with too many variables in relation to the number of cases, researchers measure the same variables and cases at different points in time, which provides the analysis with more observations.

11 Falleti and Mahoney use the term "comparative sequential *method*" to describe this type of research design. We prefer "comparative sequence design", since the former term signals that there is, indeed, a single method for analysing temporal-spatial interdependence.

References

Alapuro, R., 2012. Revisiting microhistory from the perspective of comparisons. In: S. Fellman and M. Rahikainen, ed. 2012. *Historical knowledge. In quest of theory, method and evidence.* Newcastle upon Tyne: Cambridge Scholars Publishing. Pp. 133–154.

Almond, G. and Verba, S., 1963. *The civic culture: Political attitudes and democracy in five nations.* Princeton: Princeton University Press.

Anderson, P., 1974. *Lineages of the absolutist state.* London: NLB.

Askarov, Z. and Doucouliagos, H., 2015. Spatial aid spillovers during transition. *European Journal of Political Economy*, 40(1), pp. 79–95. https://doi.org/10.1016/j.ejpoleco.2015.10.005

Balland, P-A., Boschma, R. and Frenken, K., 2015. Proximity and innovation: From statistics to dynamics. *Regional Studies*, 49(6), pp. 907–920. https://doi.org/10.1080/00343400520003 20887

Basta, K., 2018. The state between minority and majority nationalism: Decentralization, symbolic recognition, and secessionist crisis in Spain and Canada. *Publius: The Journal of Federalism*, 48(1), pp. 51–75.

Beach, D. and Pedersen, R. B., 2012. *Process-tracing methods: Foundations and guidelines.* Ann Arbor: University of Michigan Press.

Bendix, R., 1964. *Nation-building and citizenship. Studies of our changing social order.* New York: Wiley.

Bloch, M., 1952 [1928]. Toward a comparative history of European societies. In: F. C. Lane and J. C. Riemersma, eds. *Enterprise and secular change.* London: Allen & Unwin. Pp. 494–521.

Boschma, R., Maroccu, E. and Paci, R., 2016. Symmetric and asymmetric effects of proximities. The case of M&A deals in Italy. *Journal of Economic Geography*, 16(2), pp. 505–535. https://doi.org/10.1093/jeg/lbv005

Boschma, R., Martin, V. and Minondo, A., 2017. Neighbour regions as the source of new industries. *Papers in Regional Science*, 96(2), pp. 227–245. https://doi.org/10.1111/pirs.12215

Braun, D. and Gilardi, F., 2006. Taking "Galton's problem" seriously: Towards a theory of policy diffusion. *Journal of Theoretical Politics*, 18(3), pp. 298–322. https://doi.org/10.1177/0951629806064351

Caramani, D., (2008). *Introduction to the comparative method with Boolean algebra*. Quantitative applications in the social sciences, no. 158. London: Sage.

Capocci, G. and Ziblatt, D., 2010. The historical turn in democratization studies: A new research agenda for Europe and beyond. *Comparative Political Studies*, 43(8/9), pp. 931–968.

Christian, S., 2016. *What is global history?* Princeton: Princeton University Press.

Cipolla, C. M., 1972. The diffusion of innovations in early modern Europe. *Comparative Studies in Society and History*, 14(1), pp. 46–52.

Coppedge, M., 2015. *Democratization and Research Methods*. Cambridge: Cambridge University Press.

Darmofal, D., 2015. *Spatial analysis for the social sciences*. Cambridge: Cambridge University Press.

Doloreux, D., 2004. Regional innovation systems in Canada: A comparative study. *Regional Studies*, 38(5), pp. 479–492. https://doi.org/10.1080/0143116042000229267

Elkins, Z. and Simmons, B. A., 2005. On waves, clusters, and diffusion: A conceptual framework. *ANNALS of the American Academy of Political and Social Science*, (598), pp. 33–51.

Esping-Andersen, G., 1990. *The three worlds of welfare capitalism*. Princeton: Princeton University Press.

Evenhuis, E., 2016. *The political economy of adaptation and resilience in old industrial regions: A comparative study of South Saarland and Teesside*. Newcastle University: PhD thesis, Centre for Urban and Regional Development Studies, School of Geography, Politics and Sociology. Faculty of Humanities and Social Sciences.

Falleti, T. G. and Mahoney, J., 2015. The comparative sequential method. In: J. Mahoney and K. Thelen, ed. 2015. *Advances in comparative-historical analysis (strategies for social inquiry)*. Cambridge: Cambridge University Press. Pp. 211–239.

Franzese, R. J. and Hays, J. C., 2008. Interdependence in comparative politics: Substance, theory, empirics, substance. *Comparative Political Studies*, 41(4/5), pp. 742–780.

Galton, F., 1889. Discussion of Dr. Tylor's memoir. *Journal of the Royal Anthropological Institute of Great Britain and Ireland*, (18), pp. 270–272.

Ihalainen, P., 2017. *The springs of democracy: National and transnational debates on constitutional reform in the British, German, Swedish and Finnish parliaments, 1917–1919*. Helsinki: Studia Fennica Historica.

Jahn, D., 2006. Globalization as 'Galton's problem': The missing link in the analysis of diffusion pattern in welfare state development. *International Organization*, 60(2), pp. 401–431.

Joyner, C. W., 1999. *Shared traditions: Southern history and folk culture*. Urbana: University of Illinois Press.

Kocka, J., 1999. Asymmetrical historical comparison: The case of the German Sonderweg. *History and Theory*, 1(38), pp. 40–50. https://doi.org/10.1111/0018-2656.751999075

Kubicek, P., 2000. Regional polarisation in Ukraine: Public opinion, voting, and legislative behaviour. *Europe-Asia Studies*, 52(2), pp. 273–294.

Landman, T. and Carvalho, E., 2016. *Issues and methods in comparative politics. An introduction*. New York: Routledge.

Laven, D. and Baycroft, T., 2008. Border regions and identity. *European Review of History*, 15(3), pp. 255–275. https://doi.org/10.1080/13507480802082581

Lijphart, A., 1971. Comparative politics and the comparative method. *American Political Science Review*, 65(3), pp. 682–693.

Lijphart, A., 1999. *Patterns of democracy: Government forms & performance in thirty-six countries*. New Haven: Yale University Press.

Loughlin, J., 2007. Creating a "social and geographical fact". Regional identity and the Ulster question 1880–1920s. *Past & Present*, 195(1), pp. 159–196. https://doi.org/10.1093/pastj/gtm002

Martin, R., Sunley, P. and Tyler, P., 2015. Local growth evolutions: Recession, resilience and recovery. *Cambridge Journal of Regions, Economy and Society*, (8), pp. 141–148.

McCullagh, C. B., 2004. *The logic of history. Putting postmodernism in perspective*. London: Routledge.

Mill, J. S., 1875. *A system of logic: Ratiocinative and inductive: Being a connected view of the principles of evidence and the methods of scientific investigation*, Vol 1 (9th ed). London: Longmans, Green, Reader & Dyer.

Møller, J., 2013. When one might not see the wood for the trees: The "historical turn" in democratization studies, critical junctures, and cross-case comparisons. *Democratization*, (20)4, pp. 693–715.

Møller, J., 2017. A framework for congruence analysis in comparative historical analysis of political change. *Quality and Quantity*, 51(5), pp. 2337–2355.

Moore, Jr, B., 1966. *Social origins of dictatorship and democracy. Lord and peasant in the making of the modern world*. Boston: Beacon.

Naroll, R., 1965. Galton's problem: The logic of cross-cultural analysis. *Social Research*, 32(4), pp. 428–451.

O'Loughlin, J., Ward, M. D., Lafdahl, C. L., Cohen, J. S., Brown, D. S., Gleditsch, K. S. and Shin, M., 1998. The diffusion of democracy, 1946–1994. *Annals of the Association of American Geographers*, 88(4), pp. 545–574.

Overton, M., 1985. The diffusion of agricultural innovations in early modern England: Turnips and clover in Norfolk and Suffolk, 1580–1740. *Transactions of the Institute of British Geographers*, 10(2), pp. 205–221.

Peters, G., 2014. *Strategies for comparative research in political science. Theory and methods*. Basingstoke: Palgrave.

Przeworski, A. and Teune, H., 1970. *The logic of comparative social inquiry*. Malabar: Krieger.

Putnam, R. D., 1993. *Making democracy work. Civic traditions in modern Italy*. Princeton, NJ: Princeton University Press.

Reiser, M., Rademacher, C. and Jaeck, T., 2008. Präsenz und erfolg kommunaler wählergemeinschaften im bundesländervergleich. In: A. Vetter, ed. 2008. *Erfolgsbedingungen lokaler bürgerbeteiligung*. Wiesbaden: VS Verlag. Pp. 123–147.

Rogers, E. M., 1995. *Diffusion of innovations*. New York: Free Press.

Rokkan, S., 1966. Comparative cross-national research: The context of current efforts. In: R. L. Merrit and S. Rokkan, ed. 1966. *Comparing nations: The use of quantitative data in cross-national research*. New Haven: Yale University Press. Pp. 3–25.

Sewell, W. H. Jr., 1967. Marc Bloch and the logic of comparative history. *History and Theory*, 6(2), pp. 208–218.

Shipan, C. R. and Volden, C., 2008. The mechanisms of policy diffusion. *American Journal of Political Science*, (52)4, pp. 840–857. https://doi.org/10.1111/j.1540-5907.2008.00346.x

Simmons, B. A. and Elkins, Z., 2004. The globalization of liberalization: Policy diffusion in the international political economy. *American Political Science Review*, 98(1), pp. 171–189.

Simmons, B., Dobbins, F. and Garrett, G., 2006. Introduction: The international diffusion of liberalism. *International Organization*, 60(4), pp. 781–810.

Skocpol, T., 1984. Emerging agendas and recurrent strategies in historical sociology. In: T. Skocpol, ed. *Vision and method in historical sociology*. Cambridge: Cambridge University Press, pp. 356–291.

Snyder, R., 2001. Scaling down: The subnational comparative method. *Studies in Comparative International Development*, 36(1), pp. 93–110.

Strang, D., 1991. Adding social structure to diffusion models: An event history framework. *Sociological Methods and Research*, 19(3), pp. 324–353.

Taylor, E. B., 1889. On a method of investigating the development of institutions: Applied to laws of marriage and descent. *Journal of the Royal Anthropological Institute of Great Britain and Ireland*, (18), pp. 235–270.

Ther, P., 2009. Comparisons, cultural transfers, and the study of networks. Toward a transnational history of Europe. In: H.-G. Haupt and J. Kocka, eds. *Comparative and transnational history. Central European approaches and new perspectives*. New York: Berghahn. Pp. 204–225.

Volden, C., Ting, M. M. and Carpenter, D. P., 2008. A formal model of learning and policy diffusion. *American Political Science Review*, 102(3), pp. 319–332.

Wellhofer, S. E., 1989. The comparative method and the study of development, diffusion, and social change. *Comparative Political Studies*, 22(3), pp. 315–342.

Werner, M. and Zimmermann, B., 2006. Beyond comparison. "Histoire croisée" and the challenge of reflexivity. *History and Theory*, 45(1), pp. 30–50.

Weyland, K., 2006. *Bounded rationality and policy diffusion. Social sector reform in Latin America*. Princeton: Princeton University Press.

Wolff, S., 2003. *Disputed territories: The transnational dynamics of ethnic conflict settlement*. New York: Berghahn.

Part III

Empirical case studies

7 Catching the ladder

The formation and growth of the São Paulo automotive industry cluster[1]

Tomàs Fernández-de-Sevilla and Armando J. dalla Costa

Introduction

A direct connection between industrialization and economic growth has largely been established (Gerschenkron, 1962; Landes, 1969; Pollard, 1981; Allen, 2010). The automobile industry became a major driver of economic growth in late industrialized countries from the mid-20th century (Amsden, 1989; Jenkins, 1995). Likewise, regional concentration of industry has also been indicated as a source of competitive advantage in both developed and developing countries (Porter, 1990: Schmitz, 1999). However, in order to be able to overcome the difficulties to develop industrial clusters in an endogenous manner, the peripheral economies tend to have to resort to direct foreign investment, often in the form of the installation of subsidiaries of multinational companies (MNCs) (Amin and Thrift, 1994; Young, Hood and Peters, 1994). Nevertheless, it is not surprising that the result is an independent evolutionary process through which the development of the cluster in turn determines the strategies of the MNCs (Enright, 2000).

The aim of this research is to analyze the emergence and growth of an automobile industry cluster in São Paulo (Brazil) from its origins at the beginning of the 20th century until its expansion phase was completed in the mid-1970s, when production stabilized in the region at 900,000 vehicles per year for the next 25 years. The São Paulo automobile industry cluster considered in this research encompasses companies and institutions located in São Paulo city and in the areas organized around the Anchieta and Dutra motorways. The former connects São Paulo to the Port of Santos, crossing the so-called São Paulo ABC (the municipalities of Santo André, São Bernardo do Campo, and São Caetano do Sul), whereas the latter connects São Paulo with Rio de Janeiro. The cluster stretches as far as the municipality of São José dos Campos (85km from São Paulo).

The formation and expansion of the São Paulo cluster was an evolutionary process which, far from being linear or automatic, arose from the combination of premeditated decisions, historical situations and trial and error. Historical analysis therefore has great explanatory potential, making it essential to study this subject from a long-term dynamic perspective. Understanding the process of the emergence and development of the São Paulo industrial automotive district in a comprehensive manner will lead to an increase in the empirical evidence on this type of phenomena, which are currently taking place both in other regions of Brazil and in other countries which are seeking to become industrialized. This will facilitate the practice of regional policy and planning, in Brazil and elsewhere.

Greater São Paulo is one of the few tropical or sub-tropical areas in the southern hemisphere where an advanced industrial system has developed. The origins of São Paulo's industrialization can be traced to the late 19th century, when the investment of capital accumulated through coffee exportation caused the first factories to emerge (Dean, 1969; Silva, 1976; Cano, 1981; Suzigan, 1986). Although the take-off of the automotive industry took place in the mid-20th century, its roots go back to the beginning of the century. By using a historical approach, this study attempts to assess the key determinants in the formation and growth of the São Paulo auto-industry cluster.

This research will follow the interpretative models and empirical strategies defined by Markusen (1996), Catalan (2017), and Carli and Morrison (2018). Markusen's (1996) concept of hierarchical cluster, in which few big firms acted as coordinating centres or hubs of the regional economy, is used. The conceptual framework distinguishes between internal and external explanatory factors and allows for acknowledging that the different phases in the evolution of the cluster do not occur in a rigid manner but rather follow an adaptive path (Carli and Morrison, 2018). Finally, the empirical strategy used to analyze the evolution of the São Paulo automotive cluster is defined in Catalan (2017), who studied the life-cycle of the Barcelona automotive district exploring the role played by four possible factors in the explanation of the relative success attained by that cluster: the presence of external economies; the capacities provided by hub companies; the adoption of national government strategic industrial policies; and the emergence of adequate local institutions.

History matters: Cluster institutions, strategic policies and large enterprises in the formation of the São Paulo auto-industry cluster

Clusters emerge and develop due to a process of positive mutual reinforcement arising from the geographic concentration of industrial activity, their life-cycles differing from those of industries (Swann, 2009, chapter 13; Menzel and Fornahl, 2010). Bergman (2008) identifies three main phases in the cluster life-cycle: the *existence*, which includes what must happen before the cluster achieves critical mass; the *expansion*, which involves the cluster growth; finally, the *exhaustion*, which arises when maturity and saturation hinder its viability, breaking its ability to innovate. In this last phase, which is beyond the scope of this study and in which congestion costs play a key role (Maskell and Kebir, 2006), the cluster may follow a divergent path, since it either enters a lock-in phase or may experience a renaissance (Enright, 2003; Tödtling and Trippl, 2004).

However, recent studies maintain that the majority of the work on the life-cycle of clusters has focused almost exclusively on their internal dynamics, neglecting the role of external factors, socio-economic contingencies and historical situations (Martin and Sunley, 2011; Trippl et al., 2015; Carli and Morrison, 2018). The conclusion of these studies is that clusters tend to follow an "adaptive" path rather than evolving in accordance with a predefined pattern, thus revealing the importance of history. Through a historical analysis which uses a narrative structure, this study seeks to understand the role played by various economic factors, such as Marshallian externalities, local institutions, industrial policy and big companies, in the formation and expansion of the São Paulo automotive cluster.

The developmental state has been pointed out as a crucial agent of industrialization in developing countries (Johnson, 1982; Amsden, 1989 and 2003; Evans, 1995; Woo-Cumings, 1999), including Brazil (Schneider, 1991; Shapiro, 1994; Catalan and Fernández-de-Sevilla, 2018).[2] Chang (2002) recovered the protectionist argument for the defence of emerging industries in developing countries described by Friedrich List – who was in turn influenced by Alexander Hamilton – to argue that all economies in the process of modernization have employed industrial, trade and technological policies to boost their economic development. According to him, historical experience shows that the transition towards higher added-value activities does not happen naturally, but rather requires the use of a wide array of strategic policies, including protection of targeted industries. Their insistence on the need for developing countries to adopt active industrial policies is shared extensively (Cimoli, Stiglitz and Dosi, 2009; Stiglitz and Lin, 2013; Norman and Stiglitz, 2016).

Nevertheless, industrial policy alone does not explain why the automobile industry clustered in São Paulo, a region that produced practically all of the near one million vehicles manufactured in Brazil in 1974. The competitive advantages associated with the geographic concentration of industry were first characterized by Alfred Marshall, who argues that Britain was the workshop of the world in the 19th century due to certain external economies of scale present in its industrial districts. Together with a specific set of services and infrastructures – in Lancashire, for example, the regional railway system – these include a pool of skilled workers and specialized suppliers, forming a vigorous intra-district market and permitting the (almost) free spread of knowledge and information (Marshall, 1890, book 4, chapter 10).

The Marshallian district was revisited by Italian economic geographers, who pointed out that the competitive advantage of industrial districts of the so-called "Third Italy" came from an institutional environment characterized by an abundance of small and medium-sized firms with a high level of flexibility, enabling cooperation between firms and local governments in order to share risks and stabilize markets (Bagnasco, 1977; Brusco, 1982; Becattini, 1990). However, it has been argued that these works understated the role played by big firms in shaping the Italian districts (Harrison, 1994, chapter 4).

The Italian perspective has been challenged in Markusen (1996) by presenting three typologies of industrial districts articulated around large companies (the hub-and-spoke district, the satellite platform and the state-anchored district), which would better explain the flourishing and consolidation of regional economies in the USA, Japan, Korea and Brazil. Hub-and-spoke districts, the most predominant typology, are formed by a few large companies that act as anchors or hubs to the regional economy. In economic and business history, the greater efficiency of large companies has been also defended by emphasizing that their success lies in their accumulated technological and organizational capabilities (Chandler, 1977; Lazonick, 1990).

By offering access to public or semi-public goods such as infrastructures, vocational schools, universities and research centres, the cluster institutional environment, usually articulated by industrial and trade associations, could also provide part of the regional competitive advantage (Porter, 2008). According to Brusco (1982), the interaction between the productive structure, the labour market, and the local institutions to link salaries, productivity and investment in Emilia-Romagna (Italy) explained the regional competitive advantage. From a macroeconomic perspective, Marglin (1990) and Eichengreen (2007) maintain that the remarkable growth of Western European economies during the Golden Age was due to a series of neo-corporate institutional agreements between unions, employers' organizations and governments that explain why the former accepted the restriction of wage increases in return for the latter channelling the higher profit into new investment. Conversely, Olson (1982) and Acemoglu and Robinson (2012) explain that diverse groupings of industrialists or workers can be motivated to form lobbies to defend their personal interests, often pushing for the application of protectionist policies that damage economic growth.

Detailed studies have been undertaken in economic and business history on the structural transformations of central districts of the Industrial Revolution in the United Kingdom and the United States (Scranton, 1997; Wilson and Popp, 2003; Popp and Wilson, 2007). In the case of a typical industry from the second Industrial Revolution, such as the automotive sector, studies such as Klepper (2007, 2010), Donnelly, Begely and Collis (2017), and Pardi (2017) illustrate the potential of the historical analysis to understand the regional concentration of this industry, showing the rise and decline of clusters such as that of Detroit in the United States and the West Midlands in England. Likewise, Catalan, Miranda and Ramon-Muñoz (2011a) have presented an analysis that integrates the evidence presented in almost 20 case studies which offer a historical vision of the formation and growth of districts and clusters in Southern Europe. They conclude that, in this region, although cases have occurred of the emergence of competitive advantage in the framework of the neo-Marshallian district, the cluster model has been more common, with leading companies which have complemented the Marshallian externalities with the organizational capabilities characteristic of big companies (Catalan, Miranda and Ramon-Muñoz, 2011b). Outside the scope of industrial clusters, Molema, Segers and Karel (2016) indicate that, in the case of various agribusiness clusters developed in Europe in the 19th and 20th centuries, interactions between governments, entrepreneurs and associations of producers in the region played a pre-eminent role in the expansion through regulatory frameworks along with educational and scientific policies. On the other hand, disagreement and competition could also promote the clustering of activity. All of these studies reveal the potential of the historical analysis to understand an economic phenomenon such as the tendency of industrial activity to concentrate on a regional level.

The following three sections chronologically study the formation and expansion stages of the cluster, beginning with its origins, continuing with the formation of the critical mass essential for the cluster to be recognized as such, and ending with its growth until it reaches maturity. Finally, a last section integrates the three phases and the role played by the determinant factors in each of the stages.

The cluster's origins, 1900s–1929

At the same time as the wealthy coffee barons from inland were building their mansions in the first three decades of the 20th century, 1.57 million immigrants (82 per cent from abroad, mainly Europe) arrived in the city of São Paulo in search of employment in trade, construction and in its budding industry. The number of industrial establishments in the overall state went from 327 in 1907 to 4,112 in 1919 and 9,603 in 1928, with the number of employees in industry increasing from 25,000 to over 150,000, raising the weight of São Paulo's industry in the Brazilian total from 16 per cent to 37 per cent (Negri, 1996, pp. 36–37).

If in 1901 there were five cars registered in São Paulo, five years later there were 84 (Forest, 2002, p. 42). The chauffeurs that usually accompanied the imported vehicle introduced the first knowledge of mechanics to the region. They were responsible for repairing the vehicles and they taught the profession to their first Brazilian colleagues (Wolfe, 2010, pp. 21–22). The origins of the São Paulo cluster, however, lie in the small repairs and car parts manufacturing workshops that began to emerge during the 1920s to serve the automotive aftermarket. During those years, the number of cars registered in São Paulo state experienced constant growth, reaching 70,000 vehicles in 1929 (Forest, 2002, p. 31). In 1928, there were 317 establishments dedicated to the manufacture of transport material, which together employed almost 5,000 people (Negri, 1996, p. 37).

It was under this expansion that Ford, GM and International Harvester opened their first assembly lines for completely knock-down (CKD) kits.[3] After having opened a small office in the city of São Paulo in May 1919, Ford rented a large skating rink in Praça da República, right in the city centre, which became its first assembly line in January 1920. A few months later, the company decided to build a three-storey plant (which accounted for 100 employees) in the Bom Retiro neighbourhood, where it remained for several years (Wilkins and Hill, 2011, pp. 93–94). In 1925, Ford's production reached 14,861 units (Wilkins and Hill, 2011, p. 146), while sales reached 24,500 cars (Gonçalves,

1989, p. 34). According to Wilkins (1974, p. 171), Ford also tried to assemble in Recife (1925), Porto Alegre (1926) and Rio de Janeiro (1927), but without success, maintaining its assembly operations in São Paulo.

For its part, GM inaugurated a factory in the Ipiranga neighbourhood, the industrial heart of the city, in 1925. According to General Motors (1995, p. 11), the decision to set up the factory in São Paulo "resulted from an in-depth feasibility study conducted by the Corporation's management". The GM managers placed special value on the availability of electric power, petrol, raw materials, accessories and spare parts and components. A year after its inauguration, the rate of production was 40 cars per day. In 1927, having already assembled 25,000 Chevrolets, GM began the construction of a new factory in São Caetano do Sul, in the ABC region. The new factory was inaugurated in 1929, with an installed capacity of 100 units per day. The GM workforce (600 people) tripled Ford's workforce. Together with International Harvester, which also installed a small truck assembly line in 1926, many other brands established networks of representatives to import complete vehicles.

A set of related associations accompanied the first phases of São Paulo's motorization. The first car race in Latin America took place in São Paulo on 26 July 1908, organized by the Automobile Club of São Paulo, which had been founded 15 days earlier. Approximately 10,000 people gathered in Parque Antártica to see the start and finish of the race (Gonçalves, 1989, p. 24). After that, a wide range of car races took place involving São Paulo. Ten years later, in 1917, the 1st Congress of São Paulo Roadways was held, promoted by the state government. Some 70 cars circulated with relative ease along the road that connected São Paulo to the port of Santos, whose infrastructure development works, which began in 1913, were at a very advanced stage (Forest, 2002, pp. 40–42). In fact, in 1921, the four main cities in the state of São Paulo (Campinas, Jundiaí, Santos and São Paulo) were connected by road, while the connection with Rio de Janeiro did not appear until 1928. Furthermore, on 13 October 1923, the First Automobile Exhibition was inaugurated, with five shows being held during the decade (Wolfe, 2010, p. 47). In terms of worker training, it is worth highlighting that the Ford School of Mechanics and the GM School of Advanced Mechanics both geared towards training workers for the assembly lines and for the aftersales service offices (Nascimento, 1976, p. 14). Beyond the automotive industry, the creation of the Centre of Industries of the State of São Paulo (CIESP) in March 1928 and the Federation of Industries of the State of São Paulo (FIESP) in 1931, both founded by Jorge Street, Francisco Matarazzo and Roberto Simonsen, was also of special importance, as they were the first associations to call for a containment of the deindustrialization of Brazil and to defend industry protection.

During this period, neither the government nor the firms called for or tried to implement industrial policies to foster the industry's development. Ford and GM's main interest was the liberalization of trade, especially with regard to the importation of CKD kits. If both were assembling in São Paulo, this was due to their conviction that this was more profitable than importing complete vehicles. In fact, all the relations that Ford established with the Brazilian government involved rubber plantations in the Amazon basin, which was its main business in Brazil until 1945 when it was sold at a substantial loss; none involved assembly plants (Wilkins, 1974, pp. 102–122). The manufacturers from the auxiliary industry did not push for the application of industrial policies either, since they were not yet organized and did not have a unified discourse, which arrived with the deindustrialization that accompanied the impact of the Great Depression. Indeed, the creation of the CIESP coincided with the beginning of the slowdown in industrial production just before the outbreak of the Great Depression, while the formation of the FIESP took place at the height of the same. Moreover, the sectors most affected by the crisis were the chemical industry and metal products, within which the automotive industry falls. The manufacturing levels of 1929 did not recover until 1933, reaching a minimum of 72 per cent in 1931 (Baer, 2014, p. 29). Thus, in this phase, no type of industrial policy geared toward promoting the automotive industry was applied, either on a regional or a federal level.

At the dawn of the Great Depression, subsidiaries of the two biggest multinationals in the sector were operating in São Paulo and had great potential to become hub firms for the region. Ford's unsuccessful attempts to establish more assembly lines in other Brazilian regions could indicate the presence of external economies, as described by Marshall, in São Paulo. This hypothesis could be reinforced by the fact that GM also established its subsidiary in São Paulo, defined by GM as the main industrial hub in Latin America (General Motors, 1995, p. 11). Together with the Michigan giants, dozens of small workshops geared towards the spare parts market were starting to shape the cluster. This involved the formation of potential suppliers and skilled workers. They had no problem in finding as many workers as they required, not only from the roughly 150,000 industrial workers in the region, but also from immigration. Moreover, some associations were emerging and accompanying the district's first steps. However, the cluster's potential remained low, mainly because the two large firms restricted their operation to the simple assembly of CKD kits from the United States. At this stage, no industrial policy was implemented, and the degree of development achieved was not enough to consider the cluster as existent.

Looking for the critical mass: A trade association behind the cluster's first boost, 1930–1955

The Great Depression placed the Brazilian economy in dire straits. São Paulo's recovery consolidated in 1933, boosted by industrial expansion driven mainly by national capital that erected small and medium-sized plants with low capital intensity. The state's share of industrial added-value for the whole of Brazil went from 32.2 per cent to 48.9 per cent between 1919 and 1949, a percentage that reached 72.4 per cent in the case of durable goods (Negri, 1996, p. 80). This was no longer an industrialization process subordinated to the coffee industry's dynamics, but an expansion whose main driver was the city of São Paulo itself. In this period, Brazil was mainly ruled by Getúlio Vargas, who divided his sympathies between Roosevelt's New Deal, Mussolini's Charter of Labour and German-inspired dirigisme (Fausto, 2006). Vargas was appointed provisional president in 1930 by the Military Junta that led the 1930 Revolution, remaining in power first as constitutional president (1934–1937), and then as a dictator (1937–1945) by imposing a constitution that eradicated political parties, the right to vote and the right to strike. Vargas recovered the power in 1951 through a free and secret ballot, ending his presidency by committing suicide in 1954 (Fausto, 2006).

The autoparts industry boosted its development by taking advantage of the impossibility of importing autoparts during the Second World War. When the war ended, around a hundred workshops were scattered throughout São Paulo with the capacity to produce parts such as electrical accumulators, brake drums, wheel hubs, crown gears, pinions and axle shafts (Dean, 1969, p. 244). Although the liberalization of the market at the end of the war damaged the industry, most of Brazil's autoparts workshops were clustered in São Paulo in 1949 (Table 7.1), hosting 3,219 workers who accounted for 80 per cent of Brazil's total autoworkers (Nascimento, 1976, p. 27).

The externalities present in São Paulo can explain why the Veículos e Máquinas Agrícolas (Vemag) factory was established in the Ipiranga neighbourhood, although neither of its owners came from the region – the Domingos Fernandes family, established in Rio since the 19th century, where they had interests in casinos and hotels; the Swedish investor Svend H. Nielsen; and Melvin Brooks, a Studebaker representative (Sandler, 2005, p. 134). Its factory, which had one of the most important fleets of heavy-duty equipment in Latin America, assembled its first truck in 1948. Two years later, the company began negotiations with Scania on importing CKD truck kits, with the first units arriving in 1952. One year earlier, the Cia. Americana Industrial de Omnibus (CAIO), established in 1945, had started the production of chassis for its own buses, importing only engines and drive shafts (Nascimento, 1976, p. 25).

Table 7.1 Autoparts workshops in Brazil: 1949, 1953 and 1957

	São Paulo		*Rio de Janeiro*		*Rest of the States*		*TOTAL*	
	N°	*%*	*N°*	*%*	*N°*	*%*	*N°*	*%*
1949	65	65.0	3	3.0	32	32.0	100	100.0
1953	103	71.0	24	16.6	18	12.4	145	100.0
1957	118	88.1	5	3.7	11	8.2	134	100.0

Source: Authors' elaboration. For 1949 from Nascimento (1976, p. 27). For 1953 and 1957 the data corresponds to firms with displays at the Mostras da Indústria Nacional de Autopeças celebrated in Rio de Janeiro on 20 January 1953 and 22 July 1957, obtained from Gattas (1981, p. 107 and p. 249).

However, neither Vemag nor CAIO had the potential to act as anchor for the regional economy, as defined in Markusen (1996). It was GM and Ford who should have played this role, but they did not. In 1955, Ford assembled ten trucks per day and GM only half that, even adding buses and trucks, having an installed daily capacity of 125 and 200 vehicles, respectively (Nascimento, 1976, p. 53). The Brazilian economy was not attractive enough to persuade the American giants to transform their facilities into fully-fledged factories. In fact, until the mid-1950s, the main activity of GM's plant in São Caetano was fridge production (General Motors, 1995, pp. 40–45). Under these circumstances, the autoparts industry was limited to working only for the aftermarket.

The lifting of trade restrictions once the war ended (coinciding with the ousting of Vargas in 1945) once again filled the domestic market with imported parts, leaving many of the district's small companies in a critical situation. Therefore, the autoparts manufacturers took advantage of Brazil's serious foreign payment crisis of 1947, which depleted practically all of the currency reserves accumulated during the war, to promote the protection of the sector. After several meetings in the headquarters of the FIESP, the Professional Association of the Autoparts Industry of São Paulo (Associaçao, transformed into Sindipeças since September 1953[4]) was founded in October 1951 and involved the participation of 122 companies (Gattas, 1981, pp. 57–61). This association would turn out to be a key for the future of the cluster.

The Associaçao intensively demanded a protectionist programme inspired by the agenda formulated by Roberto Simonsen,[5] the direction of which recalls the nascent industry protection argument formulated by Friedrich List in 1841 and the design of which presents numerous points in common with the policies which, at the time, were beginning to be applied in developing countries, such as South Korea (Chang, 1993; Catalan, 2010) and Spain (Catalan and Fernández-de-Sevilla, 2013; Fernández-de-Sevilla, 2014). Its demands were considered favourable by Vargas's new government, which had been established after a democratic election on 31 January 1951. The government created the Sub-Commission on Jeeps, Tractors, Trucks and Cars, which reported to the Commission on Industrial Development on 20 March 1952 that it would study the viability of manufacturing cars in Brazil. One month later, the Associaçao delivered a report in which it maintained the existence of 250 companies capable of manufacturing 162 groups of parts and accessories. The rewards were reaped in August 1952 when "Aviso" No. 288 was published, vetoing the importation of the items on a list of 104 groups of parts and accessories already manufactured in the country. Because of this measure, many companies from the metal-mechanical branch began to produce parts that appeared on the list (Gattas, 1981, pp. 77–88).

In order to strengthen its position, the Associaçao promoted the holding in Rio de Janeiro, then the capital of the Federation, of the First Show of the Brazilian Autoparts Industry, which took place in Santos Dumont Airport on 20 January 1953. The geographical distribution of the almost 145 companies involved reveals that the industry was already concentrated in São Paulo (see

Table 7.1). A little later, in April 1953, "Aviso" No 311 prohibited the importation of pre-assembled motor vehicles, authorizing only the entry of CKD kits if they came without the parts specified in Decree 288. As a result, Volkswagen (VW) and Willys-Overland began to assemble CKD kits in workshops located around São Paulo, while Mercedes-Benz assembled its first units in Rio de Janeiro. However, as with Ford and GM, these initiatives were far from being fully-fledged manufacturing facilities.

The industrial development achieved by São Paulo in this period likely indicates the presence of external economies in the region, mainly the abundance of skilled workers as well as the presence of related industries. The intensification of the car parts industry clustering around São Paulo (see Table 7.1) and the establishment of Vemag also point in this direction. At the end of the period, well over 100 firms were located in the cluster, mostly in the Ipiranga neighbourhood and in the ABC. A pool of skilled workers and specialized suppliers was present in the district, where knowledge of the art moved easily from workshop to workshop. The lack of large carmakers with great demand-pull capacity was the main constraint to the cluster's expansion. Neither GM nor Ford had any desire to increase the range of their operations. To overcome this constraint, the autoparts companies created their own association to boost the sector through protectionist policies. Their demands found prompt echo in the new Vargas administration. Before the end of the year, Willys and VW had established assembly lines in São Paulo, while Mercedes-Benz installed its line in Rio de Janeiro. Soon afterwards, in June 1954, the Vargas government created the Executive Commission of the Autoparts Industry to boost the industry's development (Latini, 2007, pp. 84–97). However, after Vargas committed suicide in August 1954, the new liberal government of João Café Filho placed it on standby (Nascimento, 1976, pp. 45–49). The definitive boost for the cluster came from Juscelino Kubitschek (JK), appointed president of Brazil in 1956.

Growth: Industrial policy and hub firms, 1956–1974

Kubitschek did not hesitate to use the force of the state to boost the industrialization and modernization of Brazil (Sikkink, 1991; Shapiro, 1994). Automobiles were included in JK's flagship programme, known as the "Plano de Metas" or "Goals plan", which turned their manufacture into a priority.[6] In June 1956, the Executive Group of Automobile Industry (GEIA in its Portuguese initials) was created to accomplish the requirements of the Goals plan regarding vehicle manufacturing (Gattas, 1981; Shapiro, 1994). Its functions included setting the production targets (80,000 trucks and buses, 50,000 jeeps and light commercial vehicles and 40,000 passenger cars) and the percentages of local content (90 per cent for trucks and commercial vehicles and 95 per cent for cars and jeeps in 1960), as well as handling the acceptance and monitoring of individual investment projects. Protection was the essential tool to force the installation of big brands in the area, brands that would also gain some advantages in the exchange rate and some access to public credit. Beyond the fact that it was practically impossible to import automobiles, the central element which explains the growth of the cluster was the requirement to produce them with nationally manufactured parts and components.

The GEIA guidelines encouraged the development of the subsidiaries established in 1953 by VW and Willys, as well as causing the move of Mercedes to São Paulo, these being the companies that led the cluster's growth. The first project that VW presented to the GEIA was the manufacture of the Kombi van. Although, in the end, pressure from the GEIA led the Germans to also include the Beetle, their people's car – popularized in Brazil as the Fusca (Shapiro, 1991, pp. 911–918). Because of this pressure, VW built a new factory in São Bernardo do Campo, strongly inspired by its flagship plant in Wolfsburg (Fleury and Salerno, 1998, p. 281). At the same time, Willys erected a modern industrial complex in São José dos Campos with assembly lines, bodywork stamping and engine manufacturing (the engine block was cast in the neighbouring municipality of Taubaté), adding a research and development centre in 1962. It is important to note that, in order to accomplish its new and more ambitious goals, Mercedes-Benz moved its factory from Rua Bela in the city of Rio de Janeiro to São Bernardo do Campo. In September 1956, Mercedes inaugurated a new factory located at kilometre 15/16 of the Anchieta motorway, in the heart of the ABC region, thus further reinforcing the presence of external economies in the region.

The GEIA's requirements also forced Ford and GM, which were much more reluctant about manufacturing in Brazil (Wilkins and Hill, 2011, p. 414; Shapiro, 1991, pp. 918–933), to develop their facilities and become mass producers. GM modified its project to build only a truck assembly line in São José dos Campos by establishing a new comprehensive Chevrolet engine factory with iron casting, forging and engine block manufacturing, which was inaugurated in March 1959 (Gattas, 1981, pp. 223–224). Ford, which had no intention of manufacturing using entirely local content in its new facilities inaugurated in the Ipiranga neighbourhood in 1953, had to commit to erecting a fully-fledged engine factory next to the factory they already had (Wilkins and Hill, 2011, p. 416). Ford had only agreed to increase the domestic content of their trucks to 30 per cent, since they considered the Brazilian market too small to do so in greater depth. However, to obtain the GEIA rubberstamp, Ford built an engine and stamping factory in São Paulo and a foundry in Osasco, a municipality located a few kilometres from the factory (Shapiro, 1994, p. 76). Because of the GEIA's requirements, Ford and GM transformed their long-time Brazilian assembly operations into a real manufacturing activity.

JK's administration considered foreign direct investment to be the only way to promote the transfer of technology and capital that the industry needed (Nascimento, 1976, pp. 94–97; Shapiro, 1991, pp. 876–947). This explains why the GEIA did not promote the creation of one or two public companies to act as a '"national champion",[7] a strategy which was applied in countries such as South Korea, Spain and Argentina (Catalan, 2010). The GEIA approved 18 car manufacturing projects, of which 11 were implemented, and 154 autoparts

Table 7.2 Projects approved by the GEIA which achieved implementation (1957)

Company	*Established*	*Factories*	*Firm ownership 1962*	*Types of vehicles*
Fábrica Nacional de Motores	1942	Rio de Janeiro	*Brazilian (95%)* *Acquired by Alfa Romeo in 1967*	Heavy trucks Passenger cars
Ford Motor do Brasil	1920	São Paulo city	Ford (100%)	Light commercial vehicles Medium trucks
General Motors do Brasil	1925	São Caetano do Sul (ABC) São José dos Campos (SP)	GM (100%)	Light commercial vehicles Medium trucks
International Harvester	1926	Santo André (ABC)	*Int. Harvester (100%)* *Acquired by Chrysler in 1966*	Medium trucks
Mercedes-Benz do Brasil	1953	São Bernardo do Campo (ABC)	Brazilian (50%) and Mercedes (50%)	Medium trucks Heavy trucks Buses
Scania-Vabis do Brasil	1957	São Paulo city	Scania (major) and Vemag (minor)	Heavy trucks Buses
Simca do Brasil	1958	São Bernardo do Campo (ABC)	*Brazilian (80%) and Simca (20%)* *Acquired by Chrysler in 1966*	Passenger cars
Toyota do Brasil	1958	São Paulo city	Toyota (100%)	Passenger cars Light commercial vehicles
Vemag	1945	São Paulo city	*Brazilian (82%) and DKW (18%)* *Acquired by Volkswagen in 1965 and closed in 1967*	Passenger cars Light commercial vehicles
Volkswagen do Brasil	1953	São Bernardo do Campo (ABC)	Brazilian (20%) and Volkswagen (80%)	Passenger cars Light commercial vehicles
Willys Overland do Brasil	1952	São Bernardo do Campo (ABC) Taubaté (SP)	*Brazilian (55%) and Kaiser (45%)* *Acquired by Ford in 1967*	Passenger cars Light commercial vehicles

Source: Authors' elaboration from ANFAVEA (1961) and Gattas (1981, p. 380).

manufacturing projects (ANFAVEA, 1962a, p. 27). As Table 7.2 shows, all of the projects regarding auto manufacture located their facilities in São Paulo, except for the Fábrica Nacional de Motores (FNM), which played a residual role in the development of the industry. The FNM was a state-owned company established in 1942 to make aeroplane engines for the allied aviation that started to assemble trucks using Issota licences in 1948 and Alfa Romeo licences from 1951, with a low level of production. In 1955, the FNM assembled 2,426 of the 13,950 trucks assembled in São Paulo (Nascimento, 1976, p. 50). The industrial base of the region, with hundreds of workshops and the presence of potential supplier industries, was decisive in the choice of location. Only Simca tried to establish its factory outside the cluster.

During a European trip just after his electoral victory, JK visited Simca's factory near Paris and showed enthusiasm towards the establishment of a subsidiary in Brazil, preferably in his native state of Minas Gerais. Convinced by the direct commitment of the president of Brazil, the French became involved in the project amidst a serious lack of definition and knowledge, to the point that their plan implied importing CKD kits, which disobeyed the GEIA's rules. Simca do Brasil was founded in May 1958 in Belo Horizonte, capital of Minas Gerais, where it received land assigned and prepared by the state governor. The shareholders were the National Steel Company, a group of banks in Minas Gerais, the Banco Francês e Brasileiro, and Simca itself, in a minority position. Almost a year later, in March 1959, the company began to operate provisionally in a rented workshop in São Bernardo (ABC), 800km from Belo Horizonte. The decision was taken by the second technical authority of Simca, who had been sent to Brazil to monitor the operation. The domestic content requirements of the GEIA forced the temporary transfer to São Paulo. One year later, it was admitted that the move to Minas Gerais was unviable. Practically all of the nearly 1,000 suppliers were located in São Paulo (there were three in Rio Grande do Sul and another one in Rio de Janeiro), including Ford do Brasil, which supplied the engines (Sandler, 2005).

The case of Vemag illustrates the vibrant dynamism that the cluster experienced in the mid-1950s. Taking advantage of the GEIA's guidelines, Vemag established a joint venture with the German DKW to manufacture its vans and jeeps, producing the first vehicle in 1958. Vemag also participated in the production of trucks, this time through a joint venture with the Swedish Scania Vabis, established in 1957. Scania do Brasil installed an engine and chassis factory for buses and trucks in Ipiranga, very close to the Vemag factory where the trucks were to be assembled. The engine blocks were cast by the Companhia Fabricadora de Peças in its factory in Santo André (ABC), with the help of Swedish technicians. The factory began activity in 1959, producing 1,000 engines with 40 per cent Swedish pieces. One year later, Scania decided to take on solo production of the truck by dissolving the joint venture, after accusing Vemag of lacking the capacity to assemble for both DKW and Scania. However, it continued to use the Vemag line until December 1962, when it inaugurated its new factory. The factory was located in São Bernardo, on land assigned by Vemag in exchange for shares in the new company. With the move, Scania located itself in the heart of the ABC region, where most of its 680 suppliers were also located (Scania, 2007, pp. 50–59), although only some can be defined as autoparts makers.

The results of the policies adopted by the GEIA are clear. In 1962, production reached nearly 200,000 vehicles, with over 30,000 people employed by carmakers and another 30,000 employed in the autoparts industry. Furthermore, the percentages of domestic content exceeded 90 per cent (ANFAVEA, 1962b, p. 13). Despite that, JK's government had to face the rejection of international institutions such as the IMF, an organization the government broke with in 1959. According to the Fund, the Brazilian government could not achieve comprehensive development since it broke with its monetary and credit policies (Gattas, 1981, pp. 297–298).

The expansion of the automobile industry was interrupted by the economic and social turmoil which began in 1962 and led to a military dictatorship in 1964. Production reached 190,000 vehicles in 1962, a figure that was not exceeded until 1966. Behind this evolution, we find the political instability in which Brazil had become immersed. Janio da Silva Quadros, appointed president on 31 January 1961, proved to be a severe critic of policies to promote industrialization, particularly due to the registered inflation rates. However, amidst a serious political crisis, Quadros could not even finish the first year of his term. In August, he was replaced by Joao Goulart, his vice president, who failed to implement any consistent economic policy (Baer, 2014, p. 73). Incapable of stabilizing the situation, Goulart, who was accused of having communist tendencies after nationalizing a few small-scale refineries and announcing his willingness to carry out agrarian reform, was ousted by a right-wing military coup on 31 March 1964. Although the GEIA was taken over by the Executive Group of Machine Industries, the military maintained basic aspects of the GEIA policies, including market protection and the domestic content requirements. However, with the military governments pretty much closed to foreign capital (Skidmore, 1988, chapters 2–4; Moraes, 2016), a process of denationalization of the autoparts industry took place (Addis, 1999, pp. 108–121).

The large carmakers gradually organized the cluster hierarchically as the 1960s progressed, transferring parts of the organizational capabilities that they had been developing for years and that were at the heart of their competitive advantage (Chandler, 1977; Lazonick, 1990). In order to achieve the level of local content to which they had committed, the end manufacturers were forced to teach the car parts industry concepts of industrial organization, to give them equipment and tools, and to facilitate contact with their foreign suppliers, helping them to obtain the transfer of licences and technical assistance (Shapiro, 1994, chapter 5; Addis, 1999, chapter 3). The signing of long-term contracts (mostly supported by the GEIA and under exclusivity agreements) also allowed the long-term development of the autoparts industry. As this process expanded, the São Paulo cluster gradually adopted a similar form to what Markusen (1996) characterized as hub-and-spoke districts, although the participation in international trade was almost token – in the 1960s, 987 buses were exported, 26 trucks and 3 cars (ANFAVEA, 2016, p. 70) – and, above all, the business associations maintained their central position in the cluster.

In the 1960s, trade associations such as Sindipeças, the Federation of Industries of the State of São Paulo, and the Industries Centre of the State of São Paulo, as well as educational and vocational organizations, continued to play a central role in the development of the autoparts industry, although their function changed. In the 1950s, the main task of industry unions was to serve as a lobby to protect the industry and to establish strict local content requirements. However, in the 1960s, their efforts were focused on obtaining quality standards and on training qualified and semi-qualified workers. Technical assistance was given to the manufacturers through agreements with the institutes of technology, especially the Instituto Tecnológico de Aeronáutica (Technological Institute of Aeronautics), located in São José dos Campos, and the Instituto de Pesquisas Tecnológicas (Institute of Technological Research) located in São Paulo. Through these collaborations, they sought to maintain permanent contact with the small and medium-sized companies in order to guide them towards the obtainment of higher-quality standards. The industry union also coordinated companies with technical teaching institutions to develop courses in metalwork, mechanics and electricity, as well as to establish university degrees in engineering, economics and business administration. The semi-qualified operators were normally trained in the workplace through short-term method-based courses. Some noteworthy training centres for medium and higher-level managers include the University of São Paulo, the Technological Institute of Aeronautics of São José dos Campos and the Getúlio Vargas Foundation.

According to Teixeira, Correa and Fausto (1967, p. 160), 27 per cent of the small and medium-sized firms that manufactured autoparts in São Paulo in 1965 had requested direct help from one of the technological institutes. This research was funded by the Delft Programme, which is in itself a sign of the cluster's active institutional environment in the search for competitiveness, since it was the result of an agreement between the Faculty of Economic and Administrative Sciences at the University of São Paulo, the Industries Centre of the State of São Paulo, the Industrial Social Service of São Paulo and the Research Institute for Management Science at the Delft University of Technology in the Netherlands, its goal being the training by consultants of the SME autoparts makers of São Paulo. The land registry data analyzed in the study show that, in 1966, there were 489 companies registered as autoparts manufacturers, of which 62 were described as artisanal (less than eight workers), 309 as small (between eight and 110 employees), 104 as medium (between 111 and 550 workers), and 14 were considered large companies (over 550 employees). Nevertheless, the study detected that, of the 413 companies identified as small and medium-sized (SMEs), only 368 were effectively operating, as the rest manufactured autoparts as a secondary activity, had moved outside the cluster or were inactive (Teixeira, Correa and Fausto, 1967, pp. 8–10). This leads one to conclude that the number of SMEs manufacturing autoparts was around 400, since presumably part of the

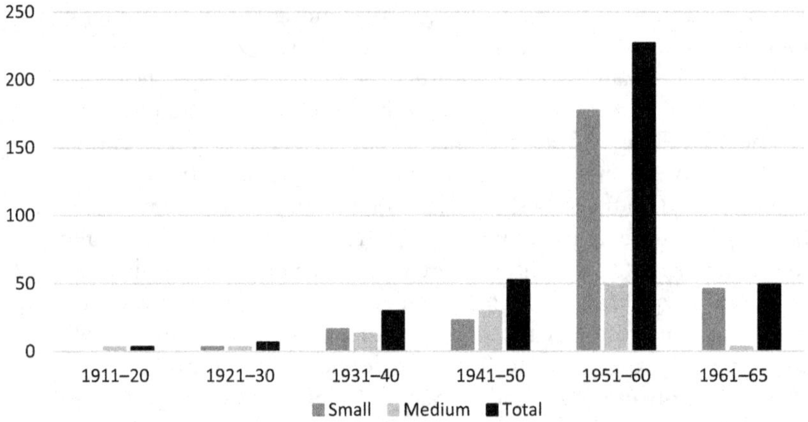

Figure 7.1 Period of establishment of the SMEs operating in the cluster in 1965

Source: Authors' elaboration from Teixeira et al. (1967, pp. 18–19). The percentages obtained for the 112 companies effectively studied have been applied to the group of 368 SMEs.

artisanal companies should also have been excluded from the sample. However, since the study does not consider companies located in São José dos Campos and Taubaté, the total number of companies present in the district would easily be over 400. In terms of activity, a little over three-quarters of the SMEs were dedicated to manufacturing mechanical parts, one-tenth to the production of electrical material, 7 per cent to manufacturing rubber parts, and a little over 2 per cent both to upholstery and to plastic parts.

Figure 7.1 shows that, of the SMEs active in 1966, only 1 per cent were established before 1920, 2 per cent during the 1920s and 8 per cent in the 1930s. The boost experienced due to isolationism resulting from the Second World War is reflected in the fact that 14 per cent of the companies were established in the 1940s. Nevertheless, the figure clearly illustrates the impact of industrial policy: over 60 per cent of the companies were founded in the 1950s, the decade in which the industrial policies that explain the cluster's growth were implemented, both by Kubitschek's and Vargas's governments.[8] The serious crisis experienced by the Brazilian economy between 1962 and 1966 is reflected in the fact that fewer companies were founded in the first five years of the 1960s than in the 1940s, and represented only a quarter of those founded in the 1950s. Moreover, as already indicated, at the heart of most of the SMEs manufacturing autoparts, we find specialized workers from other companies in the sector. At a time of considerable increase in the demand for inputs from the final assemblers, it seems logical that workers who had enough knowledge about the industry would venture to found their own companies. Therefore, while most of the 122 companies that founded Sindipeças at the beginning of the 1950s did not remain active, they were the origin of the companies established in the second half of the 1950s, which constituted the bulk of the companies operating in the mid-1960s.

The fact that a number of these SMEs were set up by specialized workers from other companies in the sector reinforces the hypothesis of the presence of Marshallian externalities, at the same time as pointing to inheritance as a key factor in the cluster's reproduction, which is in line with what Klepper (2010) indicated regarding the formation of the auto cluster in Detroit. However, the hierarchization of the cluster around the large-end assemblers adopting a hub-and-spoke form, as described in Markusen (1996), limited this model since large companies with higher salaries attracted workers trained in the medium-sized companies of the ancillary industry, which in turn did the same thing with specialized workers from the sector's small companies (Teixeira, Correa and Fausto, 1967, p. 145).

The vast majority of the companies were members of one of the business organizations in the district, which proves the importance that the institutions had in the creation of competitive advantage. Thus, only 10 per cent of the district's SMEs were not members of any association, in most cases small companies. Sindepeças was by far the largest association of the autoparts industry, with a membership percentage that reached 44 per cent of the SMEs in the district. The Federation of Industries of the State of São Paulo and the CESP had, together, a level of membership that represented 33.3 per cent of the small companies and 28.6 per cent of the medium-sized companies (Teixeira, Correa and Fausto, 1967, p. 35). Also, a third of the SMEs surveyed confirmed having received assistance from one of the trade associations in the district, a percentage which increased to half in the case of medium-sized companies. Likewise, only 14 per cent of the SMEs surveyed did not know that institutions in the cluster could offer them assistance, whether technical, administrative or financial (Teixeira, Correa and Fausto, 1967, p. 161). For their part, the end assemblers were organized in the National Association of Motor Vehicle Manufacturers, or ANFAVEA, created in May 1956, just at the beginning of Kubitschek's developmental policies.

The automotive industry led the economic recovery of the period 1968–1974. During those years, the production of vehicles grew at an average annual rate of 22 per cent (double the overall growth of the economy), exceeding 800,000 passenger cars and light commercial vehicles manufactured and close to 100,000 trucks and buses in 1974. At the end of the period, the six carmakers that were still active in São Paulo (see Table 7.2) directly generated 100,000 jobs, while the ancillary industry generated almost 200,000 jobs (ANFAVEA, 2016, pp. 44–45). The driver of growth was domestic consumption, which expanded under expansionary macroeconomic policies.

When the economic recovery of 1967–1968 began, the structure of the cluster was changing. The weight of the small and medium-sized companies was reducing, the end manufacturers were integrating more parts from the production process, and the number of companies controlled by foreign capital was increasing (Addis, 1999, pp. 93–95). With the surge in inflation, the end manufacturers pressed the ancillary industry (mainly by terminating the exclusivity contracts) to achieve price reductions. When they could, they opted to integrate production vertically, and when this was not profitable, they promoted the installation of new suppliers, especially foreign ones that tended to enter through joint ventures with local companies already in operation (Shapiro, 1994, pp. 191–215). Despite the growth in production, the structure of the district did not change much and its hierarchical organizational structure was consolidated around the large final assembly plants.

The take-off of the cluster began at the start of the 1950s and culminated at the start of the 1970s. Although, when the expansion began, the structure of the cluster could resemble that of a district with a Marshallian base, with abundant labour, specialized suppliers and the relatively simple circulation of knowledge and information through the movement of specialized workers who gradually created their own companies. When the expansion ended, its structure fitted in reasonably well with what Markusen (1996) described as the hub-and-spoke district. During this transformation, local capital lost its pre-eminence compared with international capital, and the associations of small and medium-sized companies, the true promoters of the district at the beginning of the 1950s due to their insistence on the application of policies protecting the industry, shifted their activity toward the provision of training and specialized consulting. From the mid-1970s, and for the following 20 years, both production and the number of employees remained relatively stable, indicating that the cluster was passing through its maturity stage which, in view of its characteristics, deserves a separate study.

Concluding remarks: A long-run view

The research presented reveals how the regional concentration of industry does not follow a predetermined path, but rather is affected by endogenous and exogenous factors which interact with different results, strongly influenced both by the different historical situations and by the regional area in which they are inserted. Therefore, a full understanding of the emergence and expansion of industrial districts and clusters also requires an analysis with a historical perspective which, in turn, increases in explanatory potential if it integrates theoretical and conceptual frameworks developed from multidisciplinary spheres such as regional studies, economic geography and evolutionary economics.

During the first half of the 20th century, São Paulo was the most industrialized region in Brazil, a backward and agriculture-based country. However, by the middle of the century, the production of cars in São Paulo was almost token. Twenty-five years later, São Paulo had placed Brazil in the world top ten of car-producing countries. Different leading brands in the industry agreed to transfer their knowledge and technologies, forced by a closed market situation and by strict local content requirements. They also had to do this if they did not

Table 7.3 Determinants in the development of the São Paulo auto industry cluster by stage

	Cluster life-cycle stage	*Main sources of development*	*Other sources of development*
Until 1929	Formation	*External Economies* 1. Pool of labour 2. Pool of industrial activity	*Institutional Environment* 1. Infrastructures
1930–55	Achieving critical mass	*Institutional Environment* 1. Trade associations 2. Infrastructures	*External Economies* 1. Pool of labour 2. Pool of suppliers 3. Knowledge spillovers
1956–74	Growth	*Active Industrial Policies* 1. Protectionism 2. Domestic content *Large Companies* 1. Hub firms 2. Internal scale economies 3. Organizational capabilities	*External Economies* 1. Pool of labour 2. Specialized suppliers 3. Knowledge spillovers *Institutional Environment* 1. Trade associations 2. Infrastructures 3. Education and vocational institutions

Source: Authors' elaboration.

want to abandon an empty and rapidly expanding market. However, the outcome was that the cluster evolved towards a hierarchical organizational structure headed by the large-end manufacturers under foreign control, while the weight of Brazilian capital, even in the autoparts industry, gradually declined.

The key factors in the performance of the São Paulo auto industry cluster in each stage of development are indicated in Table 7.3. The origins of the São Paulo auto industry cluster can be found in the dozens of small workshops serving the spare parts market that progressively emerged during the 1920s to facilitate the region's motorization, while Ford, GM and International Harvester established facilities to assemble CKD kits imported entirely from the US. Their activity was facilitated by the good connection – by railroad (1870s) and by highway (1910s) – between the Port of Santos and the city of São Paulo. In addition, from 1910, there was a group of associations that aimed to promote the automotive sector. Despite the fact that early knowledge of the art was widespread throughout the region in the form of semi-skilled workers and some specialized suppliers, the critical mass necessary for the cluster's existence was still far off.

The opportunity to achieve a critical mass came with the trade restrictions brought about by the Second World War. Restrictions on car part imports from industrialized nations favoured the flourishing of hundreds of workshops that were able to provide a wide range of parts and components, even though they were undercapitalized and undersized. According to Table 7.1, 65 per cent of the workshops and 80 per cent of the workers in the Brazilian automotive industry were located in São Paulo in 1949. As local producers became aware of their common interests, they joined together to push to maintain barriers to foreign competitors once the war was over. The association of autoparts makers created in São Paulo in October 1952 to obtain market protection had its first success a few months later when 108 groups of parts were protected. The importing of complete vehicles was banned shortly after, with only the entry of CKD kits and none of the aforementioned groups of parts being permitted. Forced by the new legislation, Volkswagen and Willys-Overland also established assembly lines in São Paulo. External economies in the form of specialized suppliers and semi-skilled workers, together with a powerful industry association, worked well for this location. Although the critical mass had been reached, the cluster's growth had not yet occurred.

The cluster's expansion took place once JK's government, established in January 1956, applied a broad set of active industrial policies that can be defined as infant industry protection a la List (see Chang, 2002). The high level of domestic content required forced all project facilities to be located in São Paulo, reinforcing the sector's concentration in the region, as shown in Table 7.1. If protection and, above all, domestic content requirements were key for the cluster's growth, they found fertile ground in the form of external economies made up of hundreds of suppliers and thousands of workers. Proof of this prior base can be found in the existence of an institutional framework that accompanied the industry's progress, and which worked towards the comprehensive development of the industry by facilitating the circulation of knowledge and by providing assistance in worker training and business organization. The data presented in Figure 7.1 on the year of establishment of the SMEs active in the cluster in the mid-1960s fit well with the interpretation proposed. However, since then, large subsidiaries of global carmakers have led the cluster's development, causing the district to take on a hub-and-spoke form, as described by Markusen (1996).

By targeting the auto industry for investment, placing barriers to foreign production and requiring high levels of domestic content, strategic industrial policies fostered the development of the auto industry clustered around São Paulo, as stated by Chang (1993, 2002). While the active industrial policy applied since the 1950s can explain the automobile industry's take-off, it cannot explain its concentration in São Paulo. The industry clustered in the region due to the presence of external economies and the actions of its own institutions, mainly trade associations, which led the cluster's development until the mid-1960s. Nevertheless, the cluster's path of development also presents some limitations, since the development of local carmakers did not occur. Both the Japanese and the Korean experience reveal that the goal is not only to force the introduction of an industry, but also to create domestic firms with capabilities to compete in the international arena.

This research shows how a certain region in a backward country was able to develop one of the flagship industries of the Second Industrial Revolution, proving the potential of infant industrial policy. However, the research also highlights how active policies only impacted the most industrialized region of the country. A pool of specialized suppliers and skilled workers, together with vibrant industry associations and an appropriate provision of public goods, increased the region's competitive advantage. This study has shown what factors are behind the formation and growth of the São Paulo auto-industry cluster. However, only more research on the maturity stage will tell us how the cluster has been able to sustain its activity over time.

Notes

1 The authors wish to express their gratitude to the Spanish Ministry of Economy and to the European Regional Development Fund (ERDF) for their financial support for this research through project HAR2015-64769-P, as well as to the Kurgan-van Hentenryk Chair in Business History of the Solvay Brussels School of Economics and Management. Preliminary versions of this paper have been presented at several venues including the 1st World Congress in Business History/20th Congress of the European Business History Association, the 2016 Economic History Society Annual Conference, and the XII Congresso Brasileiro de História Econômica. We especially thank organizers and audience members at the Inaugural Workshop RSA ReHi network, as well as the editors of this volume for their insightful comments. Usual disclaimers applied.

2 A nuanced point of view regarding the Brazil case is offered in Evans (1995); Amann and Baer (2005); and Baer (2014).

3 A knock-down kit is a kit containing the parts needed to assemble a product. A CKD is a kit of the completely non-assembled parts of a product and a method of supplying parts to a market, particularly on shipping to foreign nations, being a common practice in the automotive industry.

4 In September 1953, the Associaçao was authorized to register itself as a trade association, which granted it a much greater capacity for action, turning it into the powerful Sindicato da Indústria de Peças para Automóveis e Similares no Estado de São Paulo, commonly known as Sindipeças.

5 The industrialist postulates formulated by Simonsen can be found in Simonsen and Gudin (1977) and are analyzed in, for example, Bielschowsky (1988), Fonseca (2003), Cepêda (2003), and Bruzzi and Mendes (2015).

6 The *Plano de Metas* sought the industrialization and modernization of Brazil and was launched as a result of the work undertaken by the Conselho de Desenvolvimento, established by Decree No. 38.744 of 1 February 1956, the first working day of the Kubitschek administration. With the motto "50 years in five", the plan presented 31 goals organized into five main groups – energy (1 to 5), transport (6 to 12), food (13 to 18), basic industry (19 to 29), and education (30) – plus one goal called a synthesis goal: the construction of a new capital, Brasilia, which was to be located in the centre of the country. As goal number 27, automobiles were the only consumer good included in the plan.

7 Under a national champion policy, by setting policies which favour a particular national firm (whether private or state-owned), governments expect this domestic corporation to seek profit and to advance the interests of the nation. This strategy

was largely used in the Gaullist *dirigisme* in France, also inspiring some developing countries to adopt it.

8 The differences between the two administrations regarding the conditions to attract FDI are explained in Campos (2017).

References

Acemoglu, D. and Robinson, J., 2012. *Why nations fail: The origins of power, prosperity, and poverty*. New York: Crown.

Addis, C., 1999. *Taking the wheel: Auto parts firms and the political economy of industrialization in Brazil*. University Park PA: Pennsylvania State University Press.

Allen, R., 2010. *The British industrial revolution in global perspective*. Cambridge: Cambridge University Press.

Amann, E. and Baer, W., 2005. From the developmental to the regulatory state: The transformation of the government's impact on the Brazilian economy. *Quarterly Review of Economics and Finance*, 45(2–3), pp. 421–431. https://doi.org/10.1016/j.qref.2004.12.012

Amin, A. and Thrift, N., eds., 1994. *Globalization, institutions, and regional development in Europe*. Oxford: Oxford University Press.

Amsden, A., 1989. *Asia's next giant: South Korea and late industrialization*. Oxford: Oxford University Press.

Amsden, A., 2003. *The rise of "the rest": Challenges to the west from late-industrializing economies*. Oxford: Oxford University Press.

ANFAVEA, 1961. *Industria automobilística Brasileira: Novembro 1961*. São Paulo: ANFAVEA.

ANFAVEA, 1962a. *Industria automobilística brasileira: Sua contribução para o desenvolvimento nacional*. São Paulo: ANFAVEA.

ANFAVEA, 1962b. *Industria automobilística brasileira: Novembro 1962*. São Paulo: ANFAVEA.

ANFAVEA, 2016. *Anuário da indústria automobilística Brasileira 2015*. São Paulo: ANFAVEA.

Baer, W., 2014. *The Brazilian economy: Growth & development*. Boulder CO: Lynne Rienner.

Bagnasco, A., 1977. *Tre Italie: La problematica territoriale dello sviluppo*. Bologna: Il Mulino.

Becattini, G., 1990. The Marshallian industrial district as a socio-economic notion. In: F. Pyke, G. Becattini and W. Sengenberger, eds. *Industrial districts and inter-firm cooperation in Italy*. Geneva: International Institute for Labour Studies. Pp. 37–51.

Bergman, E., 2008. Cluster life cycles: An emerging synthesis. In: C. Karlsson, ed. *Handbook of research in cluster theory*. Cheltenham: Edward Elgar. Pp. 114–132

Bielschowsky, R., 1988. *Pensamento econômico Brasileiro: O ciclo ideológico do desenvolvimentismo*. Rio de Janeiro: IPEA/INPES.

Brusco, S., 1982. The Emilian model: Productive decentralisation and social integration. *Cambridge Journal of Economics*, 6(2), pp. 167–84. https://doi.org/10.1093/oxfordjournals.cje.a035506

Bruzzi, L. F. and Mendes, A., 2015. Redimensionando a contribuição de Roberto Simonsen à controversia do planejamento (1944–1945). *America Latina en la Historia Económica*, 22(3), pp. 76–107. http://dx.doi.org/10.18232/alhe.v22i3.651

Campos, F. A., 2017. Internacionalização brasileira e Instrução 113 da SUMOC. *América Latina en la Historia Económica*, 24(2), pp. 93–124.

Cano, W., 1981. *Raizes da concentraçao industrial em Sao Paulo*. São Paulo: T.A. Queiroz.

Carli, G. and Morrison, A., 2018. On the evolution of the Castel Goffredo hosiery cluster: A life cycle perspective. *European Planning Studies*, 26(5), pp. 915–932. https://doi.org/10.1080/09654313.2018.1448757

Catalan, J., 2010. Strategic policy revisited: The origins of mass production in the motor industry of Argentina, Korea and Spain, 1945–87. *Business History* 52(2), pp. 207–230. https://doi.org/10.1080/00076791003611863

Catalan, J., 2017. The life-cycle of the Barcelona automobile-industry cluster, 1889–2015. *Revista de Historia Industrial*, 26(66), pp. 77–125.

Catalan, J. and Fernández-de-Sevilla, T., 2013. Die staatliche industriepolitik und die entwicklung der automobilindustrie in Spanien 1948–1985. In: S. Tilly and F. Triebel, eds. *Automobilindustrie 1945–2000*. Munich: Oldenbourg. Pp. 254–284.

Catalan, J. and Fernández-de-Sevilla, T., 2018. Emergence and maturity of the developmental state in Argentina, Brazil and Spain, 1930-1990: An economic history approach. In: A. Ferraro and M. Centeno, eds. *State and nation making in Latin America and Spain: The rise and fall of the developmental state*. Cambridge: Cambridge University Press. Pp. 207–237.

Catalan, J., Miranda, J. A. and Ramon-Muñoz, R., eds., 2011a. *Distritos y clusters en la Europa del sur*. Madrid: LID.

Catalan, J., Miranda, J. A. and Ramon-Muñoz, R., 2011b. Ventaja competitiva y capacidades empresariales de los distritos de la Europa meridional: Evidencia histórica para tres revoluciones tecnológicas. In: J. Catalan, J. A. Miranda and R. Ramon-Muñoz, ed. *Distritos y clusters en la Europa del sur*. Madrid: LID. Pp. 367–412.

Cepêda, V. A., 2003. Roberto Simonsen e a formaçao da ideologia industrial no Brasil: Limites e impasses. PhD dissertation: Universidade de São Paulo.

Chandler, A., 1977. *The visible hand: The managerial revolution in American business*. Cambridge MA: Harvard University Press.

Chang, H.-J., 1993. The political economy of industrial policy in Korea. *Cambridge Journal of Economics*, 17(2), pp. 131–157. https://doi.org/10.1093/oxfordjournals.cje.a035227

Chang, H.-J., 2002. *Kicking away the ladder: Development strategy in historical perspective*. London: Anthem Press.

Cimoli, M., Stiglitz, J. and Dosi G., ed., 2009. *Industrial policy and development*. Oxford: Oxford University Press.

Dean, W., 1969. *The industrialization of Sao Paulo, 1880–1945*. Austin TX: The University of Texas Press.

Donnelly, T., Begely, J. and Collis, C., 2017. The West Midlands automotive industry: The road downhill. *Business History*, 59(1), pp. 56–74. https://doi.org/10.1080/00076791.2016.1235559

Eichengreen, B., 2007. *The European economy since 1945: Coordinated capitalism and beyond*. Princeton NJ: Princeton University Press.

Enright, M. J., 2000. Regional clusters and multinational enterprises: Independence, dependence, or interdependence? *International Studies of Management and Organization*, 30(2), pp. 114–138. https://doi.org/10.1080/00208825.2000.11656790

Enright, M. J., 2003. Regional clusters: What we know and what we should know. In: J. Bröcker, D. Dohse and R. Soltwedel, eds. *Innovation clusters and interregional competition*. Berlin: Springer Verlag. Pp. 99–129.

Evans, P., 1995. *Embedded autonomy: State and industrial transformation*. Princeton: Princeton University Press.

Fausto, B., 2006. *Getúlio Vargas: O poder e o sorriso*. São Paulo: Companhia das Letras.

Fernández-de-Sevilla, T., 2014. Inside the dynamics of industrial capitalism: The mass-production of cars in Spain. *Revista de Historia Económica–Journal of Iberian and Latin American Economic History*, 32(2), pp. 287–315. https://doi.org/10.1017/S0212610914000093

Fleury, A. and Salerno, M., 1998. The transfer and hybridization of new models of production in the Brazilian automobile industry. In: R. Boyer, E. Charron, U. Jürgens and S. Tolliday, ed. *Between imitation and innovation: The transfer and hybridization of productive models in the international automobile industry*. Oxford: Oxford University Press. Pp. 278–295.

Fonseca, P. C. D., 2003. Sobre a intencionalidade da politica industrializante do Brasil na década de 1930. *Brazilian Journal of Political Economy–Revista de Economia Política*, 23(1), pp. 133–148.

Forest, M., 2002. *Automóveis de São Paulo*. São Paulo: Arquivo do Estado.

Gattas, R., 1981. *A indústria automobilística e a 2ª revoluçao industrial no Brasil*. São Paulo: Prelo.

General Motors, 1995. *General Motors do Brasil: 70 years of history*. São Paulo: General Motors.

Gerschenkron, A., 1962. *Economic backwardness in historical perspective*. Cambridge, MA: Harvard University Press.

Gonçalves, V., 1989. *O século do automóvel no Brasil*. São Paulo: Iconographia.

Harrison, B., 1994. *Lean and mean: The changing landscape of corporate power in the age of flexibility*. New York: The Guilford Press.

Jenkins, R., 1995. The political economy of industrial policy: Automobile manufacture in the newly industrialising countries. *Cambridge Journal of Economics*, 19(5), pp. 625–645. https://doi.org/10.1093/oxfordjournals.cje.a035334

Johnson, C., 1982. *MITI and the Japanese miracle: The growth of industrial policy 1925–1975*. Redwood City CA: Stanford University Press.

Klepper, S., 2007. Disagreements, spinoffs, and the evolution of Detroit as the capital of the U.S. automobile industry. *Management Science*, 53(4), pp. 616–631. https://doi.org/10.1287/mnsc.1060.0683

Klepper, S., 2010. The origin and growth of industry clusters: The making of Silicon Valley and Detroit. *Journal of Urban Economics*, 67(1), pp. 15–32. https://doi.org/10.1016/j.jue.2009.09.004

Landes, D., 1969, *The unbound Prometheus: Technological change and industrial development in Western Europe from 1750 to the present*. Cambridge, MA: Cambridge University Press.

Latini, S., 2007. *A implantaçao da indústria automobilística no Brasil: Da substituçao da importaçoes ativa à globalizaçao passive*. São Paulo: Alaude.

Lazonick, W., 1990. *Competitive advantage on the shop floor*. Cambridge MA: Harvard University Press.

Marglin, S., 1990. Lessons of the golden age: An overview. In: S. Marglin and J. B. Schor, ed. *The golden age of capitalism: Reinterpreting the postwar experience*. Oxford: Oxford University Press. Pp. 1–38.

Markusen, A., 1996. Sticky places in slippery space: A typology of industrial districts. *Economic Geography*, 72(3), pp. 293–313.

Marshall, A., 1890. *Principles of economics*. London: Macmillan. 8th ed. 1920.

Martin, R. and Sunley, P., 2011. Conceptualizing cluster evolution: Beyond the life cycle model? *Regional Studies*, 45(10), pp. 1299–1318. https://doi.org/10.1080/00343404.2011.622263

Maskell, P. and Kebir, L., 2006. What qualifies as a cluster theory? In: B. Asheim, P. Cooke and R. Martin, eds. *Clusters and regional development: Critical reflections and explorations*. London: Routledge, pp. 30–49.

Menzel, M.-P. and Fornahl, D., 2010. Cluster life cycles – Dimensions and rationales of cluster evolution. *Industrial and Corporate Change*, 19(1), pp. 205–38. https://doi.org/10.1093/icc/dtp036

Molema, M., Segers, Y. and Karel, E., 2016. Introduction: Agribusiness clusters in Europe, 19th and 20th centuries. *The Low Countries Journal of Social and Economic History*, 13(4), pp. 1–16. http://doi.org/10.18352/tseg.894

Moraes, R., 2016. O Governo Castello Branco e a Federação das Indústrias do estado de São Paulo: As bases do "milagre" (1964–1967). *América Latina en la Historia Económica*, 23(2), pp. 64–90. http://dx.doi.org/10.18232/alhe.v23i2.709

Nascimento, B., 1976. *Formaçao da indústria automobilística brasileira: Política de desenvolvimento industrial em uma economia dependente*. São Paulo: USP.

Negri, B., 1996. *Concentraçao e desconcentraçao industrial em São Paulo (1880–1990)*. Campinas: Editora de Unicamp.

Norman, A. and Stiglitz, J., eds., 2016. *Efficiency, finance and varieties of industrial Policy*. New York: Columbia University Press.

Olson, M., 1982. *The rise and decline of nations: Economic growth, stagflation, and social rigidities*. New Haven CT: Yale University Press.

Pardi, T., 2017. Industrial policy and the British automotive industry under Margaret Thatcher. *Business History*, 59(1), pp. 75–100. https://doi.org/10.1080/00076791.2016.1223049

Pollard, S., 1981. *Peaceful conquest: The industrialization of Europe 1760–1970*. Oxford: Oxford University Press.

Popp, A. and Wilson, J., 2007. Life cycles, contingency, and agency: Growth, development, and change in English industrial districts and clusters. *Environment and Planning A*, 39(12), pp. 2975–2992. https://doi.org/10.1068%2Fa38403

Porter, M., 1990. *The competitive advantage of nations*. New York: Free Press.

Porter, M., 2008. Clusters and competition: New agendas for companies, governments, and institutions. In: Michael Porter, ed. *On competition: Updated and expanded edition*. Cambridge MA: Harvard Business Review Book. Chapter 7.

Sandler, P., 2005. *DKW. A grande historia da pequenha maravilla*. São Paulo: Alaude.

Scania, 2007. *Scania no Brasil: Passado, presente e futuro, 1957–2007*. São Bernardo do Campo: Scania.

Schmitz, H., 1999. Collective efficiency and increasing returns. *Cambridge Journal of Economics*, 23(4), pp. 465–83. https://doi.org/10.1093/cje/23.4.465

Schneider, S., 1991. *Politics within the state: Elite bureaucrats and industrial policy in authoritarian Brazil*. Pittsburgh PA: Pittsburgh University Press.

Scranton, P., 1997. *Endless novelty: Specialty production and American industrialization, 1865–1925*. Princeton NJ: Princeton University Press.

Shapiro, H., 1991. Determinants of firm entry into the Brazilian automobile manufacturing industry, 1956–1968. *Business History Review*, 65(4), pp. 876–947. https://doi.org/10.2307/3117267

Shapiro, H., 1994. *Engines of growth: The state and transnational auto companies in Brazil*. Cambridge: Cambridge University Press.

Sikkink, K., 1991. *Ideas and institutions: Developmentalism in Brazil and Argentina*. Ithaca NY: Cornell University Press.

Silva, S., 1976. *Expansao cafeeira e origens da industria no Brasil.* São Paulo: Alfa Omega.

Simonsen, R. and Gudin, E., 1977. *A controvérsia do planejamento na economia brasileira.* Rio de Janeiro: Ipea/Inpes.

Skidmore, T., 1988. *The politics of military rule in Brazil, 1964–85.* New York: Oxford University Press.

Stiglitz, J. and Lin, J., ed., 2013. *The industrial policy revolution I: The role of government beyond ideology.* New York: Palgrave.

Suzigan, W., 1986. *A industrializaçao Brasilera: Origen e desenvolvimento.* São Paulo: Brailiense.

Swann, P., 2009. *The economics of innovation: An introduction.* Cheltenham: Edward Elgar.

Teixeira, D., Correa L. and Fausto, F., 1967. *Pequenas e medias indústrias de autopeças.* São Paulo: Programa Delft.

Tödtling, F. and Trippl, M., 2004. Like Phoenix from the ashes? The renewal of clusters in old industrial areas. *Urban Studies*, 41(5–6), pp. 1175–1195. https://doi.org/10.1080%2F00420980410001675788

Trippl, M., Grillitsch, M., Isaksen, A., and Sinozic, T., 2015. Perspectives on cluster evolution: Critical review and future research issues. *European Planning Studies*, 23(10), pp. 2028–2044. https://doi.org/10.1080/09654313.2014.999450

Wilkins, M., 1974. *The maturing of multinational enterprise: American business abroad from 1914 to 1970.* Cambridge MA: Harvard University Press.

Wilkins, M. and Hill, F., 2011. *American business abroad: Ford on six continents.* Cambridge MA: Cambridge University Press.

Wilson, J. and Popp, A., eds., 2003. *Industrial clusters and regional business networks in England, 1750–1970.* Aldershot: Ashgate.

Wolfe, J., 2010. *Autos and progress: The Brazilian search for modernity.* Oxford: Oxford University Press.

Woo-Cumings, M., ed., 1999. *The developmental state.* Ithaca: Cornell University Press.

Young, S., Hood, N. and Peters, E., 1994. Multinational enterprise and regional economic development. *Regional Studies*, 28(7), pp. 657–777. https://doi.org/10.1080/00343409412331348566

8 Urban and regional development policy

Its history and its differences

Kevin Cox

Context[1]

The emergence of a state interest in urban and regional development in the US and in Western Europe has to be seen first in the context of the expansion of the state in the 20th century: an expansion which combined both regulatory aspects and a very, very substantial increase in state spending. There were many conditions for its appearance, but two in particular command attention. The first was an increasing socialization of production: notably the deepening of the division of labour and the growth of a shared physical and social infrastructure. These were both problematic in terms of the familiar challenges surrounding the mitigation of transaction costs, externalities, monopoly power and sectoral imbalance. The second condition was the rise of the labour movement, comprising the labour unions and the political parties that they founded or sponsored, and which would eventually result in the growth of the welfare state.

Urban and regional development would be one particular area of state intervention. There was little evidence for this as such in the 19th century but in the course of the 20th century, and as a label, it would assume increasing coherence of meaning attaching to a distinct set of state practices. It would burst forth in very clear form subsequent to the Second World War. It was a response to the same issues generated by the socialization of production and social inequalities but now projected onto a spatial plane and mobilizing space relations as a means of mitigation. There was, for instance, an urban question focusing on the externalities subsequent to agglomeration (Preteceille, 1976); and on questions of social segregation and inequality of life conditions. A regional question would emerge alongside in the form of anxieties about geographically uneven development, regional imbalance and inequalities in employment opportunities. Regional disparities would then be reflected in differences in the challenges faced by different urban areas, while resolving the urban question could be turned to resurrecting regional fortunes.

In general, policy would assume the form of interventions into the geography of things: defining where they should go and moving them around. Therefore, the approach to urban and regional crisis would be one of displacement, though with varying degrees of a mixture between public and private. The state would always be a significant actor; sometimes more passive and sometimes more active. The emphasis would be technical and the ultimately social basis of urban and regional questions that gave them a refractory character tended to be ignored. One result would be that, to a large extent, problems would be simply moved around. Capitalism inevitably produces a scarcity of jobs and unemployment somewhere, as in Marx's industrial reserve army: rising wages result in an attempt to economize on labour which then entails an increase in the numbers of the unemployed. As wages rise again, the process repeats itself. If the economy is in an expansionary phase, moving employment to areas of high unemployment may not immediately show up in unemployment in the areas from which the jobs are moving. But in the contractionary phase, as profitability is reduced, it will be: which is what happened in Western Europe in the 1970s and subsequently led to calls for an end to the policy.

The concrete shape eventually assumed by policy in response to urban and regional problematics was conditional on a number of developments of a social and technical character (Cox, 2016, chapter 2). These would then come together to form an emergent structure of social relations. I would include here at least four: the growth of city and regional planning as a state function; the rise of property capital in the form of the real estate development industry; a new mobility in the space economy; and new sorts of real estate product, as in industrial parks, planned factory districts, shopping centres, and garden suburbs.

City and regional planning were already taking shape at the beginning of the 20th century as a response to urban growth, to health problems, housing and transportation. It would provide legitimation for the sorts of state interventions that would come later under the heading of urban and regional development. Property capital as a distinct branch of the capitalist division of labour focusing on the provision of premises, on the other hand, does not emerge till the post-Second World War period, though there are earlier intimations. Under its stimulus new forms of real estate product would appear: some of them large enough to affect uneven development in dramatic fashion and imbricating with what I have called a new mobility (Cox, 2016, pp. 93–97). The latter had its own origins in the second Industrial Revolution: electricity and the manufacture of an increasing array of consumer goods. It was more footloose than the industries of the first Industrial Revolution and so auxiliary to the physical displacement that would be the state response to urban and regional questions.

In the immediate post-war period, urban and regional development policy had clear outlines which would be quite different in the countries of Western Europe than in the US. In the former, the partitioning of space and displacement of industry, housing and the like would be subject to strong central state orchestration: planning systems organized from the centre, along with state financial incentives. Policy would be legitimated as a search for the good geography: the right things in the right places. In the US it would be very different: almost a mirror image as policy would be subordinated to strong bottom-up forces. Local governments, aided and abetted by the famous growth coalitions, would take the lead while more central branches of the state, particularly the federal level, would be more passive: a source of regulatory relief and monies prompted by demands from below. The motif of planning would be displaced by one of adapting to the dictates of the market; in that case, a market in locations in which local governments acted on the supply side, facilitating the provision of premises in a struggle to alter the contours of the space economy to local advantage.[2] In turn, each of these approaches has had distinctive socio-historical conditions, which have come together to create particular structures of social relations, empowering and limiting in their different ways. The aim of this chapter is to enlarge on these themes: how urban and regional development emerged as a policy focus; and how and why this policy focus would be expressed quite differently in the countries of Western Europe on the one hand, and in the US on the other, even while they shared most of the underlying conditions.

The coming into being of urban and regional development policy

The idea of a specifically urban and regional development policy has its roots in a complex combination of urban and regional questions. The conditions for this can be traced back a long way. It is useful at the outset, though, to point to a shift in the competitive nature of the capitalist economy. As both David Harvey (1982, pp. 144–145) and John Weeks (1981, pp. 167–168) have indicated, the cut-throat nature of the capitalist economy did not spring into being, ready-made. The common notion of a pure competition (of small firms) preceding a more contemporary dominance of monopolies is deceiving. Rather it is the other way around. Under 19th-century conditions, and more so the further back one goes, firms tended to be protected from competition by the cost of transportation and by obstacles faced by would-be competitors in organizing the invasion of a particularly lucrative market. The space economy approximated more to a set of local and regional monopolies; space economies, in other words. Railroads, and later the iron steam ship, would begin to make a dent in this, along with the separation of capital into distinct industrial and financial branches. This would allow firms to raise the money to enter a market where previously there had been little competition. But in short, competitive pressures tended to intensify in the course of the 19th century, both within countries and internationally, forcing the seeking-out of competitive advantage in agglomeration, regional specialization, new products that would undermine existing geographic divisions of labour and so on.

The subsequent tensions would then assume sharp relief in urban and regional crises. An important marker here is the debate about tariff reform in the United Kingdom at the beginning of the 20th century. The impetus came from Birmingham and the surrounding Black Country in the English Midlands. The rise of German industry was severely affecting the prospects of the dominant metal-working firms of the area. This prompted demand for some modification of the free trade that had dominated British policy hitherto. But it lacked serious support elsewhere in the country and there was opposition from the City of London. The Port of London did a healthy trade in the import of goods from the rest of Europe prior to export elsewhere and City banks prospered in part on financing these movements. In the US the shift of the textile industry to the Piedmont states of the South would promote similar angst in New England, but, and significantly, was met from the 1920s on by a regional response promoting transition in the regional economy (Koistinen, 2013).

The urban question was of longer standing: issues of health, housing and urban degeneracy long blamed on the moral failures of the poor and addressed through an appropriate moralization. Temperance and social visits by the wives of the well-to-do, often based on settlement houses, were part of the common practice – a sort of missionary approach to what were seen as those in need of salvation. At the same time, particularly in Western Europe, there was a valorization of the rural, which was heavily steeped in class anxieties. The rural was regarded as healthy, a repository of traditional values and of feelings of belonging, while in urban areas alienation ran wild, church attendance lagged and market values ruled. This was the founding motif of the new academic discipline of sociology. Weber talked of tradition and modernity, Durkheim of organic and mechanical solidarity, Tönnies of *Gemeinschaft* and *Gesellschaft* and Henry Maine of status and contract, but the overlaps were striking.

Everywhere in Western Europe during the 1920s and 1930s the rural was defined in positive terms, while the urban was seen as detrimental to "national values". Founded in 1902, the German Garden City Association was active in proposals for new urban forms that would, among other things, bring people back closer to the soil in the form of settlements that would mix industry and agriculture. It also emphasized the creation of satellite cities in anticipation of some aspects of post-war planning policy in some of the Western European countries.

In France, the contributions of Jean-François Gravier (1947), the deeply conservative writer who had enjoyed close associations with the Vichy government, came later but his book, *Paris et le désert Français*, written during the war, would have a major impact on postwar French planning, even though the details of his reasoning would be rejected. As per the title of his book, Gravier railed against the concentration of people and industry in Paris and advocated a radical decentralization. This was inspired by a view of the big city as deeply injurious to the nation's moral fibre. It destroyed families, uprooted people from the communities that stabilized the social life of the country and lowered the birth rate to the disadvantage of France as a great power.[3]

Great Britain shared some similarities with these cases, particularly that of Germany (Dietz, 2008). It would also be different. From round about the turn of the century, something called distributism emerges as a set of policy recommendations (Cox, 2016, pp. 70–72). This targeted the ills of economic and political centralization and advocated a return to life in local, relatively self-sufficient communities, based on a greater democratization of property ownership. Free trade capitalism and the destruction of small-town life that it had caused were as anathema as socialism. Of these different strands of anti-urbanism, all expressing a strong decentralizing sentiment, it was this that was most apparent in the US, even when it did not adopt that label (Shapiro, 1972).[4]

Finally, in considering the issues and climate of opinion within which we must situate urban and regional policy, the fundamental assumption that inequality of outcomes was a bad thing, including those of a geographic nature, owes at least something to the advent of the welfare state and the thinking which preceded it. This in turn was giving way to a recognition that state intervention of a mitigating sort was an entirely legitimate activity. Provision for unemployment insurance was well underway in the European countries by 1930, even if highly limited in what it provided. The idea that housing for the poor should be subsidized in various ways, including through government provision of the housing itself, had been realized in programs across much of Western Europe, including in France, Germany, Great Britain and the Netherlands.

As far as the urban question was concerned, an early response would be the development of city and regional planning as a state practice, but also as a practice of those developers working on a large scale.[5] The large metropolitan area was a particular challenge, showing all the dysfunctionalities of excessive agglomeration: pressures on housing, on the ability of firms to expand, on the environment and, as the city expanded at its edges, moving people around. It was within this context that notions of reordering space through zoning controls and planning for expansion via the layout of new highway and rail lines and the development of new nodes around them would take shape. It assumed a strongly technical character – a matter of moving things, including people, around and arranging them in some rational form – even while generating an almost missionary zeal among its practitioners. The city would be reorganized so as to function more efficiently and, not least, as a competitive mechanism (Cox, 2016, p. 82). At the same time, and as part and parcel of this, class antagonisms would be mitigated. The idea of the new town or garden city was an integral aspect, but so too was aiding the expansion of the city so as to facilitate some resolution of the housing question. How these ideas and practices would be later refined and incorporated into what would be defined as urban and regional development was in the future, but not the least of their achievements was to legitimize the idea of state intervention in the space economy.

A second crucial part of the mix would be the rise of property capital: the separation out from capitalist activity as a whole sector providing premises of all sorts – acquiring the land, constructing housing, shopping facilities, offices, specialized industrial areas and then holding for rent or selling so as to provide the funds for new rounds of development. During the 19th century and continuing well into the 20th, the separation was far from clear. A good deal of housing for industrial workers and miners was owned by the employer. There was also a lot of self-build by workers (Harris, 1991; Stovall, 1989): purchasing land from a landowner, speculative or otherwise, and then building a house on it, perhaps over a fairly lengthy period of time. Retail outlets and office buildings tended to be custom-built and owned outright.

This clearly changed, particularly after the Second World War.[6] The creation of premises, often for rent, as in the case of shopping centres, office developments or industrial parks, has become a very competitive, speculative industry and for developers, a clearly identifiable social interest. Developments are highly leveraged and returns are put back into the business with a view to further expansion. They are built ahead of any buyer commitment which requires a constant attention to innovation to attract the customer. Some of this innovation is also with a view to enhancing land rent through the internalization of externalities; this helps to explain the sheer magnitude of many new developments, including ever larger shopping centres, logistics parks, ambitious residential developments incorporating lakes, green space and golf courses and so-called "mixed-use" developments. Other changes relate to the specifics of the buildings. Housing is exemplary in the transformations and changes of fashion that it has experienced: from one-car garages to two-car and upwards; differentiation into housing targeted at retirees versus that for young families and so on. Likewise with office buildings which are open-plan and now equipped with underground garages and their own recreational spaces, as in the office campus ideal. Meanwhile, the construction of modular units for industry and warehousing was at one time a novelty. Without a highly competitive, speculative impulse, it is hard to imagine these changes.

The emergence of property capital has affected urban and regional development in some obvious ways, with land extensive developments giving it a strong suburbanizing impulse, for a start, but also in some less obvious ones; not least in providing models that would then be incorporated into state practice. In the 1930s, in an attempt to lure firms into areas suffering from high unemployment, the British government created what were called "trading estates": these included ready-built factory units for rent at subsidized prices. This, however, had already been anticipated by the earlier, private ones, notably the industrial parks at Slough, west of London and Wythenshawe close to Manchester. In the US, though an extreme case, local governments would be established by developers as a tax-avoidance ruse that consisted of nothing but an industrial park. The sheer size of new developments has also been factored into development policy, sometimes something to be fought, as in the aversion of downtown retailers in the cities of Western Europe to suburban shopping centers; and also as something, as in the American case, to be welcomed because of the large and sudden impetus they can give to local tax bases.

The final condition for development policy has been what I have called "the new mobility" (Cox, 2016, pp. 93–97): a necessary one if things were indeed to be moved around into areas of high unemployment, into new towns on the edge of metropolitan areas or simply to satisfy the desires of local growth coalitions. The contrast is with conditions under the first Industrial Revolution where technologies and the nature of products tended to fix industry in highly particular places. Most notably, and given reliance on steam power, these were the coalfields and estuarine locations enjoying access to coal by relatively cheap steam navigation:[7] much cheaper than by rail. Textile industries clustered in this way, as did iron, steel and ship-building: all leading sectors of the period. The second Industrial Revolution would sow the seeds of change, though not entirely on its own.

First, the rise of electricity as motive power liberated industry from the coalfields. At the same time, the second Industrial Revolution was accompanied by the creation of a whole new set of consumption goods industries, durable and non-durable. Some of these were downstream from existing ones, like the increasing differentiation of the clothing industry. Others, like many household appliances, depended on the extension of the electricity network if they were to be bought. Meanwhile, there was the succession of new products revolutionizing personal mobility: the bicycle, the automobile and the street car and tram. The point about these new industries is they were far more indifferent in their locations than their predecessors of the first Industrial Revolution. Partly this was a matter of progressively deskilled labour needs; partly it was that they were assembly industries that brought together components from many different locations; in some cases it was a matter of market access, but in that instance, depending on economies of scale in the industry in question, that could mean a multiplication of plants in different locations. But for this new mobility to be a condition for urban and regional policy, one of which was moving them into what were judged to be desirable directions, either by a national government or a local growth coalition, there had to be changes in industrial organization.

What makes a big difference here is the emergence of the multi-locational firm, either horizontally integrated, with several plants producing the same thing; or vertically integrated, where plants were organized in supply chains, or some mix of the two. No single firm with one point of production was going to move lock, stock and barrel. That would have been highly risky, unless over a very short distance, as did indeed happen in particular urban areas. But what was now possible was the creation of a second, a third and more plants elsewhere, perhaps in accord with calculations of shifting market advantages. This would then give way to a phalanx of plants and shifts in capacity among them, even to the closure of some, along with the opening of new ones. This would in turn lay the basis for new spatial divisions of labour among places. Larger cities might lose their production functions and even their headquarter, organizing functions, to the extent that advantage in that direction lay in the capital city, or major regional centres like New York, Chicago and San Francisco. So if through the branch plant, urban and regional policy had the weapon it needed – moving them around in accord with policy goals – that self-same mobility could also challenge the economic bases of cities, re-posing the regional question in new ways.

This is to focus on one aspect of the new mobility. It also extended to workers and households. Successive revolutions in personal mobility – the tram, the street car and the omnibus, the automobile – revolutionized the possibilities of residential choice and had major impacts on the emerging development industry. It allowed greater expansion at the periphery, creating some resolution of the diseconomies of agglomeration, notably congestion and the concomitant concentration of activities that results in increasing rents. This applied both to employees seeking cheaper housing and to employers keen to expand and take advantage of the larger layouts that electric power facilitated. The progressive formation of metropolitan housing and labour markets then provided the scope for the newer, larger real estate developments: the Levittowns, the industrial and office parks and the regional shopping centres would follow.

But viewing the new mobility as a whole, the locational discretion of firms as well as of households was also to some degree problematic. Not all firms or types of activity were mobile to the same degree. Those depending on urban rents, whether landlords or developers, could be particularly vulnerable to shifts in their market as major employers closed plants and opened them elsewhere. This could be a dilemma shared by the local working class to the extent that people were, for whatever reason, locked into local labour markets undergoing a contraction as firms shifted operations elsewhere or simply went out of business.

It is this tension between mobility and a relative fixity which lies behind anxieties about local and regional economies and which is the *sine qua non* for any notion of local and regional development policy. Harvey (1985, p. 203) outlined one solution:

> The more corporations used their powers of dispersal (…) the less urban regions competed with each other on the basis of their industrial mix and the more they were forced to compete in terms of the attractions they had to offer to corporate investment as labor and commodity markets and as bundles of physical and social assets that corporations could exploit to their own advantage.

But in fact, this turns out to be a very country-specific approach: that of the US. In Western Europe it would be different. The problem of mitigating local economic disadvantage is taken in hand by central government: a much more top-down approach, therefore. But in both instances, and as Harvey implied, the new mobility would turn out to be not just a curse but also an opportunity.

National difference and national conjunctures

Accordingly, the way in which it would be exploited in development policy would vary to a very considerable degree. In the US, the bits and pieces – parts of the divisions of labour of firms, and quickly defined as up for grabs – would become objects for local growth coalitions to attract in, or ignore, depending on how they fitted into some local vision. In Western Europe, on the other hand, the rise of the branch plant turned out to be something that could be used by central governments as they sought to alter the distribution of industry for their own purposes, which they did.[8]

Indeed, in the second half of the century, the opportunities for mobilizing the footloose for purposes of local economic development would expand significantly beyond the industrial branch plant. Large corporations with multiple branches would come to be a major feature of developed economies in both manufacturing and in the so-called service industries: bank branches, hotel chains, back offices, retail chains and the shopping centres that serve as their characteristic sites. Retail chains then entailed the creation of warehouses and distribution centres, adding to the bits and pieces that could be the object of location policy in the Western European case or of policies of attracting inward investment in the American one. The expansion of the state increased the possibilities through its multiplication of military, air and naval bases and the hiving-off of routine office work from capital cities for relocation elsewhere. Eventually new residential developments, particularly the larger ones, would become objects of strategic planning for local and regional development.

But it bears repeating that how such mobility would be exploited for the purposes of advancing development agendas would vary considerably between the US and the Western European countries. In the US they would be the object of local, quite narrowly defined programs aimed at the enhancement of rents from property, which would then be subject to forces of a market-led nature and a competition between localities: for the population growth and housing demand promised by investments in office or industrial employment; and then a competition between the different local governments in a metropolitan area to land the housing developments that would result – a competition typically spearheaded by the landowners, the property companies and local government itself. Planners would play a role but they would be in the service of local government and local government in turn would find itself subordinated to the pressures of local growth interests.

In Western Europe, it would be different. The various mobilities would be drawn on by central governments as part of creating what can only be described as "the good geography": a set of roughly interlocking goals, reflecting national debates about growth and distribution. There would be attention to questions of equity over space as we have already seen in discussion of policies aimed at redistributing employment. The national geography would also emerge as a consciously conceived and planned-for productive force as in specifically national port/airport/transport policies, ensuring that housing was located where it was most needed, and in attempts to create the compact city. Here, the order of priorities would be reversed: central government rather than local, and planners, particularly those at the centre, in a dominant position.

In Western Europe, there was considerable convergence in policy (Romus, 1958), most notably in directing employment towards areas of relatively high unemployment, but also those deemed to be backward: as in Southern Italy, Western France, the Scottish Highlands and Islands, and the far norths of Norway and Sweden. Areas were designated and the state used financial incentives to persuade firms to locate there and sometimes, just to remain. In some instances, it was a matter of the investment decisions of firms in public ownership. There again areas believed to be under severe housing and labour market pressure were subject to controls over firm expansion. This applied to much of the Midlands and Southern England, and as far as office employment was concerned, to the Paris basin.

Other aspects of policy, including the dispersal of government offices from capital cities to provincial towns in areas of high unemployment were more variable from country to country: France, Ireland, the Netherlands and the United Kingdom all made use of this (Cox, 2016, p. 148). New towns were common in France and the United Kingdom with other cases in Ireland, the Netherlands and Sweden. These were in part designed to mitigate diseconomies of agglomeration by moving people and employment out of major cities. The new towns surrounding London, Birmingham, Manchester and Paris provide examples. But in the old mining areas of South Wales, Northeast England and the Pas de Calais/Nord region of France, the idea was to concentrate labour reserves in areas where population was notoriously dispersed over many small colliery villages (Hudson, 1982). Again, in the Netherlands, new towns had a different origin in the draining of the Zuyder Zee but, concomitantly, providing some relief for nearby Amsterdam.

Urban and regional development policy in the US has been quite different; in fact, the "regional" part of it barely exists at all. Rather it is cities that take the lead in promoting development, largely by attracting inward investment from outside. Accordingly, they compete with each other by offering various financial incentives and infrastructural improvements. The individual states are auxiliary to this in virtue of their responsibilities for not only their own taxation but also large swathes of labour law. These include the power to ban the closed shop and so make the organization of workplaces more difficult, as well as control of compensation for injury on the job: an important consideration that weighs on firms in the form of insurance premia. State tax policy and labour law are important contributions to what is called a state's business climate and something over which local governments bring strong pressures to bear.

The undergirding structure governing urban development and, derivatively, regional development, is what might be called a market in locations: locations are "sold" to firms who play one local government off against another, seeking the best deal. The competition in 2018 for the second Amazon headquarters, promising 50,000 jobs to the "winning" city is indicative of how this works. What is at stake is not so much development, even though that is the way in which these practices will be sold to the public – as growth. Significantly one talks about "growth machines" and they are a crucial actor in urban development policy: something for which equivalents in Western Europe are much harder to find.[9]

The growth in question is first and foremost in the demand for the products of local developers; homebuyers for housing, tenants for shopping centres and office parks, and conventioneers and tourists for hotels. Increasing demand via, most obviously, an increase in population, is absolutely crucial for developers in the American context. This is because of their heightened dependence on demand in a particular locality. Developers tend to be locked into a particular place in virtue of connections with local banks, builders and those "in the know" about what is about to happen: most importantly, the local politicians who make the decisions about new freeway interchanges, re-zonings of land and major capital projects which promise to alter accessibility relations and so the prospect of extracting rent. This is peculiarly American. The developers in one city will be different from those in another: testimony to the unique qualities of particular local markets; something connected, in turn, to the remarkable institutional differences among US cities (Cox, 2018).

Historically they were joined by other agents, some of which remain important. As a result of the anti-trust legislation at the beginning of the last century, banking was a notoriously decentralized industry. Branching out across county and state lines was forbidden until the rules were relaxed in the 1970s. This meant that banks were extraordinarily dependent on local markets: growth in deposits and loan demand in the county where they were based was fundamental to their fortunes. Involvement in local development policy and politics is now largely over for them, but not so the gas and electric utilities where there were similar restrictions on inter-state mergers. Rather they had unique service areas, so that growth in demand there was fundamental to revenues. They are still significant players: gatekeepers for inward investment in industry since any owner of an industrial site will lodge the information with them. They control the process with developers participating, and local government last of all (Cox and Wood, 1997).

The stake of local government is largely fiscal. In the US local governments are highly dependent for their revenues on local taxation: largely property and sales taxes – hence the interest in attracting large regional shopping centres – and increasingly, local income taxes. A lot rides on this: not just revenue but also the ability to raise money for capital projects. This occurs through the sale of what are called municipal bonds. But these carry ratings that determine the rate of interest, and the rating depends significantly on the growth of the local tax base (Cox, 2010, pp. 221 and 223).

Interestingly, until the 1970s, this worked quite well from the standpoint of redistributing employment to relatively backward areas, most notably the Southern states (Cox, 2016, pp. 154–155), promoting a degree of regional convergence, as in Western Europe. There were no new towns in the Western European sense. Rather the answer to diseconomies of agglomeration in the US has been the private one of massive urban sprawl and latterly the edge city. There are "new towns" but they are simply coagulations of new development around small towns slowly incorporated into a wider metropolitan area, and perhaps the basis for a new nucleus of development around some massive mixed-use project for which it is hard to find parallels in Western Europe.

Since the 1970s, there have clearly been changes in both the US and Western Europe. In the US policy largely continues much as it was: bottom-up, a market in locations. But now its effectiveness in countering uneven development, even while it was never one of its goals, has markedly deteriorated. The branch plants that were the targets of many smaller towns are now going to Mexico or China or have closed down in the face of heightened international competition. On the other hand, the possibilities of attracting some high-tech development with demands for elevated labour skills are quite poor: the skills demands of mass-assembly branch plants were modest to say the least (Veltz, 2017).

In Western Europe, there *has* been a change in policy, though there too, regional convergence has tended to go into reverse. The areas once eligible for financial assistance to attract new employment have greatly contracted, partly under pressure from an EU that wants to promote development in the more backward areas of Eastern and Southern Europe, and partly, at least in the United Kingdom, on ideological grounds and the view that market forces should prevail. Meanwhile, there have been no new towns in Western Europe since the late 1960s, though there is now talk in both France and the United Kingdom of a new generation of them. On the other hand, there is also the suggestion that the development of the single market has nudged policy more in the direction of the American model: a more "bottom-up" approach where the member governments compete for inward investment. Firms now locate with respect to the EU as a whole rather than with respect to individual countries. At the same time, the inclusion of the Eastern European countries has had a dramatic effect on the range of wage rates within the EU. Both of these factors have induced some attention to the "business climate", akin to the practice of the US states: notably national labour law and corporate taxation, but also the willingness to provide the multinationals with various sweeteners. But while in the US this is accepted as normal practice there has been greater criticism in the EU, particularly in Western Europe where anxieties about the relocation of firms to Eastern Europe has led to charges of what is called "social dumping".

Even so, there *has* been continuity, and in particular in the central coordination of policy. There is a view that powers over new development have been decentralized: a tendency in the American direction, and not just to the member states of the EU as discussed above but also to local governments. This has been exaggerated (Le Galès and Harding, 1998; Cox, 2009; Cox, 2016, pp. 171–187). Rather what is observable is a tendency on the part of central governments to discriminate between those regions seen as able to compete more effectively in an increasingly global market, and those less able. State money is targeted at infrastructural improvements in the former and most notably the bigger metropolitan areas: the emergent post-industrial cities. In some instances, this has meant directing money to capital cities (Crouch and Le Galès, 2012). If there is to be regional convergence in this policy-making environment, then it will be largely, though not exclusively, via trickle down effects: "not exclusively", since there have been other central government initiatives designed to promote development in more equalizing ways, as in the Urban Development Corporations and enterprise zones of the Thatcher era (Anderson, 1990) and France's poles of competitivity (Ancien, 2005). This does not mean that local and indeed regional governments have not become more involved in local economic development and often in ways that depart from the simple competition for inward investment: where there is a strong local IT presence, for example, local governments seeking out ways of facilitating their expansion.[10]

In short, while there has been some shift in the geographic division of state labour in Western Europe as it pertains to urban and regional development, the contrast with American practice remains a sharp one, which raises the question of exactly why that might be. A first and obvious place to look is the territorial structure of the state (Cox, 2004; Cox, 2016, pp. 295–318). The contrasts are as striking as the differences in approach to urban and regional policy that they inform. The American state is a highly decentralized one. It is a radical federation in which the states have very considerable powers, including, as we have seen, some aspects of labour law. The states have then seen fit to delegate many of their powers to local governments, including land use policy. From a developer standpoint the functions that local governments can and do perform are enviable. They include the power to:

- grant tax abatements for new developments.
- regulate land use without any superordinate supervision. Appeals to a superior body from those adversely affected by a development are not possible.
- raise money for public works from the sale of municipal bonds: for airports and new highways with the potential to alter accessibility advantages and so enhance the possibilities of new sources of land rent.
- annex land that is unincorporated. This is particularly important given the interest of developers in land-extensive projects like office parks, logistics centres and regional shopping centres.

The highly fragmented nature of the state creates other possibilities for local interests, whether organized as coalitions or even as individuals looking for a favour. For the bottom-up nature of development policy also extends to relations with state and federal governments. They are a primary source of favours, regulatory and monetary, and, in virtue of the structure of the American state, highly vulnerable to entreaties from below (Arnold, 1981). In part, this rides on the committee system. No piece of legislation can make it to consideration in houses or senates unless it has been discussed and typically amended in the appropriate committee. By and large representatives get to sit on committees relevant to their constituencies: so congresspersons and senators representing New York and North Carolina are prominent on finance and banking committees, given the importance of financial services to respective major metropolitan centres: New York and Charlotte. This puts them in a prime position to block legislation or seek amendments favourable to the industry in their home bases. Should the legislation move forward for a vote, then the weakness of party discipline means that, through horse trading and the creation of coalitions that cross party lines, it stands a good chance of success. This is made possible by the radical separation of legislative from executive branches. Failure to pass a bill can never put a government in jeopardy as it does under parliamentary systems, where it can create a crisis of confidence and a government's resignation. In fact, legislation can only be introduced by a legislator, not by the government, and then has to be subject to committee meetings. The same applies to the operations of the individual states, and with similar implications for the politics of local and regional development (Weir, 1996). Local, and to a lesser degree, state government is utterly complicit in this because of their own fiscal stakes. There are clearly government programs that channel money from federal and state branches respectively. But with the possible exception of education, they have little equalizing effect. And the fact that so much social policy is delegated or at least shared with the states, means that inequality gets built in to the geography of America's welfare state.

This is a lengthy explanation but important since misunderstanding of how the American state functions is widespread. It is very different from the centralized states of Western Europe, and even from the federal states of Belgium, Germany, Spain and Switzerland which, compared with the American federation, are quite weak, and where the separation of legislative from executive branches does not exist. In the unitary states, local governments are subordinated to central government in so many different ways: land use planning is coordinated from the top, and funding of the welfare state has a strong equalizing effect across local governments. Local governments have limited incentive to promote local development and when they do, central control of land use planning limits their scope. The conjunction of legislative and executive branches then translates into strong party discipline with scant possibility for the expression of territorial interests in the way so characteristic of the American case. The federal states are somewhat different and there is some scope for the individual provinces to develop policies of their own. On the other hand, their powers are much more limited than that of the American states and the vulnerability of governments to dismissal through a vote of no confidence puts pressure on representatives to toe the party line rather than that of the home district. And in the German and Spanish cases, there is fiscal redistribution from the more affluent provinces to the poorer ones.

Yet, and clearly, state structures do not exist independently of social formations. The United States and the countries of Western Europe are capitalist states, but, in virtue of very different histories, the values, the dominant discourses, the inherited structures, can vary and help condition the formation and ongoing reproduction of, accordingly, different state forms. For a start, the relation between state and economy is quite different. In the US the subordination of the state to the forces of a capitalist economy is striking. This is most dramatically on show in the way in which the state, through its structures of relations, mimics the market. The market in locations through which local governments compete for inward investment is one aspect of this; likewise, the way in which state policy, via the committee system and weak parties, is seen as an adjunct to competitive advantage. This in turn is underlain by a popular embrace of the virtues of the market and a suspicion of the state as a monopoly provider; accordingly, state powers are to be limited, except when they involve grants to local governments for local development purposes or some regulatory indulgence. Meanwhile, the mosaic of welfare states that feeds into business climate competition is celebrated on the grounds of expanding choice. In the countries of Western Europe, it can seem to be the other way around. Competition among local governments is more likely to be frowned on. Limits are placed on the ability of local governments to grant tax concessions to new developments. The competition of smaller airports for low cost airlines was placed under severe limits by the EU (Cox, 2016, pp. 258–260). Central government is free of the opprobrium of "big government".

In part, it is a matter of a very different balance of class relations. In terms of the subsumption of labour to capital, a process in which the working class sees its interests as coincidental with those of employers – i.e. profit and expansion – the US is *sui generis*. The labour movement is organizationally extremely weak: there is no socialist representation in party politics and union membership is relatively low. Labour unions are seemingly pragmatic bodies pursuing an interest group approach to politics, which fits nicely into the dominant view of what competitive politics should look like. They lack the ideological bite of their Western European counterparts, even while that bite is no longer what it was. This is particularly clear in the relative weakness of the welfare state and, as an aspect of it, any serious spatial policy aimed at mitigating geographically uneven development.

Crucial to understanding these differences are different histories. American capitalism developed in and across a space uncluttered by pre-capitalist residues: no peasantries, landed gentries or ancien regimes with limited interest in buying and selling. In Western Europe it was different. A nascent capitalism encountered resistances born of framings of social life that did not reduce it to market relations and the unbridled conversion of everything into commodities. Rather there were very different views of the respective claims of individual and community, and of civil society and the state. Competition and its effects on the community would be seen more critically and the state as a means of limiting as well as facilitating capital. The two different aspects of the commodity form, so central to capitalism, would be given different emphases: in the US exchange value could come to dominate use value, but not nearly so much in Western Europe. There was, rather, a moral economy[11] (Thompson, 1971) of the form absent in the US, which fortified resistance (Calhoun, 2012) A capitalist economy is seen as having dysfunctionalities that need to be countered, not least through the land use planning mechanism and a state-orchestrated reordering of the space economy.

There is also the question of inherited state forms. Certainly in the US, the creation of the radical federal structure in 1789 had very little to do with the class relations of capitalism because, for the most part, it pre-dated them. Despite this contingency of origins, it would become a condition for capitalist hegemony and express the claims of the superiority of markets and of competition, albeit to the disadvantage of the labour movement. The formation of a national welfare state would be frustrated by the competitive anxieties of the different states; something with which the capitalist class as a whole could easily ally itself (Farhang and Katznelson, 2005; Weir, 2005).

One can make analogous claims for the centralized states of Western Europe. The absolutist state is antecedent to capitalist social relations, even while it can be regarded as an important condition for them. Its centralizing institutions would accordingly be the stage for class struggle: that was where power resided and continues to reside. That the (central) state had a monopoly of power was regarded by the labour movement as an advantage. This was because it allowed a uniformity of labour law that would work against capitalist competition in terms of wages and conditions of work. Even for those not inclined to vote for parties of the left, the central state has been seen as an important counterweight to the damaging effects of market relations: testimony to a different view of the meaning of capitalism.

Concluding comments

The emergence of urban and regional development as a state preoccupation after the Second World War has first to be situated with respect to the contradictory development of capitalism and how that was projected onto a spatial plane: regional questions of uneven development and urban questions of diseconomies of agglomeration and its social implications. It would take some time before it was defined and practiced by the state but the preconditions for particular forms of intervention were emerging some time before: city and regional planning, property capital and its innovative forms of development and a new mobility of production. How these bits and pieces would be put together in policy form would vary. In Western Europe there have been strong tendencies to top-down planning: notably attempts to displace employment in the form, largely, of branch plants, to areas of relatively high unemployment or sheer lagging development; and the relief of large cities by the construction of new towns. In the US, instead, there was reliance on a market form: local governments competed for the self-same branch plants and local property development assumed a dominant role instead of its more subordinate one in Western Europe.

These differences are owing in the first place to very different state structures. The decentralized state forms of the US are an important precondition for the market in locations that is the form assumed by urban and regional development there. The much more centralized states of Western Europe on the other hand, have been a necessary precondition for top-down policies. Beyond that, state forms have to be seen as aspects of wider social formations which lend discursive underpinnings to highly diverse policy approaches.

Notes

1 For a more detailed elaboration on these points, see Cox (2016, chapter 2).
2 Compare Goodman (1979).
3 Marchand and Cavin (2007) have discussed Gravier's arguments, as well as outlining the similar views expressed by the influential Swiss planner Armin Meili.

4 See Woods (1939) for an example of this genre.
5 Whole cities, or segments of cities, have been planned by private developers: Irvine CA in the first instance, and Edgbaston, the Birmingham suburb on the other; aka the Calthorpe Estate (Cannadine, 1977). In some instances the private planning came before public and provided templates of good practice.
6 Writing in 1975 about Great Britain, Ambrose and Colenutt (1975) recognized the relative recency of this, arguing that "[b]efore the Second World War there were very few large property companies. Instead, redevelopment was undertaken by individual entrepreneurs, or by firms developing buildings for their own occupation. There were few speculative office blocks and the tendency was for firms to own freeholds to their premises rather than rent. Certainly there was no public awareness of 'developers' as such. Few property companies were quoted on the Stock Exchange, there was virtually no property press dealing with commercial development, and there was no coherent organization lobbying for the developers." (p. 37).
7 For the influence of coal mining geography on urbanization in Europe as a whole, in large part through the steam engine and its implications for the location of the iron and steel industry, see Fernihough and O'Rourke (2014).
8 On the significance of the branch plant to urban and regional policy, see Heim (1983).
9 See Cox (2017) for a critical discussion of some aspects of the growth machine idea.
10 For one example of this see While, Gibbs and Jonas (2004).
11 A social form in which economic life is not separate from moral judgment but where economic practice inevitably has strong associations of what is fair and just, and what isn't.

References

Ambrose, P. and Colenutt. B., 1975. *The property machine*. Harmondsworth Middlesex: Penguin.

Ancien, D., 2005. Local and regional development policy in France: Of changing conditions and forms, and enduring state centrality. *Space and Polity*, 9(3), pp. 217–236. https://doi.org/10.1080/13562570500509877

Anderson, J., 1990. The 'new right'. Enterprise zones and urban development corporations. *International Journal of Urban and Regional Research*, 14(3), pp. 468–489. https://doi.org/10.1111/j.1468–2427.1990.tb00151.x

Arnold, R. D., 1981. The local roots of domestic policy. In T. E. Mann and N. J. Ornstein, eds. *The new Congress*. Washington D.C: The American Enterprise Institute. Ch. 8.

Calhoun, C., ed. 2012. *The roots of radicalism: Tradition, the public sphere and early 19th-century social movements*. Chicago: University of Chicago Press.

Cannadine, D., 1977. Victorian cities: How different? *Social History*, 2(4), pp. 457–480.

Cox, K. R., 2004. The politics of local and regional development, the difference the state makes and the US/British Contrast. In: A. Wood and D. Valler, eds. 2004. *Governing local and regional economies*. Aldershot: Ashgate. Ch. 10.

Cox, K. R., 2009. 'Rescaling the state' in question. *Cambridge Journal of Regions, Economy and Society*, 2(1), pp. 107–121.

Cox, K. R., 2010. The problem of metropolitan governance and the politics of scale. *Regional Studies*, 44(2), pp. 215–227. https://doi.org/10.1080/00343400903365128

Cox, K. R., 2016. *The politics of urban and regional development and the American exception*. Syracuse NY: Syracuse University Press.

Cox, K. R., 2017. Revisiting the city as a growth machine. *Cambridge Journal of Regions, Economy and Society*, 10(3), pp. 391–405. https://doi.org/10.1093/cjres/rsx011

Cox, K. R., 2018. American cities and their institutions. *Unfashionable geographies*. Available at https://kevinrcox.wordpress.com/2018/05/30/american-cities-and-their-institutions.

Cox, K. R. and Wood, A. M., 1997. Competition and cooperation in mediating the global: The case of local economic development. *Competition and Change*, 2(1), pp. 65–94.

Crouch, C. and Le Galès, P., 2012. Cities as national champions. *Journal of European Public Policy*, 19(3), pp. 405–419.

Dietz, B., 2008. Countryside-versus-city in European thought: German and British anti-urbanism between the wars. *The European Legacy: Toward New Paradigms*, 13(7), pp. 801–814.

Farhang, S. and Katznelson, I., 2005. The Southern imposition: Congress and labor in the New Deal and Fair Deal. *Studies in American Political Development* 19(1), pp. 1–30.

Fernihough, A. and O'Rourke, K. H., 2014. Coal and the European Industrial Revolution. *Discussion Papers in Economic and Social History*, Oxford University, No. 124.

Goodman, R., 1979. *The last entrepreneurs*. New York: Simon and Schuster.

Gravier, J.-F., 1947. *Paris et le désert Français*. Paris: Portulan.

Harris, R., 1991. Self-building in the urban housing market. *Economic Geography*, 67(1), pp. 1–21. https:\\doi.org\10.2307/143633

Harvey, D., 1982. *The limits to capital*. Oxford: Blackwell.

Harvey, D., 1985. *The urbanization of capital*. Oxford: Blackwell.

Heim, C. E., 1983. Industrial organization and regional development in interwar Britain. *Journal of Economic History*, 43(4), pp. 931–952.

Hudson, R., 1982. Accumulation, spatial policies, and the production of regional labor reserves: A study of Washington New Town. *Environment and Planning A*, 14(5), pp. 665–680.

Koistinen, D., 2013. *Confronting decline: The political economy of deindustrialization in 20th-century New England*. Gainesville, FL: University Press of Florida.

Le Galès, P. and Harding, A., 1998. Cities and states in Europe. *West European Politics*, 21(3), pp. 120–144. https:\\doi.org\10.1080/01402389808425260

Marchand, B. and Cavin, J. S., 2007. Anti-urban ideologies and planning in France and Switzerland: Jean-François Gravier and Armin Meili. *Planning Perspectives*, 22, pp. 29–53.

Preteceille, E., 1976. Urban planning: The contradictions of capitalist urbanization. *Antipode*, 8(1), pp. 69–76.

Romus, P., 1958. *Expansion économique régionale et communauté Européenne*. Leyde: Sythoff.

Shapiro, E. S., 1972. Decentralist intellectuals and the New Deal. *The Journal of American History*, 58(4), pp. 938–957. https://doi.org/10.2307/1917852

Stovall, T., 1989. French communism and suburban development: The rise of the Paris red belt. *Journal of Contemporary History*, 24(3), pp. 437–460.

Thompson, E. P., 1971. The moral economy of the English crowd in the eighteenth century. *Past and Present*, No. 50. Pp. 76–136.

Veltz, P., 2017. Introduction: Regions and territories: Evolutions and changes. *Economie et Statistique*. 494-495-496. Pp. 5–17.

Weeks, J., 1981. *Capital and exploitation*. London: Edward Arnold.

Weir, M., 1996. Central cities' loss of power in state politics. *Cityscape*, 2(2), pp. 23–40.

Weir, M., 2005. States, race, and the decline of New Deal liberalism. *Studies in American Political Development*, 19(2), pp. 157–172.

While, A., Gibbs, D. C. and Jonas, A. E. G., 2004. Unblocking the city? Growth pressures, collective provision, and the search for new spaces of governance in Greater Cambridge. *Environment and Planning A*, 36, pp. 279–304. https://doi.org/10.1068/a3615

Woods, R., 1939. *America reborn: A plan for decentralization of industry*. New York: Longman, Green and Co.

9 Spatial-economic development

The effect of urbanization on education in China, 1890–present[1]

Meimei Wang and Bas van Leeuwen

Introduction

Human capital is widely recognized as an important driver of regional economic development; therefore, it is instructive to investigate the spatial differences in schooling and learning (Koscinska and Herbst, this volume). Urbanisation is a major spatial component affecting education. Because cities are generally centres of learning and educational modernisation, urban education is prominent in a wide range of academic debates, including those concerning urban economic growth and the job market, the supply of essential social services in cities, urban–rural relations and migration.

In this chapter, we discuss the relationship between urban–rural spatial differences and education in China. The Chinese case is particularly interesting for several reasons. First, urbanisation has historically drawn significant government attention in China because these urban areas are considered to have a mainly administrative role (in contrast to Europe, where urban areas have many additional functions), and also to act as drivers of economic modernisation and development. Second, China's education system was dominated for centuries by a civil examination scheme having a curriculum based exclusively on the humanities. Only since the late 19th century have more practical topics such as mathematics, technology, languages, economics and physics been included. Cities were the frontrunners in this educational reform process. Third, China experienced a political period (c. 1949–1979) during which the government-regulated relationship between urbanisation and education was reversed, and educated people moved to the countryside. Finally, the remarkable economic and urban growth experienced by China in recent decades has led to a return to the traditional, pre-1949 link between urbanisation and education.

In this chapter, the abovementioned massive changes that occurred over time and across urban and rural regions are related directly to the theme of this volume—the multidisciplinary connection between historical and regional studies. This chapter further elaborates on this topic by exploring urbanisation (as a driver of knowledge-based development of cities and regions) from the angles of history and of the social sciences relevant to regional studies (e.g. sociology and economics). However, the roles of these multiple fields vary considerably by time period. To analyse these issues, in the following section we discuss the construct of urbanisation. Sections 3–5 discuss Republican China (pre-1949), the first phase of the New China period (1949–1979) and the Reform Period (1979–present). We end with a brief conclusion.

Quantifying urbanisation

The historical dimension

Numerous studies have attempted to quantify urbanisation, most commonly by defining cities as settlements with a certain number of persons (e.g. 5,000, 10,000 or 40,000) living together. Quantification has been related partly to a desire to properly define the concept of urbanisation, and partly to the goal of creating a historically and/or geographically comparable indicator. However, this type of definition goes beyond mere academic interest because (as we will show below) it affects individuals directly in terms of allowing migration, offering job opportunities and supplying social care, among others.

Examples of key scholars involved in quantifying urbanisation include Chandler (1987), a historian; Modelski (2003), a political scientist and Bairoch (1988), an economic historian. Chandler used censuses, travel reports, and other direct and indirect information, including cities larger than approximately 20,000 before 1850 and cities larger than 40,000 after that year. Modelski (2003) updated Chandler's work by including more data and applying theories to predict missing population counts for cities. One such theory was Zipf's law which, when applied to cities, states that city sizes in a country will follow a certain "Zipf distribution", thus allowing scholars to predict city sizes.[2] Modelski focused on cities with more than 10,000 (ancient times) or more than 1,000,000 inhabitants (modern times). Similar to Chandler and Modelski, Bairoch (1988) used various sources, but took a more eclectic approach as, "when the data did not exist, he found a way to collect or construct it" (Brezis, 2008). Bairoch constructed data for a series of cities of 5,000 or more inhabitants for the period before 1850. Presently, urbanisation data are published by the United Nations as *World Urbanization Prospects*. In these publications, the definition of a city is highly detailed and varies significantly across countries. In general, however, population clusters above 2,000 to 100,000 persons are considered cities, depending on the country.

The above discussion on the population sizes of cities shows clearly that urbanisation is viewed differently according to the region, field and time period. Arguably, Paul Bairoch has been the most influential scholar in this field. His work has been modified numerous times for application in various countries (see e.g. Malanima, 2009), including China. Although numerous such studies have been performed with regard to China (Skinner, 1977; Cao, 2000a, 2000b), most have been conducted by economic historians for the pre-1949 period. Identifying the cities was a major problem faced by these studies. Yet most scholars are agreed on the definition of a city as 2,000 or more inhabitants for the pre-1900 period. In a recent study, Xu et al. (2018) provided trends by region from AD 1100 to AD 1900. Based on the above definition, the urbanisation ratio of Inner China remained stable from 1776 to 1893, at around 7 per cent. During the early stages of the 20th century, the total urbanisation in China increased rapidly, approaching 13 per cent in 1918. Growth was also rapid after 1918: for cities with 2.500 or more inhabitants, the urbanisation ratio was 34 per cent at the end of the 1920s (Xu, 1930), 32 per cent in 1933 (Ouyang, 1936) and 28 per cent in approximately 1936 according to the China Yearbook (Sun, 1946).

Urbanisation in New China

Sociologists, in particular, objected to the approach of using city size as a measure of urbanisation because many people who were counted in the urban population were actually farmers. According to an official investigation of cities and towns along main railway lines in the 1930s (with the exception of Chongqing city and Guiyang city), farmers accounted for more than 70 per cent of the urban population in all cities in the provinces of Guizhou and Sichuan. Even in Guiyang city, the capital of Guizhou Province, more than 60 per cent of the population consisted of peasants (Yin and Li, 2009).

This criticism of Republican urbanization rates led, after the establishment of New China in 1949, to a change in the statistical definition of urbanisation to exclude the farming population. After 1958, the *Hukou* (household registration) system divided the entire population into agricultural and non-agricultural segments. Those who held farmland were designated as agricultural and excluded from certain social benefits; e.g. they could not migrate to urban areas unless they had an urban spouse. Hence, prior to 1978–1982 when this system was relaxed, the strict *Hukou* system and the existence of communes almost completely separated the agricultural and urban populations, causing the officially reported urbanisation ratio to be much lower than in previous decades. Nevertheless, from 1949 to 1960, due to the demand for labour during industrialization, the share of the non-agricultural population increased quickly and drove the urbanization ratio (defined at that time as the share of persons with an urban *Hukou*) from 10.6 per cent (Bai, 2003) to 20 per cent (Zhao, 1988). However, this upward trend was interrupted by the Great Famine that struck around 1960. The government was forced to reduce the urban population because of the lack of food, and many labourers who had come to the cities from rural areas were sent back. Hence, in 1966, the urbanization rate was only 17.9 per cent. The share of the urban population further stagnated when, from the second half of the 1960s to the early 1970s, the government implemented a strategy for the development of the hinterlands, for national security reasons. Many urban students and workers were sent to rural areas to perform labour (Wang, 2001). These two factors, combined with lower fertility rates in the cities caused by the one-child policy, led to the urbanization rate declining slightly to 17.6 per cent in 1977.

After 1978, urbanisation resumed its upward trend, which has continued to the present. This occurred because, first, the institutional barriers such as the *Hukou* system became more flexible, reopening the possibility of rural–urban migration. Stimulated by more and better job opportunities created by the fast-growing urban economy, there was even an absolute decline in the rural population. A second reason for this resumption of urban growth was a change in the official definition of the urban population. Since the third population census in 1982, and as was the case before 1949, all people living in urban areas—including farmers—have again been defined as part of the urban population. The definition of urban areas remains based on administrative divisions, but the urban divisions have continuously expanded (National Bureau of Statistics of China, 2008; see also Table 9.1).

The return to the practice of including the agricultural population living in cities in the urbanisation statistics has met with the same criticism as it did in the Republican Period, with multiple scholars arguing that rural labourers who migrate to urban areas should be counted as part of the agricultural population.[3] These scholars considered the officially reported urbanisation of nearly 60 per cent in 2017 to be nominal urbanisation, with real urbanisation being no more than 45 per cent.[4]

Table 9.1 Urbanisation ratios in New China

	Note	*Urbanisation ratio*
1776	Population >2,000; including farmers living in city	7%
1851	Idem	7%
1918	Idem	13%
1933	Population >2,500; including farmers living in city	32%
1958	Population > 2,500. Only those who had non-agricultural Hukou included	16.2%
1966	Idem	17.9%
1977	Idem	17.6%
1986	All residents living in political centres of governments at all levels or other independent areas such as industrial and mining areas, science parks, research institutions, higher education facilities, the headquarters of farms and forest farms with more than 3,000 residents; including farmers living in city	24.5%
1995	Idem	29.0%
2001	Idem, with as additional criterium a population density of 1,500 or above	37.7%
2009	Idem as in 2001 with the addition that now also towns and suburban regions with links to cities are included	46.6%
2017	Idem	58.5%

Source: Xu et al. (2018; Ouyang (1936); Department of Comprehensive Statistics of National Bureau of Statistics (2010); National Bureau of Statistics of China (2008); National Bureau of Statistics of China (2018)

The pre-1949 effect of urbanisation on education

Traditional China was famous for its civil examination system, which was based on Confucian canons. However, the military defeats in the Opium Wars in the mid-19th century created a Westernisation movement that strove for the modernisation of industry and education. This resulted in accelerated industrial and commercial growth. Economic historians (Skinner, 1977) have argued that the resulting urban labour demand attracted a large-scale inflow of people to urban areas. Other scholars (Chi, 2001) added that after the 1930s, when the government became increasingly weaker, refugees who wanted to escape from famines, disasters or wars accounted for a large proportion of rural–urban migration.

This increasing urbanisation affected educational development in various ways. First, urbanisation affected education since the latter was initially funded by (and dependent on) donations from businessmen and missionary organisations, as well as by self-payment by students (Lu, 2011), who were more abundant in cities. The opening of treaty ports and the concessions granted by the Chinese government to foreign countries resulted in the further funding and establishment of numerous missionary schools in urban areas. Some of the educationalists (Zhu, 2009; Wang, 2013) who researched the development process of modern education in China viewed these missionary schools favourably. These schools' external funding meant free educational opportunities for the children of poor families, especially in elementary and girls' schools. In addition, these schools introduced flexible teaching methods and practical courses suited to the modern sciences and technology. These schools were therefore deemed to be promoters of China's modern education reform and pioneers in modern female education.[5]

The second factor driving the relation between urbanisation and education, which has been researched mainly by sociologists, concerns the availability of potential students. Indeed, urbanisation was driven at least partly by better income and job opportunities for migrants. The population inflow to cities contributed significantly to the expansion of educational resources in urban areas, particularly for relatively higher-level education and in private education. Taking Nanjing as an example, local students accounted for only 52 per cent of the total number of pupils attending primary schools established by the local municipal government in 1930. Around 15 per cent of these students came from other regions of Jiangsu Province, and the remaining students (approximately 30 per cent) came from other provinces. However, in private general secondary schools, only 17–20 per cent of the students were locals (Nanjing Education Bureau, 2010). After the 1930s, as noted above, refugees started to account for a disproportionate share of rural–urban migrants, resulting in a large influx of low-skilled, cheap labour into urban areas and leading to a further decline in the share of locals in urban schools (Liu, 2009).

The third channel through which urbanisation affected education, which has been discussed in detail by economists, is the creation of a completely new, Western-style education system. From the late-19th century onwards, the Chinese education system moved slowly away from the traditional "civil examination system" based on Confucian canons, towards a more modern system. This shift was a long and relatively slow process but was led by cities because of the demands of modern industry and commerce in terms of the knowledge and skills of the labour force. According to contemporary curricula recorded in *Zhongguo Jindai Xuezhi Shiliao* (Zhu, 1983), courses that were suitable for urban industrial and commercial development were dominant in urban schools. In contrast, in the less-developed regions, although required by the government to update their curricula to those of modern schools, most traditional schools did not modernize because of a lack of teachers and teaching equipment. The resulting gap in quality between urban and rural education motivated even more people to send their children to schools in urban areas. This effect was aggravated by various government policies, which, despite being designed to support and encourage the development of modern education overall, were nevertheless directed mostly at cities.[6] Although educationalists were excited about the substantial progress in the development of modern education, sociologists and economists argued that the scale and structure of education developed faster than did the demand arising from economic growth. Particularly in pre-1949 China, the job market in some fields quickly became saturated. For example, according to the statistics recorded in the first education yearbook of Republican China, a total of 553, 986 teachers and staff members were working in all primary schools in 1930, but the number of graduates from secondary normal schools in 1929 and 1930 combined was 580, 304 (Wang, 1934), meaning that the new graduates for only two years outnumbered the total number of existing staff members. The shortage had been replaced by overproduction.

The 1949–1979 period

In the first phase of the New China period, debates on the relationship between urbanisation and education changed fundamentally, from being the domain of historians, sociologists and economists to being that of contemporary political scientists. First, as discussed in Section 2, the definition of urbanisation transformed from a static historical understanding to a more flexible *Hukou*-based definition. Second, the government's goal moved away from balancing educational training and economic demand towards a focus on enlarging the industrial base. The First Five-year Plan (1953–1957) established that urban areas should be developed as bases for implementing the national industrialisation strategy and that the primary function of cities should be production (The National Planning Commission, 1995). All of the new industrial projects in the First Five-year Plan were distributed among 120 cities, with a focus on 18 key cities (Kirkby, 1985), resulting in strong urban demand for skills. However, because of the resulting rapid expansion of urbanisation (Cao and Chu, 1990), in 1955 the government decided to decentralize industrial production units to small cities to take full advantage of the existing infrastructure in these settings.

Third, there were mixed benefits of the migration that occurred in 1949–1979. To ensure the smooth progress of its large-scale industrial projects, the government transferred economic surpluses from rural areas to urban areas via "price scissors". Agricultural products were sold forcibly at low prices, causing farmers to become poorer. At the same time, urban residents had their food supply guaranteed by the government and also benefited from social welfare benefits such as health security (Liu and Wu, 2006). The large gap in living conditions between rural and urban areas attracted many rural migrants to the cities. The decentralisation of industrial projects beginning in 1955 was beneficial to rural migrants because they did not need to move far away from their hometowns. Consequently, urbanisation accelerated after 1955. During 1957–1960, the net increase in the urban population was 30–40 million, and the number of workers in industrial enterprises more than doubled (Cao and Chu, 1990). Peak migration from rural areas occurred in 1958, and rural migration contributed at least half of the increase in the urban population during that period (Kang, 1966).

As urbanisation placed demands on education, the expansion of education was also included in the government's strategy. The first step was to increase its scale, and the second step was to modernize higher education to match the demand from industry. Indeed, from 1951 to 1953, three-quarters of all universities were converted to exclusively technological universities (The Editorial Office of the China Education Yearbook, 1984).

Despite the rapid growth of education, still only around 30–40 per cent of junior secondary school graduates had the opportunity to attend senior secondary school, and after graduation from senior secondary school, only 5 per cent had the possibility to enrol in higher education (Gu, 2009). Consequently, a large number of secondary school graduates required placement in various economic sectors after leaving the education system. Despite its rapid growth, urban economic development was insufficient to offer enough job opportunities for these graduates. The urban situation was aggravated after 1960, when a large famine struck the entire country and it became increasingly difficult for rural areas to supply cities with sufficient food. Due to the oversupply of graduates and the effects of the famine, the government decided to reduce the urban population, imposing restrictions on rural–urban migration using the *Hukou* system. As well as restricting migration from rural areas to cities, a large number of young, educated students, as well as staff members and managers of government agencies and state-owned enterprises, were moved to rural areas (known as the "Rusticated Youth" programme). However, de-urbanisation did not stop at the end of the Great Famine because the Cultural Revolution swiftly followed, lasting until 1978. The programme was most active during 1966–1972, when 41.8 per cent of secondary school graduates in urban areas (7.15 million) were sent to rural regions with the aim of increasing rural production and reducing the pressure on the cities. In addition, secondary and higher education was severely limited, and regular higher education stopped recruiting altogether in 1966–1970 (see Figure 9.1). It was not until 1969 that

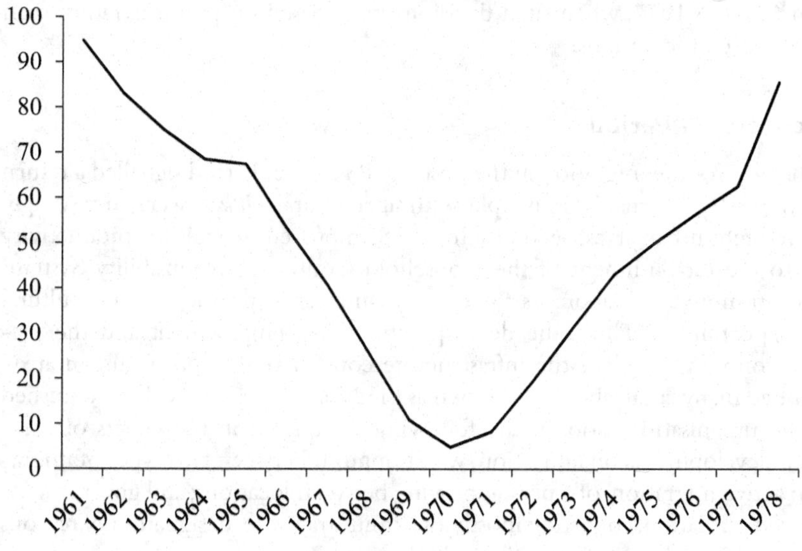

Figure 9.1 Number of students in higher education (10,000 persons)

Source: China Education Yearbook ca. 1949–1981

the economy began a gradual recovery, and higher education resumed. This improvement can be attributed mainly to the industrial sector, which had a growth rate of 30.6 per cent (Xi and Jin, 2006). The urban economic recovery offered many opportunities to educated urban youths who had been sent to the countryside in the 1960s, and many returned to the cities (Gu, 2009).

Although the debate on the 1949–1979 period has mostly been approached from a policy point of view, economists, sociologists and educationalists have recently joined the debate, focusing on the situation of the many students involved in the Rusticated Youth project. Li, Rosenzweig and Zhang (2010) found a negative relationship between the number of years these people spent in rural areas and their total years of education. Giles et al. (2015) argued that, in addition to the direct impacts of not attending school for several years, the delay in schooling caused by their transfer to rural areas under this programme increased the opportunity cost of continuing in school, because "children were older, prior learning depreciated with time out of school, and returning students faced increased competition for placement in the educational system because of accumulated cohorts of students competing for a limited number of slots". This negative effect was mitigated for students whose parents were party cadres. For example, Zhou and Hou (1999) argued that children whose parents were party cadres were usually sent to better rural locations, and then returned to cities earlier, compared with other children. Furthermore, these children had a background more conducive to self-study, which increased their chances of passing the college entrance exam. Finally, some of these parents might even have been able to directly influence college admissions decisions from 1972 to 1977, when such decisions were based on political, rather than academic, considerations.

The Reform Period

In many ways, the migration in the post-1978 Reform Period signalled a return to pre-1949 patterns. First, people with agricultural *Hukou* were increasingly allowed into urban areas. Second, after 1978, improved agricultural productivity due to the establishment of the Household Contract Responsibility System[7] freed up more rural labourers to go to urban areas to pursue non-agricultural job opportunities. Third, the development of self-employment and the private economy, as well as the infrastructure construction boom in urban areas, absorbed many rural labourers (known as the *Nongmingong*, 农民工) and pushed up the urbanisation ratio. In the following discussion on the effects of these urban developments on education, we distinguish between two types of migration: active migration, of a person moving between locations; and government-induced migration, consisting mostly of administrative re-designation of regions from rural to urban, without physical relocation of the person.

Active migration

The active movement of large numbers of migrants to urban areas affected education in various ways. First, most public primary and secondary schools prioritized local urban students because of limited urban educational resources. The children of migrant workers could access these schools only if seats remained after enrolling all of the local students, and only after paying high additional fees. In certain large cities, schools created mainly to accommodate the children of migrant workers were of relatively poor educational quality. Some educationalists found that these students felt ignored or discriminated against by teachers and by fellow students because of their rural family and educational background (Yuan, 2011). In cases where an urban school was open to the children of migrant workers, it was common for local urban students to leave the school because of a reluctance (of the student and the family) for them to attend school with the children of migrant workers. Hence, according to educationalists, migrant children were confronted with a "ceiling" in upward social mobility via education (Xiong, 2015). The government allocated special funding to alleviate these problems, but initiatives were focused mainly on how many and what proportion of children from migrant families were absorbed into urban schools. These children's educational results and whether they were able to adapt to the new environment after entering these urban schools were ignored. Moreover, these children were allowed to attend urban schools only until the end of senior secondary school. Taking the entrance examinations required to enrol in universities was possible only at the registered residence recorded in their *Hukou*. It has been shown in Shanghai, for example, that this kind of educational institutional inequality can lead to the re-production of social classes (Zhang, 2012).

Second, the large number of migrant families in urban areas led sociologists to also consider the distribution of educational resources between rural and urban areas. Yao (2017) found a linear relationship between the level of urbanisation and the numbers of schools and students at the compulsory education stage in both urban and rural areas in Ningxia Province. From 2002 to 2014, the total number of schools and the number of pupils per school expanded in urban areas. However, the increase in the number of schools was far outpaced by demand, causing a serious shortage of educational resources (Li, 2013). In contrast, the number of schools and students in rural areas decreased rapidly. Hence, for rural children, the average distance to a school increased.

Third, a large proportion of children of migrant workers did not move to cities with their parents.[8] These children were educated in rural areas and were cared for by their grandparents or other relatives, and there is an intense debate on the effects of this situation on their education. The majority of scholars, mainly educationalists, have concluded that leaving children in rural areas under the care of others has obvious negative effects on the quality of their education. For instance, Ye et al. (2006) found that these students received worse examination results, compared with their results before their parents left to work in the city. However, economists and demographers have disagreed with the assessment that leaving children in the countryside when their parents go to the city to work inevitably leads to negative effects for the children. For example, Hu (2012) showed that income sent back to rural areas by migrant workers improved the educational status of their children who remained in these areas. Likewise, Duan and Yang (2008) found that the enrolment ratio of these children was higher than that of children who moved to the city with their parents. Providing a more nuanced picture, Zheng and Wu (2014) combined both the advantages and the disadvantages, finding that the absence of the father and the mother had various effects on their children's education. They performed probability proportional to size sampling among primary school students in the fourth and sixth grades, and in first- and third-year junior secondary school students, in the provinces of Gansu, Ningxia, Yunnan, Sichuan and Guangxi for the years 2006 and 2008. They found that the positive effect of a father moving to the city and generating more family income exceeded the disadvantage caused by the lack of companionship and effective supervision of the child in terms of education. However, if a mother left her children to work in the city, the net effect was the reverse, partly because women generally earn less compared with their male counterparts. In addition, if the mother went to the city, the role of decision maker would often be played by the father, who, it is argued, would attach less value to education, especially for girls. In cases where both the mother and the father left for the city, most of these children lived with their grandparents. Most existing research related to intergenerational education is from a psychological or pedagogical perspective (Huang and Chen, 2007) and tends to agree that, although grandparents have more parental experience, more spare time and more patience, children's education is harmed in these situations because of the grandparents' low educational level, outdated educational experience and indulgence of their grandchildren. These arguments are supported by the fact that children who were raised by their grandparents have been shown to be more likely to receive worse examination results and to suffer psychological problems such as being self-centred, being psychologically fragile, having poor self-control and being introverted.

A fourth effect of urbanisation on education in terms of active migrant workers concerns decision-making within the household. Some sociologists have compared decision-making across generations of migrant workers, showing that urbanisation had different influences for different groups. Xia and Chu (2014) conducted a binary logistic regression analysis using a database on more than 1,000 rural households in north Anhui Province. Their research showed that compared with their parents, the younger generation of migrant workers (born in the 1980s and 1990s) was more willing to settle in cities. Their prime motivation was to pursue a better education for their children. Yang (2007) explained that well-educated labourers, compared with the migrants of past generations, have steadier, more sustainable and higher incomes. They also face fewer institutional barriers to rural–urban migration and are able to promote and help many other family members, relatives or even neighbours to move to urban areas.

As a fifth effect, consumer theorists have researched the impact of urbanisation on education from the perspective of consumer decision-making. Yu (2015) conducted a field investigation in Qingdao and found that migrant workers who had never enjoyed the benefits of education found it difficult to correctly value education. Their decisions about whether to educate their children thus depended on external factors, such as following urban residents' high educational investment, rather than on economic maximisation. This difficulty causes irrational investments in the field of education (Niu, 2017); accordingly, the contrast between high educational cost and low economic return has resulted in the increasingly popular belief in rural areas of the uselessness of study. In addition, He (2014) found that the influence of urban lifestyle and consumerism has resulted in the spread of hedonic, conspicuous and competitive consumption throughout rural areas, and that this change in expenditure pattern has sharply reduced the amount of money available for educational investment. Moreover, the government's efforts to activate rural consumption and the rural real estate market have stimulated consumerism, and expenses related to marriage and social networks have increased. These shifts in spending patterns have increased the financial burdens for migrant families and weakened their capability to invest in education.

Government-induced migration

In addition to the migrant workers who participated actively in urbanisation, many people have been urbanized by the government. As cities expand, rural areas have increasingly been merged into cities as new districts, where their inhabitants obtain a non-agricultural *Hukou*. Following the government's desire to increase the urbanisation ratio and consolidate areas of farmland to stimulate large-scale farming, disenfranchised famers have been forcibly relocated to resettlement areas, usually in rural–urban fringe zones, to live in high-rise buildings that have urban status. This policy, along with increases in the numbers of migrants to cities, have caused expansion in both the urban population and the urban area.[9] Economists have criticized this rapid urbanisation forced by land conveyance and concentration of land, and suggested that the urbanisation is merely an illusion because without the support of industrial development, there are insufficient non-agricultural job opportunities for rural workers who appear to have been simply re-categorized by the government.

Many scholars have directed their attention to rural workers who became absorbed into urban populations because of the loss of their farmlands, and to the education of their children. Distinct from "active migrants", these people were not outsiders; rather, recently urbanized people. Their economic situation seemed to have improved, if only temporarily, as they received compensation from the government. However, unlike the active migrants who entered cities with good preparation, clear plans and the support of their farming families in their hometowns, government-induced migrants were relocated to urban areas without any preparation or means of escape. Liu (2009) conducted a survey in a new district of Huainan city in Anhui Province, which was converted from a rural area to an urban district in 2005. More than 80 per cent of the land was expropriated by the government. Farmers received either cash or a job in return, but 70.8 per cent of those surveyed were dissatisfied with the compensation. Ultimately, 55 per cent of these landless rural workers had to survive by working as manual labourers or engaging in small business. Having lost the stable income from their farmland, they were forced to spend more time working and therefore had less time to take care of their children. Because they no longer had a source of guaranteed survival (i.e. farmland),[10] 63.7 per cent considered education the only way out for their children, and began to pay more attention to their children's education. They were willing to invest, but if they reached a point when they felt that their children were not academically promising, they would stop their support and allow their children to enter the labour market. Yao's (2008) comparative research showed that this phenomenon occurred only many years after a region was urbanized, because the initial mission for peasants who had just lost their farmland was to adapt to a new lifestyle and new methods of making a living. Therefore, they initially spent less money and time on their children's education.

Conclusion

In this chapter, we assessed the connection between historical and regional studies in China using the effect of urbanisation on education as a case study. Three threads run through this chapter. First, how urbanisation is estimated depends to a great extent on the particular academic field of the author and the current political situation. Second, because of the significance of the government throughout the history of urbanisation, connections with policy and political perspectives need to be made. Third, different effects of urbanisation on education are discussed in various academic fields, including history, education, sociology and economics.

From the 1890s to the 1930s, the development of the modern urban economy brought more educational funding and increased the number of migrant students. More importantly, this development promoted the transition from an education system that was based on the humanities and dominated by the civil examination towards the modern system of education, which emphasizes modern technology and sciences. However, the structural imbalance of the modern economy led to the uneven development of different types of schools and different specialties. Hence, discussions began about the overproduction of students, which was aggravated by refugees during the wars in the 1930s and 1940s.

In the period from 1949 to 1979, the situation changed fundamentally. Before the 1960s, the government's strategy of rapid industrialisation was dominant. Strong demand from the modern industrial sector led to a boom in educational specialties related to mining, mechanism, construction and manufacturing. However, during the 1960s and continuing through 1979, economic stagnation caused de-urbanisation to become the main focus of the government. Access to urban education, especially higher education, became severely restricted. Although some people gradually returned to urban areas beginning in the early 1970s, political factors continued to have a strong effect on education through the regulation of rural migrants' access.

The Reform Period was, in many ways, a return to the pre-1949 situation. Generally speaking, the new requirements of the labour market, awareness regarding the significance of education and increasing income helped in promoting the expansion of education. However, the final results are more complicated due to many other factors, which include the difficult situations faced by children left behind by their parents in rural areas, land-deprived rural workers and the children of migrant workers; the increasingly wide gap between rural and urban education caused by population mobility; and the labour market saturation and consequent class solidification.

Notes

1 The research leading to these results received funding from the European Research Council under the European Union's Horizon 2020 Programme (ERC-StG 637695 – HinDI) as part of the project "The historical dynamics of industrialization in Northwestern Europe and China ca. 1800–2010: A regional interpretation".

2 According to this distribution, the second-largest city in a country has about half the inhabitants of the largest city, the third-largest city has about one-third the inhabitants of the largest city, and so on.

3 In 2010, the sixth census showed that 49.68 per cent of the total population lived in urban areas. However, the demographic data published by the Ministry of Public Security recorded only 34.17 per cent as non-agricultural households. The National Bureau of Statistics (2010) acknowledged that around one-third of the urban population consisted of migrant rural workers and their family members. These people were engaged in non-agricultural production and lived in urban areas but did not have the same access to social welfare and public services as did urban households. Some of these migrants migrated regularly between urban areas and rural areas. Some scholars have argued that this part of the population was only semi-urbanized (see, e.g. Li, 2013).

4 In 2017, 42.35 per cent of the population had non-agricultural *Hukou* (see National Bureau of Statistics of China, 2017). This implied that "real urbanisation" was much lower. However, other scholars argued for different ways of estimating urbanisation. For example, Li (2010) argued that urbanisation should be calculated based on the occupational structure, where the total non-agricultural population made up the urban share. If this approach were adopted, urbanisation would have been more than 60 per cent because, at that time, many people with agricultural *Hukou* made their living in urban areas or worked in secondary or tertiary industries in rural areas.

5 In addition to educationalists, economic historians also noticed the role of educational funds, but these scholars focused mostly on modern factories in urban areas, which also started an apprentice education system to train labourers (see, e.g. Wang and Xue, 2016). On average, the number of apprentices in Beijing accounted for roughly 25 per cent of the industrial workforce (Gamble, 1921).

6 For instance, to cultivate more teachers for modern education, the government offered a tuition exemption and subsidies, as well as guaranteed jobs, to normal school students.

7 This system gave farmers the right to make independent decisions on the use of a small plot of contracted land. The production and management were entrusted to individual farming households through long-term contracts. During the contract period, the farmers paid taxes to the state and kept all the other proceeds for themselves. The system resulted in a steep increase in agricultural productivity.

8 According to the results of the sixth census, conducted in 2010, there were a total of 69.7 million children who were left behind by their parents. Of these children, 61 million were in rural areas. Children who were left behind by their parents accounted for 28.52 per cent of all rural children (Duan et al., 2013).

9 From 1990 to 2000, urban land expanded by 90 per cent, and the urban population increased by 52 per cent. In the following ten years, urbanisation expanded at a slower pace, but urban land increased by 83.41 per cent (Huang, 2016).

10 Before they became landless, 47.2 per cent of the peasants believed that, if their children could not continue to move forward in education, their survival would still be guaranteed by their farmland.

References

Bai, N. S. (白南生), 2003. The urbanization in China (中国的城市化). *Management World (管理世界)*, 11, pp. 78–97.

Bairoch, P., 1988. *Cities and economic development: From the dawn of history to the present.* Chicago: University of Chicago Press.

Brezis, E., 2008. Bairoch, Paul (1930–1999). In: S. N. Durlauf, and L. E. Blume, eds. *The new Palgrave dictionary of economics*. London: Palgrave Macmillan. Pp. 332–333. https://doi.org/10.1007/978-1-349-58802-2_85

Cao, S. J. (曹树基), 2000a. *China's population history (中国人口史)*, 4. Shanghai (上海): Fudan University Press (复旦大学出版社).

Cao, S. J. (曹树基), 2000b. *China's population history (中国人口史)*, 5. Shanghai (上海): Fudan University Press (复旦大学出版社).

Cao, H. T. (曹洪涛), and Chu, Ch. H. (储传亨), 1990. *Urban construction in contemporary China (当代中国的城市建设)*. Beijing (北京): China Social Sciences Press (中国社会科学出版社).

Chandler, T., 1987. *Four thousand years of urban growth: A historical census*. Lewiston: The Edwin Mellen Press.

Chi, Z. H. (池子华), 2001. *History of refugees in China (中国流民史), the modern period (近代卷)*. Hefei (合肥): Anhui Renmin Press (安徽人民出版社).

Department of Comprehensive Statistics of National Bureau of Statistics (国家统计局国民经济综合统计司), 2010. *China compendium of statistics 1949–2009 (新中国六十年统计资料汇编)*. Beijing (北京): China Statistics Press (中国统计出版社).

Duan, Ch. R. (段成荣), and Yang, G. (杨舸), 2008. A study on the situation of left-behind children in rural areas of China (我国农村留守儿童状况研究). *Population Research (人口研究)*, 32, pp. 15–24.

Duan, Ch. R. (段成荣), Lü, L. D. (吕利丹), Guo, J. (郭静), Wang, Z. P. (王宗萍), 2013. The general situation of survival and development of left-behind children in rural areas of China: An analysis based on the data of the 6th census (我国农村留守儿童生存和发展基本状况——基于第六次人口普查数据的分析). *Population Journal (人口学刊)*, 35, pp. 37–46.

Gamble, S. D., 1921. *Peking: A social survey conducted under the auspices of the Princeton University Center in China and the Peking Young Men' s Christian Association*. New York: George H. Doran Company.

Giles, J., Park, A., and Wang, M.Y., 2015. *The great proletarian cultural revolution, disruptions to education, and the returns to schooling in urban China*. The Institute for the Study of Labor. Discussion paper No. 8930.

Gu, H. Zh. (顾洪章), 2009. *The "rusticated youth" program (中国知识青年上山下乡始末)*. Beijing (北京): China Daily Press (人民日报出版社).

He, X. F. (贺雪峰), 2014. *The urbanization path of China (城市化的中国道路)*. Beijing (北京): Oriental Press (东方出版社).

Hu, F., 2012. Migration, remittances, and children's high school attendance: The case of rural China, *International Journal of Educational Development*, 32, pp. 401–411.

Huang, X. F. (黄晓芳), 2016. Ministry of Natural Resources of the People's Republic of China: Permanent basic farmlands around 89 cities have been delimited (国土资源部：89城市周边永久基本农田划定). *Economic Daily (经济日报)*, 05–26.

Huang, Sh. (黄姗), and Chen, X. P. (陈小萍), 2007. Literature review of intergenerational education (隔代教育研究综述). *Modern Education Science (现代教育科学)*, 2, pp. 63–65.

Kang, Ch., 1966. Industrialization and urban housing in communist China. *The Journal of Asian Studies*, 25(3), pp. 381–396. https://doi.org/10.2307/2051997

Kirkby, R. J., 1985. *Urbanization in China: Town and country in a developing economy 1949-2000AD*. New York: Columbia University Press.

Li, A. M. (李爱民), 2013. A study into semi-urbanization in China (中国半城镇化研究). *Population Research (人口研究)*, 37, pp. 80–89.

Li, H. Q. (李焕勤), 2013. An analysis of the effect of new urbanization factors and counter-measures on the balanced allocation of resources in the urban and rural compulsory education: A case of Henan Province (新型城镇化对城乡义务教育资源均衡配置的影响及对策探析). *Value Engineering (价值工程)*, 10, pp. 240–242.

Li, X. L. (李迅雷), 2010. Urbanization in China is underestimated (中国城市化率被低估了). *New Fortune (新财富)*, 11, pp. 36–39.

Li, H. B., Rosenzweig, M. and Zhang, J. S., 2010. Altruism, favouritism, and guilt in the allocation of family resources: Sophie's choice in Mao's mass send-down movement. *Journal of Political Economy*, 118(1), pp. 1–38. https://doi.org/10.1086/650315

Liu, E. M. (刘恩民), 2009. *The strategy and the education plight of the landless farmers' children in the development of the urbanization* (城市化进程中失地农民子女的教育困境及对策研究——以安徽省淮南市三和乡为个案. Southwest University (西南大学).

Liu, Sh. (刘胜), 2009. Correlations of modern refugees and urbanization in Kuomingtang Regime (浅析民国时期流民与城市化关系). *Journal of Wuhan Polytechnic (武汉职业技术学院学报)*, 8, pp. 15–17.

Liu, Y. T. and Wu, F. L., 2006. The state，institutional transition and the creation of new urban poverty in China. *Social Policy & Administration*, 40(2), pp. 121–137. https://doi.org/10.1111/j.1467-9515.2006.00480.x

Lu, Ch. (卢川), 2011. Urban education in Jingzhou during the Qing Dynasty (略论清代荆州的城市教育), *Journal of Yangtze University (Social Sciences) (长江大学学报社会科学版)*, 34(6), pp. 6–8.

Malanima, P., 2009. Decline or growth? European cities and rural economies. In: M. Cerman and E. Landsteiner, eds. *Zwischen land und stadt. Jahrbuch für geschichte des ländlichen raumes*, 6, pp. 2–29.

Modelski, G., 2003. *World cities: -3000 to 2000*. Washington: FAROS.

Nanjing Education Bureau (南京特别市教育局), 2010. Educational statistics of Nanjing City in 1929, 1930 (民国十八年度、十九年度南京特别市教育概况统计). In: Y. Wang, ed. *Compilation of archives and statistics of education in Republican China (民国教育资料统计汇编)*, 13. Beijing (北京): National Library of China Publishing House (国家图书馆出版社).

National Bureau of Statistics of China (国家统计局), 2008. *Provisions on the statistical division of urban and rural areas (关于统计上划分城乡的规定)*.

National Bureau of Statistics of China (国家统计局), 2018. *Statistical communique of The People's Republic of China on 2017* (2017年国民经济统计公报).

National Bureau of Statistics of China (国家统计局), 2018. *China statistical yearbook 2018*. Beijing(北京): China Statistics Press (中国统计出版社).

Niu, W. X. (牛文学), 2017. Analysis of individual decision-making mechanism in urbanization (城镇化中个体决策机理分析). *Special Zone Economy Issue (特区经济)*, 343, pp. 70–73.

Ouyang, D. X. (欧阳德修), 1936. Problems and comparison of urban and rural population in China (中国都市人口和乡村人口问题及比较). *South Wind (南风)*, 1, pp. 5–6.

Skinner, W., 1977. *The city in late imperial China*. Stanford CA: Stanford University Press.

Sun, B. W. (孙本文), 1946. *Social problems in China (现代中国社会问题)*, 2. Beijing (北京): The Commercial Press (商务印书馆).

The editorial office of the China Education Yearbook (中国教育年鉴编辑部), 1984. *China education yearbook ca 1949 - 1984(中国教育年鉴1949–1984)* Beijing (北京): Encyclopedia of China Publishing House(中国大百科全书出版社).

The National Planning Commission. (国家计划委员会), 1955. *The 1st five-year plan of China (中华人民共和国发展国民经济的第一个五年计划)*. Beijing (北京), People's Publishing House (人民出版社).

United Nations, Department of Economic and Social Affairs, Population Division, 2018. *World urbanization prospects: The 2018 revision*. United Nations.

Wang, Sh. J. (王世杰), 1934. *The first education yearbook of Republican China (第一次中国教育年鉴)*. Shanghai (上海): Shanghai Kaiming Book Store (上海开明书店).

Wang, T. (王涛), 2013. Missionary schools and modernization of Chinese education (教会学校与中国教育近代化). *Journal of Ningxia University (Humanities and Social Sciences) (宁夏大学学报（人文社会科学版）)*, 35(2), pp. 178–180.

Wang, Y. Zh. (王远征), 2001. The options and obstacles in China's urbanization path (中国城市化道路的选择和障碍). *Strategy and Management (战略与管理)*, 1, pp. 31–37.

Wang, J. D. (王季点) and Xue, Z. Q. (薛正清), 2016. An investigation report of factories in Beijing (调查北京工厂报告). In: Ch. Zheng (郑成林), ed. *The third collection of economic data of Republican China (民国时期经济资料调查三编)*, 20. Beijing (北京): National Library of China Publishing House (国家图书馆出版社), pp. 167–208.

Xi, X. (席宣), and Jin, Ch. M. (金春明), 2006. *A brief history of the Cultural Revolution (文化大革命简史)*. Beijing (北京): Chinese Communist Party History Publishing House (中央党史出版社).

Xia, Y. J. (夏永久), and Chu, J. L. (储金龙), 2014. An inter-generational comparison of peasants' willingness to migrate to urban areas: Evidence from northern Anhui Province (基于代际比较比较视角的农民城镇化意愿及影响因素——来自皖北的实证). *Urban Development Studies (城市发展研究)*, 21(9), pp. 12–17.

Xiong, Y. H. (熊易寒), 2015. The education of children of migrant workers is still affected by institutional discrimination (农民工子女教育仍面临制度性歧视). *China Youth Daily (中国青年报)*, 5(4), pp. 10.

Xu, Sh. L. (许仕廉), 1930. *The population issue in China (中国人口问题)*. Beijing (北京): The Commercial Press (商务印书馆).

Xu, Y., van Leeuwen, B. and Van Zanden, J. L., 2018. Urbanization in China, ca. 1100–1900. *Frontiers of Economics in China*, 13(3), pp. 639–664. https://doi.org/10.3868/s060-007-018-0018-9

Yang, G. K. (杨公科), 2007. The transfer of the rural labour force and the career orientation of persons with rural education (谈农村劳动力转移与农村教育的职业取向). *Education and Vocation (教育与职业)*, 24, pp. 173–174.

Yao, B. T. (姚宝亭), 2008. *Analysis on the educational dilemma and accordingly causes of the children of landless farmers in the process of urbanization (城市化进程中失地农民子女的教育困境及成因分析)*. Shanghai Normal University (上海师范大学).

Yao, Y. Zh. (姚银枝等), 2017. An empirical study of the impact of urbanization on the scale of compulsory education in urban and rural areas in Ningxia Province (城镇化对宁夏义务教育城乡办学规模影响的实证研究), *Journal of Ningxia University Humanities & Social Sciences Edition (宁夏大学学报（人文社会科学版）)*, 39(1), pp. 149–158.

Ye, J. Z. (叶敬忠等), Wang, Y. H. (王伊欢), Zhang, K. Y (张克云), Lu, J. X. (陆继霞), 2006. The influence of parents' going out to perform labour on the study of left-behind children in rural areas (父母外出务工对农村留守儿童学习的影响). *Rural Economy (农村经济)*, 7, pp. 119–123.

Yin, M. X. (殷梦霞), and Li, Q. (李强), 2009. *A compilation of economic investigations along the railway lines in the Republican China (民国铁路沿线经济调查报告汇编)*, Vol. 14. Beijing (北京): National Library of China Publishing House (国家图书馆出版社).

Yu, J. (于洁), 2015. Rural migrant workers' decision-making behaviour on education expenditure: Based on field work in city of Qingdao (进城农民工家庭教育支出决策行为分析——基于山东省青岛市的实地调查), *Education Research Monthly (教育学术月刊)*, 2, pp. 56–61.

Yuan, L. X. (袁立新), 2011. A comparative study of discrimination against middle school students in public schools and schools for migrant workers (公立学校与民工子弟学校初中生流动儿童受歧视状况比较). *Chinese Journal of School Health (中国学校卫生)*, 32(7), pp. 856–857.

Zhang, Y. H. (张银海), 2012. Children of migrant workers: How to escape from status reproduction (农民工子弟：如何逃离阶层再生产). *South Reviews (南风窗)*, 1, pp. 64–66.

Zhao, Y. Q. (赵燕青), 1988. A review of theories of the urbanization path in China (中国城市化道路理论述评). In: Ye, W., ed. *A preliminary study on the urbanization path in China*. Beijing (北京): China Prospect Publishing House (中国展望出版社).

Zheng, L. (郑磊), and Wu, Y. X. (吴映雄), 2014. The impact of parental migration on educational development of left-behind children: Evidence from western rural area of China (劳动力迁移对农村留守儿童教育发展的影响——来自西部农村地区调查的证据). *Journal of Beijing Normal University (Social Sciences edition) (北京师范大学学报社会科学版)*, 2, pp. 139–146.

Zhou, X. G., and Hou, L. R., 1999. Children of the Cultural Revolution: The state and the life course in the People's Republic of China. *American Sociological Review*, 64, pp. 12–36. https://doi.org/10.2307/2657275

Zhu, L. P. (朱利培), 2009. A brief analysis of the impact of missionary schools on the modernization of Chinese education (浅析教会学校对中国教育近代化的影响). *Knowledge Economy (知识经济.)*, 10, pp. 176–177.

Zhu, Y. H. (朱有瓛), 1983. *Historical materials of modern educational system in China (中国近代学制史料)*, 1(1). Shanghai (上海): Eastern China Normal University Press (华东师范大学出版社).

Conclusions

10 Setting an agenda for a "New Regional History"

Marijn Molema

Introduction

You might recognize the critical voice in your head which accompanies you as you work on a project, repeatedly asking the same irritating, basic questions. For me it was Bugs Bunny – the Warner Bros cartoon rabbit who outsmarted everyone in animated films such as *Looney Tunes* – who delivered a running commentary in my head for a number of years. Every now and then he would stop rushing around and provokingly ask his famous question: "Eeh… What's up, doc?" If we translate this question to the theme of this edited volume, we would ask: what is the use of spanning the gap between regional studies and history? Luckily, the essays collected in this book helped me to find the straightforward answer needed to convince an impatient and restless character like Bugs Bunny. First, bridging the gap revitalizes an older theme in the study of history, that of regional development, and also increases its societal relevance. Second, pulling history into regional studies strengthens the explanatory power of this multidisciplinary field.

This is the short answer to the Bugs Bunny question. However, the last chapter of this edited volume is not the script of a cartoon movie. Here, I take the opportunity to elaborate again on the interrelationship between history and regional studies and construe some research perspectives which emerge from that by using the individual contributions to this book. My work is also based on the presentations and discussions from five workshops which I co-organized in 2017 and 2018 as the key contact person from the RSA Research Network on ReHi. These workshops had an explorative character and yielded (too) many themes and questions (Molema et al., 2017; Parrish et al., 2017). It would have been completely unfeasible to design a conceptual framework which included all the phenomena and questions that we touched upon. Instead, this chapter is more of a personal vision of a fruitful direction for future research, inspired and strengthened by the ideas of others.

To begin with, let us imagine a field of research in which regional historians exchange knowledge with colleagues from the social sciences, such as geographers, economists, political scientists and sociologists. Imagine this field to be a football field demarcated by four corner flags. Each corner flag stands for a basic principle which is shared by both historians and their social scientific colleagues. The field's demarcation causes the interplay between historians and social scientists to be more effective, because it offers an overview of the area within which the two scientific domains can interact. I will sketch the four corner flags in the four following sections, in order to shape a multidisciplinary field of future research. My contribution will end by naming this field "New Regional History".

Societal challenges

The first "corner flag" argues that every multidisciplinary exchange should begin from a *societal* problem or challenge. Closer inspection of regional studies and history reveals the phenomenon of "academic drift" at work in both scientific domains. With this, I mean an inborn tendency of scientists to seek inspiration for new research questions within the academic field of their research itself. Discussions with and reading the work of colleagues are the sources of scientific renewal. There is nothing fundamentally wrong with the drift away from the more practically oriented world outside academia. Criticism of the utilitarian view of science is in many cases perfectly understandable (Collini, 2017). Many innovative ideas and most ground-breaking discoveries were made in isolated academic systems.

However, this begins to become problematic when fields of research ignore the societal problems that call for academic reflection and new knowledge production, and which help societies to deal with complex situations and challenges. When it comes to regional development, the field of regional studies cannot be accused of paying no attention to societal constraints. The Regional Studies Association (RSA) was founded by engaged academics in 1965. Its founding members wanted to assist policymakers by discovering new opportunities for regional development, and they contributed to regional policies by assessing its instruments and theories. In the early years of its existence, the RSA frequently engaged in public debates and was heard as a collective voice which praised or criticized political decisions. Critical observers claim that the RSA has evolved from its beginnings in the 1990s into an international community, primarily based on the services, products and networks that it provides towards its members (Hopkins, 2015). As a result, the association's "collective voice" function diminished. Nevertheless, it is without doubt that regional studies as a field still concentrates on the problems discussed among policymakers, politicians and citizens involved in regional development.

The historical sciences are also great suppliers of public intellectuals. Although many historians avoid speaking about the future because they "understand only the past", there are a lot of scholars who endeavour to help the public grasp current events with their historical knowledge. However, the core of this discipline consists of academics with a nationalist view of history. The nation state has been a safe haven of historians for more than 150 years now, only recently being defied by "global history". Regional perspectives lie more towards the fringes of the discipline, although there are countries, such as Germany, where federal structures support the production of conferences, journals and books about regional history. Regional history is generally regarded as a piece of a national mosaic. Regional history in most cases relates to national history by presenting a different view, or by explaining why national developments took the course they did. Again, there is nothing wrong with this kind of regional history – it enriches our knowledge and provides inspiration for many. Be that as it may, many societal challenges take place at the regional level. The significance of these regional phenomena is not grounded in some higher level of scale; it is the very *regional* nature of these challenges themselves that legitimizes a regional view. Current challenges within regions, however, are almost off the radar of regional and other historians.

What then are these "problems and challenges"? In order to answer this question, it is instructive to look at how our ideas about regional development have been changed from the post-war period to the present day. In the 1950s and 1960s, most Western countries embraced industrialization as the impulse for economic development. Regional industrialization policies were established to give vulnerable regions an impulse and spread welfare across the country. The industrial development perspective lost its dominance in the 1970s however, because of factors including market saturation, competition from low-wage countries and emerging environmental awareness. From the 1980s onwards, innovation became the key word – innovation which could occur in all sectors and across economic activities, and not only in industry. The consequence was that regions had to find their strengths within their own economic structures. A new "endogenous growth" perspective also emphasized other economic opportunity factors, such as the local work ethic, favourable knowledge institutions, effective cooperation between regional stakeholders, etc. Growth incentives had to come from within, instead of the exogenous state subsidies for industrial development.

It is however quite difficult to define and identify clearly the aspects of economic potential which might serve as starting points for future development. These aspects of potential are deeply interwoven into an area's ecosystem (Stam, 2015). As something which is part of an evolutionary and path-dependent process, regional economic potential is not always visible on the surface. The difficulty is to first recognize the opportunities for regional development, then to acknowledge them and finally to find ways to strengthen their economic potential. Policymaking on the basis of the endogenous development opportunities is even more difficult for regions which are vulnerable and/or are situated at the periphery of a country's economic and political core areas. The economic structure of such regions might be historically weak and their "potential" could therefore be harder to find. The weaknesses of such areas are a reality which cannot be washed away with a discourse of bottom-up development. Moreover, these areas quite often lack the expertise and human resources to recognize, acknowledge and strengthen their economic chances. These resources are absolutely necessary: reflecting on a regional economy and formulating strategic development plans is quite difficult, at least if you compare it with the *one-size-fits-all* model of regional policies in the post-war era. Meanwhile, cities and metropolitan areas do have the means to draw up attractive development plans and assign lobbyists to raise funds for the implementation of these plans.

With an exhausting range of long-term statistics on income, financial assets and purchasing power, Thomas Piketty (2013) showed how inequality increased from the 1980s. Piketty collected his data mainly as averages at the nation state level. From a bird's eye view of these nation states, however, inequality also acquires a spatial dimension. In his impactful article, the economic geographer Andrés Rodríguez-Pose (2018) stressed this spatial dimension of inequality and connected it to political populism. This phenomenon has, according to Rodríguez-Pose, strong territorial foundations and is a real societal challenge: "the populist wave is challenging the sources of existing well-being in both the less-dynamic and the more prosperous areas" (p. 189). Vulnerable regions are accompanied by societal risks of social and economic deprivation, demographic decline and, as a result of this, the loss of cultural variety. These regions might turn their backs on the establishment, and retain popular and/or extremist views and convictions.

To recap: driven by structural transformations, ideas about economic development shifted away from the primacy of industry and embraced the endogenous, specific opportunities presented by a territory instead. However, as a probably unintended consequence of this paradigm shift, state policies for economically vulnerable regions lost their prominent position in most modern countries. Because of the electoral repercussions, the problem of left-behind areas is regaining its significance in societal and political debates. This problem is too complicated to be tackled by a single discipline. Instead, we need close cooperation between history and regional studies.

The added value of historians is their holistic view and their tendency to understand problems in an evolutionary sense (Molema and Van der Zwet, 2017). For historians, the theme of regional development also has the potential to reach a new public. A new regional history offers great opportunities to load this old sub-discipline with new energy and enhance its societal impact. Regional historians gain the opportunity to come into contact with people and organizations which need historical knowledge and insight in order to find the right direction for the future. The consequence of this is a concentration on themes connected to societal challenges: territorial inequality, regional population decline and the economic renewal of cities and regions.

Construction of regions

A second point of departure or corner flag represents the idea that history and regional studies should together raise our understanding of how regions were constructed, by whom and on the basis of what kind of arguments. The areas studied by most regional historians are delineated pragmatically: they determine the borders fixed by constitutional law. Sponsors such as regional governments or regional cultural funds support regional historians to write the history of these regions or districts. This is at least the case in my country, the Netherlands, where impressive works have been published in this way about several of our provinces. The social, cultural and economic characteristics of regions such as the Dutch provinces, however, do not necessarily coincide with the geographical space of such administrative entities. Commuting to work and economic exchanges between companies are examples of daily practices which transcend the official borders of regions. There are many more such examples, like participation in sports activities or the receipt of specialized healthcare, the experience of a landscape and cultural values, collaborative initiatives to support economic innovation – all these illustrate activities which frequently have a *regional* character and which are not confined to a particular administrative district. Such insights persuaded geographers decades ago that regions are not fixed, but have a *relational* character (Tomaney, 2009). The relational character of regions refers to individual phenomena connected to each other within a given area. In other words, viewing regions as objects of research which exist principally in the sense of their administrative function has been superseded as an approach by the analysis of regions through studying the geographical scales at which people, towns, cities, companies, institutions, landscapes, etc. are interrelated. The geographical area of a region is fundamentally open and in fact part of the research question. The only convention which needs to be accepted is the idea that the size of regions resides somewhere between a town and the national territory.

The relational bases for regions have been theorized by geographers from diverse backgrounds. The German geographer Blotevogel (1996) drew a theoretical distinction between three types of region. The first type comprises regions which are principally understood as analytical categories ("Analytical Regions"), in which specific characteristics define what the region is. A region can be perceived as a territory which is densely populated. Another example can be seen in the idea of a region as an area in which a more or less coherent labour market functions. Blotevogel's second type is the Activity Region. Activities can be economic, such as a region which presents itself as a unity, for example because of its marketing goals. Activities can also have a political character: regions are then delineated by their administrative boundaries or the area on which a specific development plan focuses. A third type is the Identity Region. The social, cultural and political identities of individuals or groups are frequently connected to a specific territory, which forms the spatial framework into which feelings of regional belonging are loaded. Anssi Paasi (1991) elaborates on the theme of regional identity. His impactful interpretation of the region as a sociocultural and historical category stresses the evolutionary character of the construction of regions. The institutionalization of these regions is a result of four stages. A region needs: 1) a territorial shape; 2) symbolic aspects connected to a specific area; and 3) an institutional shape. Stage 4 requires that the result of the first three stages becomes embedded into a society's political and societal consciousness.

Blotevogel and Paasi are among the academics who have provided a terminology for understanding regions as constructed by human action. This insight gives way to a critical investigation of the agents and processes which lie at the basis of certain regional categories: are they scientists, politicians, entrepreneurs or a combination of the three? We should also investigate how regions change: with Blotevogel, we can look into the dynamics within and between Analytical, Activity and Identity Regions. Such a deconstruction of the region is especially valuable with respect to the goals of historically informed regional studies. These studies, as we have noted in the "societal challenges" section, should impact on current debates about regional development. However, if a researcher aims to inform future decisions for a specific region, they must understand the genesis of the region. In other words: the conscious or unconscious political, economic and cultural interests which affected the construction of a region should be integral to the investigation. Problematizing the regional level prevents the researcher from taking regions for granted, and helps them to situate the regional level in a wider perspective.

Multidisciplinary exchange

So far, we have planted corner flags which demarcate new regional history as a field in which research projects are connected to societal challenges, and where the construction of regions is part of the questioning. A third corner flag should introduce multidisciplinary exchanges between regional and historical studies as a rule of conduct. Regional studies is a relatively young and multidisciplinary field in itself which belongs to the social sciences, whereas history has a longstanding tradition within the humanities. Molema and Tomaney, in their contribution to this edited volume, analysed the distinctions between the two academic fields in terms of the methodological differences in which history, broadly understood, applies a narrative approach while regional studies seeks general theories. They sketched how the social and historical sciences have diverged since the late 19th century, and converged again during the closing years of the 20th century. There is therefore a tradition of crossover between the humanities and the social sciences, a tradition on which we can build our research agenda. Moreover, the research objectives of both regional and historical studies are situated in a regional *society*, which makes the overlap obvious.

As obvious as this overlap may be, it is impossible to transfer theories, methodologies and concepts from one field to the other without further exploring its compatibility. This edited volume can be regarded as such an exploration, which offers us insights into what we gain by connecting regional and historical studies. From an analytical perspective, we can distinguish several routes for multidisciplinary exchange, such as the research perspective, the concepts used or the methodology applied. Where Huggins and Thompson's chapter is an example of the first, Fernández-de-Sevilla and Costa's contribution illustrates the second route. The third and methodological perspective has been demonstrated by the chapters on quantitative measurement and their implicit or explicit connection to qualitative methodologies.

In their chapter, Robert Huggins and Piers Thompson touch upon the structure–agency problem which smoulders in both the humanities and the social sciences. How much *agency* does one person or a group of persons have? Can they change a historical process, or is this impossible, because historical processes are embedded in the collective, behavioural patterns that structure human action? The British sociologist Anthony Giddens (1984) answered these questions by finding a middle ground: human behaviour is structured by social forces, but these structures can be changed by human action. A similar rejection of extreme structuralism can be found in the philosophy of history as well. Studies of the past in which structures dominate historical explanations, and in which people are reduced to background actors, remain static: they do not reveal the experiences and indentation of our ancestors (cf. Ankersmit, 1994, pp. 182–238). Indirectly intervening in these broad and to a certain extent philosophical discussions, Huggins and Thompson argue for a behavioural approach in which we take the role of ordinary people into account. Like every other kind of development, regional development is connected to individuals who are able to inspire their urban or regional society to change. Illustrated with the seminal work of Peter Hall (1999), *Cities in Civilization*, their examples are manifold: from entrepreneurs and inventors, to mayors and leaders of civil society movements. These people, who have a great impact on their societies, become woven into urban and regional cultures. The reciprocal relationship between leading individuals and these cultures is an interesting and important theme for future research.

Multidisciplinary connections can be established by the transfer of concepts from regional studies to historical studies. These concepts can offer tools to make historical studies more analytical, and help to compare different regional economic development histories with each other. Regional studies is a rich field when it comes to theoretical ideas which help to grasp the regional development process. Recent decades have seen the emergence of several concepts which impacted on scientific reflection as well as on policymaking practice. These include the learning region (Morgan 1997), smart specialization (McCann and Ortega-Argilés, 2013) and economic resilience (Martin and Sunley, 2015). However innovative these concepts may be, the ongoing introduction of new terms into the academic debate is not without controversy. Critical scholars have accused academic proponents of concepts such as "learning region" of sacrificing their academic independence and prioritizing their relationships with politicians and policymakers over obtaining a true understanding of how regional and other economies work (Lovering, 1999). Judgements which are more fundamental because they criticize the heuristic value of this conceptual abundance, also come from scholars who point to the vagueness of many regional studies (Markusen, 2003). Such discussions within regional studies underline the importance of empirical research. A longer time perspective can be very helpful here, because it helps both with theory construction based on the new phenomena which are revealed, and with strengthening the practical application of theoretical concepts. The chapter by the economic historians Tomàs Fernández-de-Sevilla and Armando J. dalla Costa is an illustration of this added value. They embrace the cluster concept and describe how the growth of an automotive cluster around São Paulo also simultaneously fundamentally transformed it. Small repair and car parts manufacturing workshops popped up spontaneously, and formed the basis of a cluster which was gradually – especially after the Brazilian government's Foreign Direct Investment (FDI) policies in the 1950s – taken over by a few large companies. As such, the chapter shows that the evolution of clusters is not only dependent on market circumstances; economic policies also play a crucial role. It is therefore important to look at those policies, and explain their origins with reference to the history of the societies in which they were developed.

A third route towards multidisciplinary exchanges between regional and historical studies has a methodological character. The combination of qualitative and quantitative research deserves our special attention here. Economic history has a particularly rich quantitative tradition in which theories and methodologies from the social sciences, especially economics, are a source for inspiration. Cliometric approaches can prove the evolution of historical events, processes and structures. However, the underlying explanation also requires a qualitative route, through which the historical context, the crucial variables and the contingent factors are explained. Multidisciplinary exchanges between regional studies and regional history thus requires a combination of quantitative and qualitative approaches. This edited volume therefore presents two chapters on this subject. The economic historians Kerstin Enflo and Anna Missiaia clarify methodologies on measuring Gross Domestic Product (GDP) in regions. The measurement of regional GDP is a spinoff from major projects within economic history which resulted in national accounts and provided insight into the long-term development of countries. The regionalization of these quantitative approaches provides more insight into the concrete development of individual regions, and stimulates interregional comparisons. Enflo and Missiaia summarize some of their results on Swedish regions, which also offer an opportunity to consider regional inequalities. With their time series, they show how a decrease in regional equalities coincided with the Industrial Revolution in the latter half of the 19th century. Only in the later decades, from 1980 onwards, did regional inequalities arise again. Such long-term insights stimulate a search for explanations and thus a combination of quantitative and qualitative approaches. Mixed methods are also applied in the chapter by Justyna Kościńska (sociologist) and Mikołaj Herbst (economist). They look primarily at educational achievements, because education is an important driver of regional development. First, on the basis of secondary school mathematics test scores, they show that the regions of Poland that were formerly parts of the Austro-Hungarian Empire performed better than those regions which had belonged to Russia, and substantially better than the former Prussian regions. Second, they explain these differences with the help of questionnaires and in-depth interviews with the students' parents. The differences are bound up in different forms of social capital, differences in the levels of trust of education and variation in the perception of educational goals. Combining these methods constructively, this chapter optimally illustrates the benefits of multidisciplinary exchange applied from a long-term perspective.

Comparison and transfer

There is nothing wrong with a regional history that is not invoked by societal challenges, which does not question the regional borders set by constitutional law and which does not strive for a multidisciplinary exchange with the field of regional studies. As already stated, the traditional method for conducting regional history raises our knowledge of the past and is a source of inspiration to many. However, it is problematic if regional history remains limited to traditional themes and does not innovate with new themes and approaches, in spite of societal developments which revive the importance of the regional level for dealing with questions of economic, social and cultural sustainability. In that case, regional history runs the risk of becoming a marginal sub-discipline entangled with itself, and thus limited to the history of a region's past, which can result in increasingly sophisticated stories, but can also lack reference to a regional society's present or future. A final corner flag, in addition to the three already mentioned, helps regional history to avoid these marginalizing effects. This fourth corner flag argues for a comparative approach and a preference for analyzing the transfer of people, ideas and commodities between regions.

Regions and their past, present and futures must be compared for similarities and differences and mechanisms of adaptation, change or lock-in to be analysed. The broad comparison between Europe and the United States presented by Kevin Cox in his chapter demonstrates the merit of juxtaposing different categories. Cox shows how different political approaches towards regional economic development are rooted in a continent's history and society. Whereas European states took a leading role in economic and spatial policies in the development of vulnerable regions, this was not the case in the United States. There, the involvement of the centre was reduced to a minimum; local governments, competing with each other for market locations, took the lead instead. The bottom-up approach in America is connected to the development of capitalism in that country and the absence of deeply entrenched pre-capitalist structures, as was the case in European societies. Meimei Wang and Bas van Leeuwen illuminate a very different tradition of state involvement with their chapter on China. These two economic historians, like Kościńska and Herbst in this volume, considered education, and especially its relationship with urbanization. After a discussion of how urbanization can be measured and how this relates to different disciplinary approaches, the two authors reveal how the Chinese state impacted the education process through prohibitive and permissive policies.

The contribution of Martin Åberg and Thomas Denk provides the methodological basis needed to employ comparative methods properly, and in a way that opens new heuristic possibilities. Comparative Sequence Design (CSD), as they call their method, can be used in any research design, first, because the method captures both synchronic comparisons (focused on the similarities and differences between certain periods) and diachronic comparisons (focused on the parallel analysis of different cases). Second, CSD provides the tools for analyzing one case study separately, but also for examining the interdependence between case studies. As such, it backs the emancipation of regional level analysis: the logic behind CSD values regions as independent geographical entities which can directly impact each other. This is why the emphasis on regional interdependence releases the region from the national straitjacket. Contrary to mosaic thinking, in which the significance of regions is closely aligned to the national whole, regional developments stand for themselves and can impact each other without intervening national governments. This makes the chapter by Åberg and Denk an inspiring contribution which stimulates the discovery of regions which impact each other across national borders.

"New Regional History"

At the beginning of these concluding remarks, I used the metaphor of a playing field demarcated by four corner flags, which set some basic rules for the interplay between historical and regional studies. The first flag required that every research question should start from a societal problem or challenge. The second flag required that researchers view how regions were constructed critically. The third rule embraces multidisciplinary exchange, in which long-term analysis goes together with concepts and theories from regional studies. Fourth, research should be comparative in nature. From a bird's eye view, we can call the playing field "New Regional History".

What is new about this kind of history? New is that a region's history is not viewed as part of a larger (national or European) whole. We are not proposing mosaic thinking, as though regions only have significance as part of a larger whole. Instead, we want to emancipate the regional view of history as a perspective which has considerable value in its own right. Its value resides in the societal challenges which need to be grasped in the context of their historical genesis.

The title of this essay was "setting" an agenda. This verb, setting, makes clear that the agenda is not yet set. The basis of this edited volume is also not strong enough to act as a foundation for a new approach which offers new scientific opportunities and provides scholars a method for doing research which is relevant and important with regard to societal challenges. We need more time and experience for communities within both regional studies and history to create a research tradition of their own, with a common set of research themes, questions and approaches. This edited volume sketched some angular points for such a tradition. Hopefully, it will encourage research into regional challenges, and I hope it inspires the long-term investigation of regional growth and adaption, regional inequality and policies which help find ways to prevent social, economic and cultural deprivation.

References

Ankersmit, F., 1994. *History and tropology: The rise and fall of metaphor*. Berkeley, Los Angeles and London: University of California Press.

Blotevogel, H. H., 1996. Auf dem Wege zu einer 'Theorie der Regionalität': Die Region als Forschungsobjekt der Geographie. In: G. Brunn ed. *Region und Regionsbildung in Europa*. Baden-Baden: Nomos Verlag. Pp. 44–68.

Collini, S., 2017. *Speaking of universities*. London and New York: Verso.

Giddens, A., 1984. *The constitution of society. Outline of the theory of structuration*. Cambridge: Polity Press.

Hall, P., 1999. *Cities in civilization: Culture, innovation, and urban order*. London: Phoenix Giant.

Hopkins, J. A., 2015. *Knowledge, networks and policy: Regional studies in postwar Britain and beyond*. London: Routledge.

Lovering, J., 1999. Theory led by policy: The inadequacies of the 'new regionalism' (illustrated from the case of Wales). *International Journal of Urban and Regional Research*, 23(2), pp. 379–395. https://doi.org/10.1111/1468-2427.00202

Markusen, A., 2003. Fuzzy concepts, scanty evidence, policy distance: The case for rigour and policy relevance in critical regional studies. *Regional Studies* 37(6 and 7), pp. 701–717. https://doi.org/10.1080/0034340032000108796

Martin, R. and Sunley, P., 2015. On the notion of regional economic resilience: Conceptualization and explanation. *Journal of Economic Geography* 15(1), pp. 1–42. https://doi.org/10.1093/jeg/lbu015

McCann, P. and Ortega-Argilés, R., 2013. Smart specialization, regional growth and applications to European Union cohesion policy. *Regional Studies*, 49(8), pp. 1291–1302. https://doi.org/10.1080/00343404.2013.799769

Molema, A. M. and Van der Zwet, A., 2017. Research network on regional economic and policy history. *Planning Perspectives*, 32(3), 459–466. https://doi.org/10.1080/02665433.2017.1331753

Molema, A. M., Reeploeg, S., Åberg, M. and Van der Zwet, A., 2017. Report on the inaugural workshop of the RSA Research Network on Regional Economic and Policy History. *Regions*, 308, pp. 29–30.

Morgan, K., 1997. The learning region: Institutions, innovation, and regional renewal. *Regional Studies*, 31(5), pp. 491–503. https://doi.org/10.1080/00343409750132289

Paasi, A., 1991. Deconstructing regions: Notes on the scales of spatial life. *Environment and Planning A: Economy and Space*, 23(2), 239–256. https://doi.org/10.1068/a230239

Parrish, M., Molema, A. M., Svensson, S. and Reeploeg, S., 2017. Report on the second workshop of the RSA Research Network on Regional Economic and Policy History. *Regions*, 308, 31–32.

Piketty, T., 2013. *Le capital au XXIe siècle*. Paris: Éditions du Seuil.

Rodrìguez-Pose, A., 2018. The revenge of the places that don't matter (and what to do about it). *Cambridge Journal of Regions, Economy and Society*, 11(1), pp. 189–209. https://doi.org/10.1093/cjres/rsx024

Stam, E., 2015. Entrepreneurial ecosystems and regional policy: A sympathetic critique. *European Planning Studies*, 23(9), 1759–1769. https://doi.org/10.1080/09654313.2015.1061484

Tomaney, J., 2009. Region. In: R. Kitchin and N. Thrift eds. *International encyclopedia of human geography*, vol. 9. Oxford: Elsevier. Pp. 136–150.

Index

Printed in the United States
by Baker & Taylor Publisher Services